PSYCHOLOGY LIBRARY EDITIONS:
COMPARATIVE PSYCHOLOGY

Volume 12

ANIMAL AND HUMAN
CONDUCT

ANIMAL AND HUMAN CONDUCT

WILLIAM E. RITTER

Routledge
Taylor & Francis Group

LONDON AND NEW YORK

First published in Great Britain in 1928 by George Allen & Unwin Ltd.

This edition first published in 2018
by Routledge
2 Park Square, Milton Park, Abingdon, Oxon OX14 4RN

and by Routledge
711 Third Avenue, New York, NY 10017

Routledge is an imprint of the Taylor & Francis Group, an informa business

British Library Cataloguing in Publication Data
A catalogue record for this book is available from the British Library

ISBN: 978-1-138-50329-8 (Set)
ISBN: 978-1-351-12878-0 (Set) (ebk)
ISBN: 978-0-8153-6735-2 (Volume 12) (hbk)
ISBN: 978-0-8153-6747-5 (Volume 12) (pbk)
ISBN: 978-1-351-25740-4 (Volume 12) (ebk)

Publisher's Note
The publisher has gone to great lengths to ensure the quality of this reprint but points out that some imperfections in the original copies may be apparent.

Disclaimer
The publisher has made every effort to trace copyright holders and would welcome correspondence from those they have been unable to trace.

ANIMAL AND HUMAN CONDUCT

By

WILLIAM E. RITTER

Professor Emeritus of Zoology & Director Emeritus
Scripps Institution of Oceanography,
University of California

WITH THE COLLABORATION OF
EDNA WATSON BAILEY

LONDON
GEORGE ALLEN & UNWIN LTD.
MUSEUM STREET

*This book was published in the U.S.A. under the title
" The Natural History of Our Conduct "*

First published in Great Britain in 1928

PREFACE

THIS book and one to come are intimately connected with my long and close association with that remarkable man, E. W. Scripps. Realist, student, philosopher, successful journalist and business man, and above all humanist, Scripps was quick to see important implications in the biological idea of "the organism as a whole" for humankind, once that idea had gained secure foothold in his mind. As a consequence, even before he had read any comprehensive biological exposition of the idea, he began to wonder what a thorough-going study of human beings from this standpoint would bring to light; for the enigma of man with his infinite capacity for noble thoughts and deeds and his equal capacity for ignoble thoughts and deeds harassed Scripps beyond measure.

By the time my mind and hands had worked themselves free from enthrallment with *The Unity of the Organism*, his demands to know what this "damned human animal is, anyway," became so insistent that I could hardly escape taking them seriously, even though they were not usually leveled at me personally.

These demands, superimposed upon rather strong humanistic and philosophic tendencies of my own, must be put down as the "effective environmental factor" in the production of this book and a companion soon to follow.

The other book will have as title *The Natural Philosophy of Our Conduct*. Despite the circumstance that the product of my task is wrapped up in two packages, the task itself was a unit and not twofold. This follows from the unitary point of view implied by the organismal conception.

Adequate acknowledgment of all to whom I am indebted,

v

more or less personally, for help in carrying forward the undertaking, it would be impossible to give in the narrow bounds of a foreword. It seems, consequently, that my only course is to attempt nothing whatever of the kind. I must trust that my unmentioned helpers will be satisfied with having taken the chance in this case that all of us must and do take constantly, of getting reward for some of our helpful deeds from the vast stores of general but undefinable good which constitutes so large a part of human culture.

I must presume that some at least of the readers of the books would be made uneasy by an entire absence of information concerning the rôle of the collaborator in the enterprise. To Dr. Bailey's own contention that she has not contributed a single fact or idea or argument, at least wholly, I can assent only with much reservation. But whatever dubiousness I may have about what she has not done, I have none about what she has done. Any merits the books may have as to organization, readableness, and cogent presentation of the relevancy to human welfare of the subjects treated, are due far less to me than to her.

WILLIAM E. RITTER.

TABLE OF CONTENTS

CHAPTER 1

INTRODUCTION

THE best part of my life has been devoted to the study of nature. Nature, for me, has always encompassed man in the fullness of his being. This largeness and inclusiveness of nature as it has stood in my conception are largely due, I think, to my having been unwilling to suppress the emotional aspect of my response to nature to any such extent as many scientists seem to do. The emotional part of man has seemed to me no less natural than the coldly rational part. To suppose that in order to deal adequately with nature all emotion must be suppressed appears to presuppose the superior validity of a partial response to nature, as compared with the fullest response of which human beings are capable. This fallacious view concerning the influence of emotion on reason in the study of nature probably has arisen through failure to distinguish between the suppression of emotion and the guidance of it.

I have never been able to find proof that man is apart from nature, is over against and above nature in such a sense as is held by much of philosophy and especially of theology. Never have I had the feeling that there exists an implacable and irreconcilable hostility between man and nature such as sorely harasses many persons and has strongly influenced many religious doctrines. Neither the terrible calamities which befall man occasionally, nor the lesser injuries which he frequently receives at the hands of nature, nor yet the misfortunes, disasters, and miseries which he brings upon himself, have seemed to me to require such doctrines or to be explained by them. The absence of such sentiments from my general consciousness is justified by my maturer, more critical thoughts about the whole scheme of the world and man's place therein. I find no way of conceiving a true Universe, a state of things that is unified through and through, if the human spirit is not inseparably and essentially identified with it all.

The theory according to which man is divine in a sense that nothing else in the world is divine seems to have arisen because many men in many ages have sensed the uniqueness of the powers accruing to them through their possession of conscious rational minds, but have failed to perceive the way in which these powers are connected with the scheme of things by which we live from day to day. There are two aspects of man's relation to nature revealed by scientific study that go far toward explaining the origin of these separatist doctrines. One of these aspects pertains to man's physical make-up; the other to his mind. In these two aspects man must be recognized as the most surprising and marvelous of all natural productions. The most surprising product is he, because of certain of the combinations of his bodily parts; the most marvelous, because of his being conscious, rational, and, at his best, highly intelligent.

The bodily parts to which reference is particularly made are his brain and his hands. That forelimbs terminating in structures called hands should occur in man is not surprising since these structures are almost universally present in land vertebrates. That both hands *and* brain in so high a state of perfection should be man's possession is cause for genuine surprise.

Head and hands, which represent in a sense the developmental and functional climaxes of the nervous system and the muscular system, can be shown to hold such a reciprocal relation to each other that neither could have come into being, nor continue to be, without the other. The powers of knowing which characterize man could never have been acquired, nor could they continue to exist wholly apart from the powers of doing with which his hands endow him. It is the uniqueness of the anatomical combination here presented that is surprising.

While this physical combination of brain and hands is a surprising phenomenon, the consciously knowing and thinking mind is a marvelous phenomenon. The fact that a natural object should be able not only to enter into such relations with other natural objects as that called by us knowing, but should be able also to establish a similar relation with itself, is so distinct from all other natural facts with which we are acquainted and is so far beyond our present powers of analytic description as to entitle it to be characterized as marvelous. Man's supreme glory is not only that he can know the world, but that he can know himself as a knower of the world.

During recent years discoveries and speculation concerning the structure of the stellar universe have been attracting much attention. The facts, certain and highly probable, are justly characterized as wonderful, marvelous. Surely the numbers and sizes of the celestial bodies are wonderful. Wonderful too are the radiations from them, especially in the form of light, by which knowledge is gained. But this wonder comes solely from the augmentation of what is very familiar to us. Sizes, distances, and radiations are around us on every side. No absolutely new kinds of phenomena enter nature by these newly discovered sizes and distances and vast journeys of light. The knowledge obtained by the investigations leading to these discoveries constitutes a kind of relation between man and the celestial objects concerned. A purely physical relation existed before as well as after the knowledge was gained. Stellar gravitation and light act on the child and on the savage just as certainly as on the astronomer. But the moment the physical facts become part of man's knowledge, another sort of relation between him and the objects is established. It is the nature of this new relation and of man's ability to establish it that seems to me to constitute not merely the central wonder of human nature, but the central wonder of all nature.

The doctrines of man's apartness from nature have encouraged an easy-going manner of knowledge-getting which has largely destroyed the sense of the wonderfulness of the ability of an organism to think and reason. By conceiving mind as belonging to a wholly different realm from that to which the other phenomena of nature belong, the realm of the supernatural, we cut ourselves off from any basis of comparison, any standards by which to appraise the powers and capacities of the human mind.

The recognition of man as a part of nature makes it necessary to adopt a different attitude toward his knowledge-getting processes. By such recognition these processes are brought down from the realm of the supernatural into the everyday world of phenomena-which-can-be-known. Like other activities of living things, mental processes must be scrutinized as to their stimuli, their courses, and their fruitfulness. That is to say, they become proper subject-matter for the naturalist. Certain highly respectable thinkers have recognized the possibility and the desirability of a "natural history mode of philosophizing," contrasting such a way of thinking about the universe with the professedly subjective mode on the one hand, and the quantitatively exact or mathematical mode, on the other.

The naturalist's way of working is a different way from that of the theologian, or the metaphysician, or the pure mathematician. It is even a different way from that of many modern biologists who restrict the term biology to knowledge gained from experimentation, and who seek only to explain all organic phenomena in terms of physics and chemistry. In other words the naturalist whose realm of study is living nature, as contrasted with the biologist in the modern, restricted sense of biology, seeks all the knowledge and understanding he can possibly get of organisms, regardless of whether he can express or explain all he observes in terms used in other realms of nature or not.

The naturalist begins his career when he begins his life, and hence has no presuppositions, postulates, and axioms at the outset. These come later. They grow out of his experiences and are not basic for them. His work and his interest date from a time when he has very little else, mentally speaking, than ability to respond to stimuli.

If he should decide to make a professional career of studying some segment of the universe for the purpose of understanding it and helping himself and others to live in it more successfully than they otherwise could, he might find that career taking on two sharply different phases. On the one hand he might be occupied with the job of gathering and interpreting facts about the universe external to himself, and with making them useful to himself and other people. This would make him a thoroughly objective naturalist. His single-minded devotion to his career might be greatly productive of good. Because of its sincerity and simplicity of devotion to ideas and ideals this phase of his career could well be characterized as naïve. While working in this way he might be spoken of as a naïve naturalist, and the phase itself might be called naïve naturalism. Then, should he further determine to study minds and what they accomplish as seriously as he studies the phenomena of the Universe external to himself, he would find himself launched into a quite different undertaking. But since he would find nothing to make him doubt that his newly assumed tasks were any less natural than all he had been doing as a naïve naturalist, he would consider himself as passing into a different phase of his career as a naturalist. This new phase he might well characterize as philosophical,

or critical. He would become a critical naturalist as well
as a naïve naturalist.[1]

My starting-point, my motive, and my procedure in this
book have been strictly that of the naturalist in the twofold sense just defined. Neither as psychologist nor philosopher in the specialized sense of these terms, do I make
any claim for myself. Recognizing that searching and
potent understanding of mind is impossible apart from such
understanding of body, I have attempted to describe the
working of mind-and-body in human beings and in other
living things; to examine critically the mental technique involved in such descriptions; and to reason broadly as to
the bearings of the facts and processes on human life.

A disparaging remark frequently made about certain
persons is that they "do not know their own minds." The
assumption seems to be that all really normal and capable
people do "know their own minds." As a matter of fact
very few people know their own minds even moderately well
in a technical sense, and none know their minds fully.
Neither do people know their own bodies, so far as that goes.
Most of our bodily processes run on quite independently
of our knowledge of them. The organs of digestion do their
work quite as well in the new-born babe as they do in that
same person after he has become a full-fledged physiologist
with digestion as his specialty. It is demonstrable that
many of the processes involved in acquiring knowledge and
in knowing, which are certainly dependent upon the nervous
system, run on as independently of our knowledge of those
processes and their organs, as is the case with the digestive

---

[1] The terms naturalist and naturalism as here used have only a remote connection with those terms as used in traditional philosophy. The
naïve naturalist never seriously doubts either the reality of the objects
with which he is occupied or the trustworthiness of his knowledge of
those objects, once this has been fully verified. Every astronomer,
chemist, botanist, psychologist, or sociologist whose observational knowledge does not permit him to be diverted by dogmatism in one direction
or skepticism in the other, is a naturalist in this sense.

processes and their organs. The mere fact that we have minds and can use them is no evidence that we understand them. If we would know our own minds we must acquire knowledge of them in much the same ways that have made us know our own digestive or circulatory systems.

No one who has considerable acquaintance with any of the biological sciences can have failed to note the constancy with which the comparative method is resorted to. In any good modern treatise on the digestive or circulatory or nervous system of man, the discussions are based upon observations on animals of very diverse rank in the zoological scale, with as little question about the trustworthiness of the facts for elucidating the human problem under treatment as those based on observations on man himself. Within limits which the investigator should know well, the structures and functions of the lower creatures are so similar to the corresponding human structures and functions that the conclusions drawn from them can be applied without hesitation to man also.

This similarity between man and inferior animals in so many physical particulars makes it possible for man to know many things about himself and to do to himself many advantageous things that he could never know and do but for his knowledge concerning these less complex creatures. Such a measure of knowledge of the human circulatory and nervous systems as we now possess could not have been reached but for the opportunity of studying them in their varied and much simpler expressions in the lower orders and particularly in the embryos of these orders. Our enterprise aims to utilize the activities of the lower animals as effectually for enabling us to know our own activities and to control our own conscious acts, as we now utilize the bodies of such animals for enabling us to know our own bodies and to control our purely vegetative functions.

It has long been recognized on the basis of their activities

that many animals possess minds, and that these are similar
in a considerable number of respects to human minds.
Great progress has recently been made in the comparative
study of these two orders of minds, each order having been
made to contribute much to an interpretation of the other;
but no such pronounced success has attended these studies
in the direction of closing the gap between the minds of
brute animals and the minds of men, as has attended the
comparative morphological and physiological studies.   In
consequence of this, although men are well aware of their
supremacy over all other living creatures, we do not yet
possess a thoroughly critical presentation of exactly in what
this supremacy consists.   Such presentation this book will, I
trust, go far toward furnishing.

CHAPTER 2

THE ABILITY OF LIVING BEINGS TO EXIST AND DEVELOP
DESPITE ADVERSE CONDITIONS: THE PHENOMENON
OF ADAPTATION

AMONG the myriads of bodies in the world there is one
great class whose individuals are able to perform a considerable number of acts upon which their continued existence depends. All such bodies we call living, or organic.
There is another great class, the individuals of which we
call non-living, or inorganic, whose continued existence does
not depend on any such actions of their own. One great
subclass of living bodies has greater ability for acting than
another subclass. The more active subdivision we call
animal, the less active vegetable. This way of classifying
the world of bodies is rough-and-ready but unquestionably
true as far as it goes, and useful for our present purposes.

One of the surest tests we can apply toward deciding
whether a strange body is an animal is to touch it and see
whether it moves after the manner familiar to us as animal
movement: movement due to contraction induced by stimulation. So characteristic of animals is action of this kind
that for most ordinary purposes positive results of such an
experiment satisfy us. We conclude it is an animal because
of our wide knowledge that no other bodies than animals
move in that fashion and under such circumstances. This
presents in terms of common experience the familiar generalization as to what essentially characterizes an animal
organism. What animal organisms essentially are, that
plant organisms are also in some of their deepest attributes.
Living beings are fundamentally set apart from non-living
beings by their activities and by what these activities accomplish. Man's way of doing things, especially his ra-

tionally conscious activities, distinguishes him within living nature as a distinct kind of living body, and the very thing that separates man most decisively from nature in general identifies him most closely with living nature.

The undertaking upon which we are entering is grounded in the conviction of the essential correctness of the evolutionary view of man's origin, and his kinship with the whole living world. The soundness of this point of view is examined in Chapters 3 and 4, "The Problem of Man's Origin and Kinship." Accepting it for the present without question, such acceptance implies that any study of man must proceed as a two-fold task: first, to point out those of his characteristics which ally him with the living world generally; and second, to establish with equal clearness those characteristics peculiar or specific to man. This involves special emphasis on the comparative method of Louis Agassiz and the older naturalists; but since it is in man's activities, rather than in his bodily structure that we find his most sharply distinguishing characteristics, our task also resembles that of the student of animal behavior.

The point of view maintained here differs from that of many comparative psychologists in requiring us to consider, not only wherein man's activities resemble those of other animals, but wherein these activities are different. The net result of comparative psychology has tended to dehumanize our conception of man, to throw us back on his possessions held in common with the brutes. The treatment in this book starts with the common heritage of man and brutes, but carries the comparison throughout the range of his endowments and activities, to examine closely wherein he differs from the brutes. The base line for our comparison is found in the unique ability of living things as compared with all other things to fit themselves into different environments. This ability is known as adaptation and is widely recognized in the treatment of man and all other organisms.

There appears to be no human activity whatever that does not have to submit to the question: How well is it done? It is in the very nature of mankind's knowledge of its own activities to recognize that these are of different degrees of excellence. Some carpenters, some lawyers, some base-ball players, are better than others. The good, better, best criterion is applied down to the smallest elements that enter into the various activities. Some generally good carpenters are specially good at inside finishing or perhaps at shingling. Some lawyers are excellent counselors but indifferent advocates. A star out-fielder may be rather poor as a base runner; and so on without end. This perception of difference in excellence of our own acts seems to be as deep seated as our knowledge of the acts.

May the activities of creatures below man be judged in the same way? As to all domestic animals, we surely do judge them thus. With horses, mules and oxen, the good, better, best criterion is applied to their human-service activities. Concerning such activities as egg-laying by hens, milk-giving by cows, and meat-production by hogs, the regular "performance" records kept by farmers tell the story.

But what about wild animals? Any one who has lived by the seaside where he could watch pelicans, cormorants, and other fish-eaters at their fishing, will not hesitate to pronounce these all successful, and hence good fishers. Nobody's observations in this connection would warrant him in supposing the excellence of their fishing to be entirely faultless. Whether the members of any one of the species differ from one another as individual humans differ in fishing ability is by no means easy to decide, so difficult is it to observe in detail, and thus to compare the performances of a large number of individuals. But as to wild animals generally, we now have a sufficient mass of trustworthy observations to make it clear that diversities in quality of performance occur here also. This evidence we hold to be fundamental to our undertaking. It has never been brought together and systematically studied to get at its meaning in relation to human activities.

How effective are those activities of animals by which they solve their problems of getting food, securing mates, protecting themselves from injurious things in their surroundings and securing their welfare generally? This question is the essence of the problem of adaptation as applied to the activities of animals. The larger part of all that has been written about adaptation has referred to the structure of organisms only. When one speaks of birds as being adapted for locomotion in the air, what he thinks of is the structure of the forelimbs, of the feathers, of the shape of the body, and so on. The acts involved in flying are not often thought of as adaptive. Birds are more apt to be spoken of as adapted for than as adapted in flight. As a matter of actual observation, organic activity is far and away more adaptive than is organic structure. Many organic parts, particularly of the higher animals, can act in a variety of ways with little effect on the structures concerned. No one would suppose that the magpie's acquired habit of getting its food from the flesh of live sheep would have any perceptible effect on the bird's beak during an individual life time, and perhaps never for the species as a whole. Yet the change of activity might be very important for the welfare of the individuals concerned. The fact that a mule can use his hind limbs to good effect for kicking does not prove at all that this particular form of action has had any part in determining the form of the hind limbs. So far as we can judge, the mule's hind legs have been developed for one kind of action and he has found he can use them for an additional kind. The variety of acts that every normal human hand performs may be taken as representing the highest exemplification of the general principle that one and the same structure may be used by its possessor in more than one way.

The ordinary knowledge of life contains the idea of adaptation in both structure and activity as essential to life. The idea is inherent in the facts of death and injury as opposed to life and health. Latterly a considerable number of biologists have expressed the view that ordinary knowledge is wrong in holding this idea. It ought either to be applied to both non-living and living bodies or to neither. Living bodies are constituted, just as non-living ones are, of "matter" and "energy" and nothing else. If the idea of adaptation is not needed for lifeless beings (composed of energy-yielding matter) no more is it needed for living ones (also composed of energy-yielding matter), according to these biologists.

We are fundamentally opposed to this view that adaptation is a useless conception for the description and interpretation of vital activity. It is impossible to describe living beings with anything approaching fullness, without constant reference to attributes of them the very existence of which is inseparable from this idea of adaptation. All living beings must have constant supplies of substances called foods; otherwise they die. All such beings must reproduce their kind, or they become extinct as a kind. There is always the possibility of their failing to get food or to propagate. To a very great extent successes and failures in these and various other ways depend on particular structural features of the organisms, and upon what they do or fail to do. This being constructed in such-and-such ways, and acting so-and-so relative to success or failure is what common knowledge calls adaptation. The proposal to eliminate the idea from the biological sciences is tantamount to proposing the elimination from these sciences of the ideas of food-taking, of propagating, of dying, and of all the other ideas best established in all knowledge of organisms. If organisms come into living existence at all and continue to live, doing these things is prima facie proof that they are at least partially adapted to do them.   The alternatives would be that they would never become living, or would not continue to live. The final meaning of adaptation is the continuance of individual life to its wonted end.   The final meaning of maladaptation is the discontinuance of individual life before its wonted end.   Life-or-death for the individual is the final criterion of adaptation.

While adaptation and adaptability in the human species will be the central interest in this book, we shall be obliged to devote much time to adaptation in animals generally. Their successes and failures in solving their life problems will occupy us in Chapters 5 to 14.   The significance of this mass of material for the interpretation of human conduct depends on the assumption that human animals and brute animals belong to one great family by common descent, and that brute activity lends as much assistance to the understanding of human activity as does brute structure to the understanding of human structure.   While the kinship of humans and brutes in bodily structure is generally recognized, their equally significant kinship in mentality as manifest in their activities is not.   To many honest and reverent men, such kinship is open to serious question.

If established, there is no doubt whatever that our conception of Man, and of Nature conceived as including Man, will be changed.   Therefore our next undertaking, in Chapters 3 and 4, will be a careful examination of the evidence available as to the origin and kinships of human beings, giving attention both to the factual evidence and to our mental technique in dealing with it.

CHAPTER 3

THE PROBLEM OF MAN'S ORIGIN AND KINSHIP: FACTUAL EVIDENCE AND ITS PROPER TREATMENT

Our primary interest throughout this book lies in the study of the way in which man's adaptive activities are superior to those of other animals. The value of such a study for human affairs lies in indicating the most effective lines of development, of conscious improvement, of conduct.

Man is, in general, more than a match for the beasts. In the words of the Hebrew Scriptures, the Lord has given him dominion over the earth, beasts and all. In just what manner is this "dominion" made secure? The answer to this question is not to be found in his structure alone. Slow of foot, naked, shivering, short-sighted, dull of ear, on the basis of structure alone man possesses no primacy. When the use of his bodily parts is considered, we find that in the realm of reflexive and instinctive activities, he is still far from establishing superiority. It is only when we come to deal with that group of activities consciously directed toward securing his own well-being, which we call intelligent, that we find man the unquestioned superior of all other living things. Our study therefore becomes psychobiological; and concerned primarily with the development of psychical activities as adaptive agencies.

HOW WE THINK ABOUT EVOLUTION

Our mode of treatment, which may be characterized as that of comparative psychobiology, involves an assumption of the kinship of man with the rest of the living world, and of an especially close kinship with the upper levels of the animal world. "Kinship" as used here is not figurative but literal, carrying the idea of "blood-kin," of common descent, or genetic relationship.

This is too large an assumption, on a matter vital to human welfare, to be taken for granted. It therefore becomes necessary to examine the basis of the assumption in facts and in logic. The degree of probable truth revealed by this examination is a measure of the usefulness of the comparative method for the psychobiological study of man and of the trustworthiness of the generalizations which may be made from the descriptive material to be presented later.

COMMON SENSE AND THE EVOLUTION THEORY

Rational human beings living as part and parcel of animate nature have always known a great deal about and have accepted evolution quite independently of any formal theory of evolution. If any one doubts this let him turn to *The Origin of Species*. "Variation under Domestication" is the title of the first chapter. "Under *domestication*"! what a body of ordinary experience this connotes; and how skillfully Darwin made use of it!

The main classes of facts and principles upon which rests the evolution theory are well-known and unquestioningly accepted. Such knowledge while positive enough and implicitly trusted does not reach much beyond the bounds of immediate observation and experience. With reference to every one of the basic principles considered, the question arises as to whether or not they do hold good beyond the scope of common experience and knowledge. A serious attempt to answer the question would, if the answer were affirmative, result in a general hypothesis and theory, or doctrine of evolution.

As is well known, such an hypothesis and theory were

ushered into the modern world by the publication about sixty-five years ago of *The Origin of Species by Means of Natural Selection*. This epochal book dealt, not with the all-embracing problem of organic development, but with one specific though crucial aspect of it, namely that of how new species originate; and it proposed and defended with great ability a casual explanation of such origin. This is the point at which man's understanding of the phenomena of development in living nature may be considered to have passed from the realm of common knowledge to that of technical knowledge, and marks the beginning, in modern times at least, of study by the methods and for the purposes of science of the origin of those species or kinds which compose the vast world of living things.

From the broad outlook to which we have been led by the progress of knowledge since Darwin's great book was written, we see that instead of defining the evolution theory as being a theory of the "origin of species" merely, it should be defined as the theory that the well-known principles governing the origin of the comparatively few organisms with which the common life of man has made him familiar, govern also the origin of the whole living world. Common knowledge now accepts evolution as the mode of the origin of individual men and all other organisms, animal and plant. There is no longer any question that men and animals and plants originate from parent organisms. The idea of "spontaneous generation," the origin of organisms without parents, widely prevalent up to seventy-five years ago, is now wholly discarded in common teaching and experience no less than in technical teaching and experience.

Nor does the common acceptance of evolution stop with its application to the growth of individuals, and the causation of individuals by other individuals. Such acceptance has now gone far into the more obscure realm of the origin of *kinds* of individuals. In agriculture, in horticulture, in floriculture, in animal husbandry, and in pet-animal culture, new kinds are so numerously produced that they are much more commonly seen than are the original or parent kinds. The principles upon which such producing depend are widely known and applied, even more so by non-technical persons than by professional biologists. New varieties of potatoes, tomatoes, corn, and wheat; of roses, dahlias, daisies and irises; of chickens, sheep, pigs, cats, dogs, and rabbits, are so commonplace as to attract little attention except for their usefulness or beauty. So far as the evolution or development of a great variety of kinds of organisms is concerned, common sense not only accepts it in knowledge and faith but goes much further than that. It actually lives by it, thus applying to it the supreme test of all knowledge and faith in conduct.

THE PRINCIPLE OF IDENTITY IN THE EVOLUTION THEORY

One of the things which makes the problem of origin of new kinds or species peculiarly difficult, no matter from what angle it be approached, is the fact that it inevitably involves the problem of the origin of man himself. As was fully recognized by Darwin and practically every other naturalist or philosopher or theologian who has tried seriously to understand the nature of man, his resemblance to other living beings, especially the higher animals, has been obvious enough to arouse the strong conjecture that the ultimate origin of man was involved with the ultimate origin of all the rest of the animate world. The tremendous hold on men's minds and the influence upon their lives exerted by *The Origin of Species* was only secondarily due to the purely scientific problem of how new kinds of plants and inferior animals originate. The power of the book lay and still lies in its emotional impingement upon man's own life as dependent upon how he came into being. This vital truth it is necessary to take full cognizance of in such an undertaking as we are engaged upon.

Why is it that men have so generally desired a mode of racial origin wholly different from and presumably superior to the well-known mode of individual origin? Why have men felt that a supernatural or divine mode of racial origin would be better for them than any natural mode would be, even though they were obliged to be satisfied with a natural mode of individual origin?

Broad information about man in different stages of his culture shows him to be more solicitous about the character of his origin in advanced than in lowly states of his development. Many savage peoples are apparently well satisfied with the idea that they originated from animal or from even more lowly subhuman ancestors. On the other hand, most of the highly cultivated peoples, as those of Christian nations, have been and still are sorely disturbed by any questioning of their supposed supernatural origin. Why is this? An element in the explanation is the fact that men are strongly given to believing their own present natures depend upon the source from which they came in a sense close examination finds not to be correct.

No one now doubts that in general "like produces like" in organic propagation, that the nature of organisms is determined in some sense by the nature of their parents and other ancestors. From the standpoint of the knowledge-processes involved in our knowing anything about the nature and origin of natural bodies, we recognize that in another sense the nature of the organism is quite independent of its origin. Neither the reality of any object nor the certainty of our knowledge about it depend upon what we know or do not know about the origin of that object. The sugar with which you sweeten your breakfast coffee is sugar and not salt or anything else, regardless of whether it originated from sugar-cane or sugar-beets. It makes not the slightest difference in your certainty that you have put sugar and not salt into your coffee, whether you have any information about where the sugar came from and how it originated. Knowledge of form, structure, activities of any object, and knowledge of the origin of that object are wholly distinct so far as actual knowledge in itself is concerned.

According to the principle of identity, a man is a man regardless not merely of any hypothesis or doctrine which may be held concerning his origin, but regardless of his actual origin. If I meet *A*, a person whom I have never before seen or heard of, and if upon becoming more or less personally acquainted with him, I decide to call him "a man," it would be a violation of this principle for me to deny later that he is a man, merely on the strength of something I might have learned in the meanwhile about his origin.

The history of man is filled with violations of this principle. Every prophet, taking the word in its usual meaning of a person held to be something more than human, illustrates such violation. A famous instance from "profane" history is that of Alexander the Great and his episode with the Egyptian god Zeus Ammon. We take in substance the story as told by Grote. During the three years just preceding the entrance of the Conqueror into Egypt, his achievements "had transcended the expectations of every one, himself included—the gods had given to him such incessant good fortune, and so paralyzed or put down his enemies—that the hypothesis of a superhuman personality seemed the natural explanation of such a superhuman career. This caused him to recur to the heroic legends which connected his own ancestral line with Perseus and Herakles. He resolved to ascertain the fact about his own real nature by questioning "the infallible oracle of Zeus Ammon" at a temple to the god on a remote oasis in the desert. After a hard journey the temple was reached and Alexander was addressed by the priest "as being the son of the god" (probably quite to Alexander's surprise!). Grote bases his acceptance of the genuineness of Alexander's faith in his own supernatural origin and nature partly on "that exorbitant vanity which from the beginning reigned so largely in his bosom." Today, with wider knowledge of the development of the human mind, we can accept it as not so much a display of excessive vanity as a fairly typical manifestation of human nature in a particular developmental stage.

Of the numerous examples which could easily be cited in which men and women of our own day have made themselves and others believe they possessed supernatural powers of one sort or another, we mention only Joseph Smith, the founder of Mormonism. In *The Book of Mormon* Smith "was declared to be God's 'prophet' with all power and entitled to all obedience." According to the system of the doctrine of the Mormon church, not only Joseph Smith but also Brigham Young are listed with Christ and Mahomet as "partaking of divinity." [1] The history and present state of Mormonism are very illuminating as to what is possible today, in a modern civilization, in the super-naturalization of human beings.

Critical attention to the history of man's understanding of himself shows conclusively that in the systems of positive knowledge and theory which he has built up on the subject, he has tried in various ways to make himself something different from what he actually is by conceiving a mode of origin for himself specially favorable to what he desired to be.

The effort in all such cases is to gain some advantage for or through the person held to be specially endowed by attributing to him powers over and above any thing he could be supposed to possess as "mere man." Such en-

[1] "Mormonism," *Encyclopædia Britannica*.

dowment must be supposed to have originated somehow, sometime. A common way of conceiving this origination has been to impute it to the birth of the person. The case of Alexander illustrates this. Another way of conceiving the origin of the unique endowments has been that of supposing the persons to have been the recipients, sometime after birth in the ordinary manner, of special Gifts or Visitations from on High. The Joseph Smith case is an example of this.

THE PROBLEM OF NAMING A DEVELOPING THING

Our decision to attempt to answer the question of whether evolution is universally as well as narrowly true by expanding into technical knowledge our already-possessed common knowledge of organic origin and development gives this effort a peculiar character. If the attempt should lead us to an affirmative answer we should find ourselves in the wholly unique position of an organism trying to discover, by its own processes of getting knowledge, how the organism itself came into existence. We should be involved in the curious undertaking of directing our own knowledge processes, which can be such only while they are going on, to finding out when and how they went on sometime in the past. Does the effort decided upon involve such absurdity? Undoubtedly many philosophers have thought so. Certainly the great rank and file of ordinary mortals have felt so, though they have not raised the feeling into expressible thought. That is the reason why so much of mankind has believed itself in need of, and to have received, Divine Revelation touching matters which concerned it most vitally. Man has not been willing to trust his own ordinary knowledge-getting ability to furnish him with all he has desired to know about himself: his ultimate origin, highest earthly welfare, and final end. If we make up our minds to trust our own knowledge-getting powers in our effort to answer the question of our own origin, we ought to give careful attention to the character of those powers and the processes by which they work. Many a professed evolutionist has launched boldly upon the sea of evolutional theory as applied to man, whose fitness for the task so far as concerns knowledge of the working of his own mind was distinctly questionable.

Our enterprise of applying technical knowledge to the evolution theory must therefore begin by learning something about the nature of that knowledge itself. We must attend to the knowledge processes involved in acquiring, arranging and connecting facts, as well as to the facts themselves. Every objective fact like every other fact is just itself and nothing else, and cannot change into any other fact. The moiety of an objective fact that inheres in the object or body observed can disappear and be replaced by the corresponding part of some other fact, as when the green of summer foliage is replaced by the brown or red of autumn foliage. Each fact has another moiety belonging to the mind, and the permanence of this latter does not depend on the single objective fact. If we are to understand and trust facts, we must consider their subjective as well as their objective moities.

Let us notice, therefore, how we think about or reason about some of the simplest, most common cases of "organic evolution." Take the case of the evolution of the adult man or woman from the new-born babe. That the development up to adulthood consists not merely in increase in size but in many pronounced changes, structural and functional, is obvious. Reflect on how we think and talk about such evolutions. To be very specific take a boy baby a month old. Let us "name" him Robert. When he is a year old he is still Robert, is he not? And when he is ten, or fifteen, or one-and-twenty, Robert he still is, despite all that he was not on the christening day. Is the Robert of *Tam O'Shanter* really the same as the month-old Robert of the rude Scottish home? And the Robert of victory at Chancellorsville, is he truly the same as the just-christened Virginian Robert?

One is tempted to answer these questions negatively by trying to think out too fully how it can possibly be that such frail and inconsiderable bits of flesh and blood as were these two infant Roberts should become the great forces in the world they did become. In reality, the name Robert E. Lee was never intended by those who gave it to the infant Virginian to fit the infant merely. It was given with the full intention that it would be as applicable to the mature man and all the stages intervening between infancy and maturity as to the infant stage. Names, as proper names of individual humans, are in their very nature expansive enough to cover not only potentiality and actuality but also different stages and kinds of actuality. The infant, the lad, the youth, are all actually what they are as well as potentially what they are to become.

Notice what we do in thinking and talking about such cases, for the purpose of conforming ourselves to what actually occurs in nature and in history, even though we are greatly perplexed as to just how and just why it occurs. At the outset we designate one indubitably observed natural object with the label "Robert Burns" and another with "Robert E. Lee." In doing this we commit ourselves to applying these designations to the respective objects just as long as we can observe them and identify them as continuations of what we have observed before, no matter how little or how much they may change from the one time of observation to another. Robert Burns is Robert Burns and Robert E. Lee is Robert E. Lee exactly as sugar is sugar.

How can this be so in view of the fact that we have accepted the famous Robert as an observational reality, just as unquestioningly as we have accepted the infant? It "can be" so by our making it so. We make it so by a kind of mental sleight of hand always practiced in connection with our naming such objects. That sleight of hand consists in stretching somewhat the mark whenever we need to in order to make it cover or include the whole of the object marked. While the object bearing the mark, Robert Burns, is unquestionably quite different in the Tam O'Shanter period of its life from what it was in the month-old-infant period, the mark itself remains the same. Consequently the capacity, or as we ordinarily say the definition of the mark must be enlarged. It will be useful to compare the names applied to persons with the names applied to clothes worn by them. While we do not enlarge a man's name [2] with his advancing years so definitely and consciously as we do his clothes, that we do it as certainly there is not the least doubt.

In common practice nobody ever thinks of the name Robert E. Lee as having exactly the same scope and content when applied to the great commander as when applied to the infant; just as nobody ever questions that Robert E. Lee is Robert E. Lee whether in the infant, school-boy, West Point Cadet, or Commanding-General stage of his life. Common sense never goes wrong among highly civilized peoples in these matters. Proper names of individuals as ordinarily used are really general names the scope of which is over the series of developmental stages in time as contrasted with general names the scope of which is over groups of individuals; that is in space.[3] So far as any name

[2] The whole matter of naming objects presents great complexity among all peoples, especially among those of primitive culture. "No more strange and fascinating study of the vagaries of the human mind is supplied," writes Edward Clodd, "than is furnished by this phenomenon of the written and spoken name; and in the early stages of society it played no small part in the identification of the human with the non-human" ("Primitive Man on His Own Origin," *Quarterly Review*, July, 1911, p. 117).

[3] If this is correct, Mill's statement, "Proper names are attached to the objects themselves, and are not dependent upon the continuance of

can be applied to an individual organism, especially to a developing organism, it must be general or "it would be useless as a guide to action." [4]

ACTUALITY AND POTENTIALITY IN EVOLUTION

Another aspect of the evolution problem which adds to its complication both in its phenomenal phase, and in its psychological-logical phase is the difficulty of including in our conception of an organism the potentiality or latent capacity which every organism has in any one of its developmental stages to pass into the next stage. The evolution of the oak from the acorn, of the hen from the egg, and of every other organism from its germ, are illustrations. Here again common knowledge, because of the commonness of the phenomenon and the absolute dependence of human existence upon it, always goes right so long as it is contented to operate within its own proper sphere, but is in constant danger of getting into rational difficulties when it tries to go beyond that sphere.

In behalf of thinking correctly as well as merely noticing correctly let us consider a particular instance. Take the development of the silkworm moth. Recall the sharply set-off stages into which the individual life history of this insect divides itself—egg, larva, pupa, imago. These stages are so different from one another that were each studied only by itself it could hardly be suspected that each comes from the other in the order mentioned. Since, however, a great many persons have raised silkworms, there is not the least question that the various stages originate thus, and that each individual moth lives for a time in these distinct forms.

---

any attribute of the object" (*A System of Logic*), would not be true. By what means could the parents of Robert E. Lee recognize their son upon his return after months of absence if there were no "continuance of any attribute" of the son?

[4] Carveth Read, *The Origin of Man and His Superstitions,* p. 99.

No silkworm raiser has any more doubt about the sameness of an individual from egg to winged adult than has the human mother about the sameness of her child from infancy to middle life.

What do we do in our ordinary thinking and talking about such evolutionary phenomena as that of the ability of the egg to transform into the larva, of the larva into the encased pupa, and of the pupa into the imago? There are two things in particular which we take on faith every time we say or do anything involving such cases. We recognize the latent capacity of each stage to undergo just the transformation it actually does undergo. We take it for granted it will do so, and our faith is of such kind and degree as to cause us to base on it common and very important actions. Every seed-planting by the farmer, every egg-hatching by the poultry man, every moth-imago production by the silk raiser is an act of faith. Farmer, poultry-man, and silk-raiser base their actions to only a slight extent on what they can observe in the particular kernels of wheat, hen-eggs, and cocoons from which they expect to get wheat-plants, chickens, and moth-imagoes. Nor yet do they base them upon certain knowledge of the outcome. They rely on hundreds of thousands of instances in their own and other people's past experiences that such kernels, such eggs, and such pupæ actually do give rise to plants, chickens, and moths of the desired kind.

When the farmer or poultryman examines his seed grain and breed eggs he does this merely to discover whether they are "good," i.e., are the kind, as grain and as eggs, that he wants. The farmer has no expectation of discovering anything in the kernel of wheat that will of itself reveal to him what kind of plant it will produce or indeed if it will produce a plant at all. Had no one ever before seen kernels of wheat and wheat plants, no amount of examination of such a kernel could yield the slightest hint as to what it would transform into. It is a striking limitation on man's knowledge-acquiring ability that he has no sensory equipment for apprehending directly what is only potential in natural bodies. Observation on a piece of ice gives us no direct information about water as fluid and steam.

The second thing taken on faith is our belief that any full-grown plant or animal with which we have to do was produced from a germ and passed through developmental or evolutional stages of some sort whether any one has ever actually seen these germs and stages or not. The experiences of other persons and of ourselves that plants and animals do arise in this way, and the complete absence of experience that they arise in any other way, is the sole basis of this faith. The literalness and force of the truth that faith is the evidence of things not seen, are rarely recognized. How often and how closely do any of us examine the grounds of our belief that every person we see was born of a woman? As a matter of fact, with the great majority of us the belief rests on no direct experience at all. Only a small portion of us have actually observed a single birth. How much direct evidence is there that you and I and most other people came into existence in this way? It is not surprising that despite the overwhelming probability that all human beings are "born of woman," great and varied confusion should have arisen on the subject in early ages among lowly people.[5] In dealing with any organic development we always, consciously or subconsciously, recognize potentialities of some familiar pattern; and we similarly recognize that whatever structures or activities are observable have sometime been merely potential, i.e., present though not in the form or activity in which we now observe them. The

[5] Although the doubts and confusions to which the human mind has been subject in connection with the origin of individual humans have been largely removed for modern men, they are not wholly things of the past by considerable. That cases like those of Alexander the Great and Joseph Smith (p. 23) are remnants of the same old confusion there seems to be no question.

young infant's teeth we know to be present in germ long
before they are cut and brought into active service.

The reasoning involved in our common knowledge of the
evolutional origin of the individual man leads us to believe
in the evolutional origin of the species man. As an individual, he probably originated from some other individual; as
a species he probably originated from some other species.
Even in the case of individuals concerning the origin of
whom we are without direct, positive knowledge, our conclusions that these were born of mothers can be only probably true even though the probability be so great as to
leave no room for serious question. The factual and logical
conditions involved in the problem of the origin of the
species man are such as to make the probable truth of the
evolutional origin as much as we shall ever be able to
attain. We are able to conclude that the evolutional origin
of the species is more probably true than is its origin by any
other mode that has been suggested.

We saw the indubitability of stages in individual evolution, every one of which presents a certain amount of actuality and a certain amount of potentiality. Every stage
is being something and doing something now, and also is
capable of becoming something somewhat different, and doing something else later. Metamorphosis, or change of form
and of ability to act despite a certain degree of continuous-
ness and sameness, constitutes the very fabric of our lives.
Not the obscurity but the familiarity of all this blinds us.

Finally, we dwelt upon the naturalness with which our
every-day thought and speech adapt themselves to the situation so far as our own practical lives are concerned. The
word Man, as it is used in all ordinary experience, includes
the whole developmental series from babyhood to full man-
hood, not only of some one or a few human beings but of all
human beings. With equal legitimacy, it is applied to all
the innumerable kinds and stages and ages of men revealed

by history and anthropology. The term "Man" is one of our most common and useful generic terms, "generic" having its logical meaning, a term applied to many things sufficiently alike to warrant combining them into one group but at the same time enough unlike to warrant dividing the groups into subgroups, these subgroups again having individuals of still other likenesses.

THE PRINCIPLE OF RESEMBLANCE AND THE EVOLUTION THEORY

"The evolution problem" conceived as applying to the origin of species is only part of the whole problem. For surely individuals orginate and develop as well as do species. The knowledge processes involved in the two parts of the problem must have much in common. Applying the same reasoning to the part of the problem dealing with the origin of the human species as to the part dealing with the origin of the individual led us to conclude that the species must have originated from some other species. But this conclusion suggested no more as to what the parent species may have been than that it most probably resembled rather closely the offspring species.

Nothing is more crucial for sound reasoning on the problem of origins in living nature, including the origin of species, than the use we make of, and the reliance we place on, resemblance. If I see in a zoölogical garden an adult gorilla recently captured in an African forest, how do I affirm with so much confidence that it was born of gorilla parents? Many elements enter into the how; absolutely basic and indispensable is the resemblance of the creature before me to other creatures which in common practice have been called gorillas. No amount of knowledge of the laws of animal reproduction and heredity would of itself enable me to make this assertion or would increase my confidence in its truth.

The first man who cultivated regularly any crop, as rice or maize, was in as little doubt about what he would have to do at every seed time in order to get a crop as any scientific farmer or geneticist can be. His recognition of resemblance between crop after crop at the harvest time was the most fundamental element in his confidence. Resemblance plays an indispensable part in knowledge of any developmental series. If I have before me a developing animal embryo concerning the identification of which I am doubtful, I watch the changes it undergoes from day to day. As soon as I become satisfied that the upper and lower jaw regions of its head are being drawn out and encased in peculiar hard epidermal sheaths, one large block of my doubt instantly vanishes. Bird! What is it that thus drives away my doubts? It is my recognition of the resemblance of the newly arrived part to what, from an abundance of past observation by myself and others, I know as "bird's beak."

That the principle of resemblance plays a much more important part in all biological reasoning, especially in all reasoning about development, than is ordinarily appreciated, has been disclosing itself to me little by little from the years when I taught embryology and comparative anatomy. With this gradual disclosure has come increasing surprise at the inadequacy of treatment the subject receives in such textbooks and treatises on logic as I have been able to consult. Being a naturalist, I have been occupied primarily with problems of the living world and only secondarily with the problems of mind as the chief means through which I and my fellow naturalists are thus occupied. Such excursions as I have made into the field of theory of knowledge and of logic have been mainly in search of aid to my efforts at knowing the world. These excursions brought very slight

success until *A Treatise on Probability* by J. M. Keynes
came into my hands and I had read the portion dealing with
analogy (which the author seems to regard as essentially
the same thing as resemblance). I had supposed that the
kind of aid I needed was available somewhere, and that my
failure to secure it had been due to an unfortunate choice
of authorities. In this book we read: "Inductive processes
have formed of course at all times a vital, habitual part of
the mind's machinery. Whenever we learn by experience,
we are using them. But in the logic of the schools they
have taken their proper place slowly. No clear or satisfactory account of them is to be found anywhere. Within
and yet beyond the scope of formal logic, on the line, apparently, between mental and natural philosophy, Induction
has been admitted into the organon of scientific proof, without much help from the logicians, no one quite knows
when." [6]   No one is quite so well able as the thoughtful
student of biological development to appreciate the truth
and the force of this paragraph. It is surprising and significant, both for the attitude of logicians toward science and
for the attitude of scientists toward their own mental processes, that nothing adequate for the present state of advancement of natural knowledge has been done, especially in the
domain of induction and analogy, the very domain in which
the principle of resemblance chiefly operates.

[6] P. 217.

CHAPTER 4

THE PROBLEM OF MAN'S ORIGIN AND KINSHIP (*con.*):
CERTAINTY AND PROBABILITY AS TO MAN'S EVOLUTION

WE have previously recognized that there is not the least prospect of our ever knowing absolutely from what ancestral species we descended. The best we can do is to increase as much as possible the probabilities in the case. We have also found that resemblance plays a great and indispensable part in establishing such probabilities. Let us now turn to this specific task: Where in the whole subhuman animal series do we find the most numerous and closest resemblances to man?

If resemblance has played as large a part in man's speculations about his own kinship and origin as we have assumed we should expect modern science to seek with special eagerness among the primates for human likenesses. We should also expect that those primitive peoples who have inhabited portions of the earth likewise inhabited by primates would fix upon some of their primate neighbors as being their own closest kindred. There are numerous legends involving the confusion of monkeys and men in all lands occupied by both. The illustrations selected are taken from E. B. Tylor. "One of the most perfect identifications of the savage with the monkey in Hindustan," we read, "is the following description of the *bunmanus,* or 'Man of the woods' (Sanskr. *vana*=wood, and *manusha*=man). 'The bunmanus is an animal of the monkey kind. His face has a near resemblance to the human; he has no tail and walks erect. The skin of his body is black and slightly covered with hair.' That this description really applies not to apes, but to the dark-skinned non-Aryan aborigines of the land, appears further in the enumeration of the local dialects of Hindustan, to which it is said 'may be added the jargon of the bunmanus or wild man of the woods.' " [1]

And further: "In the islands of the Indian Archipelago, whose tropical forests swarm both with high apes and low savages, the confusion between the two in the minds of the half-civilized inhabitants becomes almost inextricable." [2] So much for the recognition of resemblance between apes and men in Asia.

For Africa and South America we have: "To people who at once believe monkeys a kind of savages, and savages a kind of monkeys, men with tails are creatures coming under both definitions. Thus the Homo caudatus, or satyr, often appears in popular belief as a half-human creature, while even in old-fashioned works on natural history he may be found depicted on the evident model of an anthropoid ape. In East Africa, the imagined tribe of long-tailed men are also monkey-faced, while in South America the *coata tapuya,* or 'monkey-men,' are as naturally described as men with tails." [3]

Would any present-day anthropologist who interprets *Pithecanthropus* as a connecting link between man and ape contend that he has at his command some principle of interpretation other than that of resemblance, which gives his conclusions a probability of truth entirely different from that which has been producing imaginary connecting links through the ages of man's observations upon himself and his anthropoid contemporaries? Who is so bold as to deny that the connecting links reconstructed today on the basis of the fragmentary paleontological information we possess may at some future time be characterized as "old-fashioned works on natural history"? This reflection is not designed to

[1] *Primitive Culture,* Vol. I, p. 380.
[2] *Ibid.,* p. 381.
[3] *Ibid.,* p. 383.

imply that these modern efforts at closing up evolutionary gaps are unjustifiable and useless, but to emphasize their hypothetical and tentative nature; to focus attention on the fact that resemblance (structural resemblance alone at that) is basic in them; and finally to remind ourselves that logically similar efforts have been made for thousands of years and by numberless observers.

In the combined light of our present-day factual knowledge of organic beings and our insight into the operations of our minds in getting and using this knowledge, what are we justified in believing as to the ancestry of the human species? Our examination has revealed that neither do we know absolutely, nor is there any likelihood that we ever shall know exactly, from what other species we originated. It is in the highest degree more probable that we originated in such a way than that we originated in any other way that has ever been suggested. The probability of our having originated from some other species is very much greater than the probability that we originated from any particular species which we can specify.

There are only two kinds of evidence upon which we rely for proof of the origin of anything whatever. Most fundamental is the evidence of knowledge through direct experience. Beyond this is probability dependent at bottom on resemblance. Our task is that of sifting from the vast body of factual knowledge we now possess, those portions which will enable us to decide what subhuman species the human species most closely resembles.

Part of this task has already been performed, not by science in the strict sense of today, but by the common knowledge of innumerable peoples and ages. That man's resemblance to the animal creatures below him, especially to the "beasts of the field" is closer than to any other natural objects has been recognized always and everywhere in human history. Many people have gone much further in the task than the mere recognition of these resemblances. They have designated particular animal kinds as being originative of man, if not his actual ancestors. Many of the myths and legends of primitive peoples which implicate animals in the origin of man are, from the standpoint of the theory of knowledge, in the nature of hypotheses involving the genetic kindred of many of the animals concerned. Stories of direct origin of man from animals are extremely common. Students of California Indians dwell on the part which the coyote plays in the origin and lives of these people. We read: "The present mode of life is determined by the results of the activities of the beneficent Creator and the tricky Coyote." A point deserving special notice here is the conception of coöperation between Creator and coyote in doing the job. Many such instances might be cited from the mythology of human origination.

No single group of superstitions is more striking than is totemism. Certain facts suggest the warrantableness of looking upon this institution as a sort of prescientific stage of the evolution theory. The word totemism "was first applied at the end of the last century . . . to the Red Indian custom which acknowledges human kinship with animals." [4] One of the highest developments of totemism, certainly its highest expression in art forms, is among the Indians of Northwest America, familiar in the totem poles of many museums. Apparently all authorities agree that the idea of kindred between the totemites and their totems is common, if not universal, and that the most common totems are animals. From Clodd's endorsement of Lang's theory of the origin of totemism we read: "We feel bound to say that . . . if there be any approach to a solution of the origin of totemism, Mr. Lang's theory most commends itself as having valid ground in certain world-wide savage conceptions which supply sufficient material for tracing the

[4] Andrew Lang, *Myth, Ritual and Religion*, Vol. I, p. 59.

development of that institution. These are, belief in kinship between man and brute, and in the names of things as integral parts of things." [5]

It is impossible to contend that all the varieties of totemism known to exist now depend directly upon resemblance and kinship between the totemists and their totems, but a general survey of totemism shows clearly that animals, especially mammals and birds, are the predominant totems. Out of a total of 202 such objects enumerated by these authors, 164 are animals, 22 are plants, and 16 are inanimate things.[6] "Animals," Read says, "lend the greatest plausibility to any notion of blood-relationship. . . ." "To hunters animals must have been of all things the most interesting." [7] Why should animals be the most interesting of all things to hunters? The reply which comes to one's mind first, that it is because they are the objects of the hunter's pursuit and largely his sustenance, does not tell the whole story. The evidences are innumerable that animals have been among the most interesting things to most people whether hunters or not. This interest has been due largely to the recognition of resemblance of the animals to men.

Man at all levels of his culture tends to respond emotionally to animals somewhat differently in both quality and intensity from what he does to any other natural objects. Even our modern interest in animals is by no means circumscribed by the economic use we can put them to or the fears we have of them. Our way of companioning with them and making pets of them in certain cases, and of standing in mortal fear of them and making them symbols of the worst of evils in other cases, is quite without parallel outside the animal kingdom. The zoölogy of toydom is an unmistak-

[5] "Primitive Man on His Own Origin," by Edward Clodd, *Quarterly Review*, July, 1911.
[6] Appendix B, Spencer and Gillen.
[7] *The Origin of Man and His Superstitions*, p. 296.

able witness to mankind's fundamental relation to animal life. The great vogue in modern times of effort against cruelty to animals, manifesting itself at times in the highly commendable societies having this designation, and at other times in the highly condemnable crusades against experimentation on animals for the furtherance of scientific knowledge, may be interpreted in the same way.

It is not difficult to recognize something of the psychobiology of this peculiar interest of man in animals. The fact that so many of the most common of them have two eyes much like our own and a face that can be "looked into," tells a large part of the story. Man's association with the dog is especially significant. Full of meaning are such familiar remarks about this animal as "he looked up into my face with an almost human expression." But the dog is by no means the only creature the face and eyes of which make a peculiar appeal to man. Indelibly stamped upon my own mind are the faces, with their strange eyes, of the first sheep I as a very small child ever saw at close range.

Writing on totemism, A. A. Goldenweisser [8] has the following on the point before us. "While plants and inanimate things have long since been relegated to the realm of the matter-of-fact, animals still inhabit a region where fact and fancy are peacefully wedded together. As between the animal and its human master, verbal usage reveals a common range of physical and psychic qualities. One thinks of the eagle eye, the leonine heart, the dogged perseverance, the bull-neck. Current metaphor, half earnest half jest, has introduced the fox and the beaver, the bear and the rabbit, the cat and the cow, the ape and the shark, as characters of the human scene." Surely this is not due to pure fancy. It rests on a basis of some resemblance. The effect of these unescapably recognizable likenesses between humans and inferior animals upon the minds of people very low

[8] *Early Civilization*, 1922, p. 289.

in the cultural scale must be especially intense and difficult for us of higher culture to appreciate.

The kinship recognized in totemism is of at least three quite distinct kinds. The most important of these from the evolutionary standpoint is that which assumes descent in the strict meaning of the word. This is found in many parts of the world. A typical example is furnished by the creation story of some of the natives of Australia. "The origin of the first-formed human beings is ascribed to two individuals named *ungambikula* who lived in the western sky, and, seeing far away to the east a mob of *inapertwa,* creatures who were the incomplete transformations of animals and plants, came down to earth, and with their knives released their half-formed arms and legs, cut open their mouths, bored holes for nostrils, slit the eyelids apart, and thus out of the *inapertwa* made men and women. . . . The totemic ancestors who originated in this way marched in groups across the country, every one of them carrying with him, or her, not only a personal *Churinga,* but often many others also." [9]

A second variety of kindred recognized in totemism is what may be called kindred by adoption. Persons of one totem may upon occasion be adopted into another totem otherwise than through the regular avenue of marriage from one totem into another. This involves a change of name, the name borne by a totemic group being usually a vital matter. A process of adoption, of bestowing a group name (in logic a generic name) with an appropriate ceremony, establishes a kind of heredity and kindred which may be superior in power to actual genetic heredity. Nor is it essential that this kindred by adoption shall be based on any known blood kindred. There are many cases in which adopted children of no blood relation whatever enjoy all the bonds in affection,

[9] *The Northern Tribes of Central Australia,* by Baldwin Spencer and F. J. Gillen, 1904, p. 150.

social and family advantages and legal benefits enjoyed by blood kindred. There is not the slighest question that resemblance contributes greatly to the possibility of forming these relations. White people might adopt negro or Indian children and become very fond of them. I doubt if any one would contend that parental feeling could ever go out quite as strongly and inclusively to such children as to adoptions within the same race.

A third form of kindred resulting from the custom of totemism might be called animistic kindred. In our modern English terminology, this is an affair of spirits or ghosts. The kindred assumed in totemism may sometimes be through the mediumship of spirits, and have little or no reference to lineage in the sense of modern genetics. According to the meaning of animism which rests upon the most indubitable observation, any object whatever may have something in it (a spirit) which is not the thing itself but is the real cause or explanation of the thing, or at least of some of its attributes. A stream, a mountain, a stone, may have each its appropriate spirit. There is always some sort of correspondence or resemblance between the object and its spirit. The closer the resemblance between man himself and any particular object the closer would be the resemblance between the human spirit and that of the object. As to animals, especially the higher animals, the resemblance of which to man is so striking in many respects, the resemblance between these spirits and man's spirit would naturally be correspondingly close.

A main attribute of spirits is their ability to separate themselves upon occasion from the objects they inhabit and enter into other objects; thus, the stage is well set for all manner of mix-ups among the spirits of animals and men. Hardly anything plays a larger part in the lives of primitive peoples than this very matter of their own commingling, largely via their spirits, with their animal neighbors. One

of the most learned of all writers in this field tells us:
"The sense of an absolute psychical distinction between man
and beast, so prevalent in the civilized world, is hardly to
be found among the lower races. Men to whom the cries of
beasts and birds seem like human language, and their actions
guided as it were by human thought, logically enough allow
the existence of souls to beasts, birds and reptiles, as to men.
The lower psychology cannot but recognize in beasts the
very characteristics which it attributes to the human soul,
namely, the phenomena of life and death, will and judgment,
and the phantom seen in vision or in dream. As for believers, savage or civilized, in the great doctrine of metem-
psychosis, these not only consider that an animal may have
a soul, but that this soul may have inhabited a human being
and thus the creature may be in fact their own ancestor or
once familiar friend." [10]

We have, I hope, now gone far enough in our study of
man's world-wide and eons-old efforts to satisfy his curiosity about his own origin to recognize three basic things
about these efforts: The great majority of them have linked
man in some organic, vital way with the rest of living nature,
especially with the animals assigned by zoölogical science to
a place in the system of classification not far below man:
what we moderns call the logical principle of analogy (positive and negative) or of resemblance and difference, has
played a very great part in these efforts; that the conception
of immaterial entities (shadows, ghosts, spirits, souls) similar to but independent of and often separable from man,
other animals and plants and natural objects generally, have
been very widely invoked, always to the detriment of clear
understanding and effective treatment of the objects concerned.

Our modern problem of the origin of man is the same old
problem by which man has been confronted in all his history.

[10] *Primitive Culture,* by Edward B. Tylor, sixth ed., Vol. I, p. 469.

All peoples have had some sort of explanation of their own origin, embodied for the most part in religious tradition and cherished as a precious part of the racial heritage. It seems a question we cannot let sleep, this matter of whence and how we have come. We moderns are able to state it more exactly than any of our predecessors, and have vastly more information upon which to base our conclusions than they have had.

THE WORTH AND THE LIMITATIONS OF PALEONTOLOGICAL EVIDENCE

Our task of sifting factual evidence which will enable us to decide what subhuman species the human species most closely resembles has now completed a very inadequate survey of the contribution made by the common knowledge of common folk of many lands and times. Our next task is to look at the facts which science presents as evidence for the truth of evolution, and examine the way in which that evidence is used. To many evolutionists the paleontological evidence is most convincing. It furnishes an order or kind of evidence not found in any other direction. So numerous and well worked-out are the evolutionary series and lines of descent in many animal groups possessing fossilizable parts, that there can be little doubt in the mind of any person who uses his observational and logical powers correctly, that the completest of these are phylogenetic and not merely pieced-together resemblance series. Our concern is more with the observed facts as evidence than with them as facts. We are taking for granted a vast mass of facts. What do they prove?

The famous horse series will serve well as a basis for our examination. There are few educated persons to-day who are not informed as to the evolutionary history of this one of man's closest, most useful subhuman companions. Despite the fact that the fossils which constitute the observational evidence in the case have been well known for a full half century, and have been accepted as conclusive evidence in favor of evolution by a long line of distinguished scientists, there have been from the outset and still are many educated, rational persons to whom the admitted facts do not prove evolution at all. How are such differences of conclusion possible? Is it really true that the minds of highly cultured men are so fundamentally different that from the same body of unquestioned objective evidence irreconcilably opposed conclusions can be drawn? Until a satisfactory answer to this question is found there can be no prospect of agreement either as to the origin and nature of man or as to what his conduct should be.

Let us apply to the fossils so widely held to be the remains of horses the common principles of interpretation which, in the earlier portions of this discussion, we found to lead to universally accepted conclusions relative to the most familiar cases of evolution.

Everybody knows that these fossils are found in great variety and in many parts of the earth, the western portion of North America abounding in them especially. It is well known, too, that they are found at very different geological levels. The earliest animals of which they are the remains are estimated on the basis of evidence giving considerable probability of truth, to have lived from eight hundred thousand to one million years ago.[11] From this far-away time and deep geological level (the eocene or beginning period of the tertiary era) the fossils are scattered in America through the intervening geological levels up to near the present time (the pleistocene); above which, however, none have been found. Whereas America appears to have been extensively

11 *The Horse Past and Present*, by H. F. Osborn.

populated with horses in earlier geological times, no living ones existed on the continent when it was discovered by Europeans.

What put into anybody's head the idea that all these fossils are racially related to one another and all in turn are ancestral to the familiar animal known to us as the horse? The only answer is that the fossils look like certain of the parts, the bones, of the horse. We undoubtedly violate a fundamental principle of inductive knowledge if we suppose ourselves absolutely certain that any fossil bones whatever are the remains of a horse or any other animal our original knowledge of which comes from observations on living representatives of the species in question. That the fossils upon which the supposed evolutionary history of the horse is based were once parts of horses or any other living animals is only inferential knowledge and hence can never emerge from the class of probable truth into that of certain truth. If any one questions this let him ask himself if he can possibly be as certain that a skull or other bones he may chance upon in some pasture, or even a complete mounted skeleton he may see in a museum, were once part of a horse, as he would be were he to dissect a dead horse and find in in it the corresponding skeletal parts.

I doubt if any paleontologist will contend that he is quite as certain of the derivation of fossil horse remains from horses or any other living animals as he is of the derivation of a given skeleton he has himself prepared from some animal body; or that he is quite as certain of the derivation of any one of the fossil species from some other species of the series as he is of the derivation of some adult frog from a tadpole he has kept under constant observation.

If this be granted, the whole conception of an evolutional horse series as based on the evidence available falls inevitably into the category of probable truth, the degree of probability being determined by the valuation placed upon the similarities and differences brought to light by the critical comparison of bone with bone of the entire mass of the fossil material; and of all these with the corresponding bones of the horse actually known to us. Concerning a particularly complete skeleton of *Equus scotti* found in a pleistocene deposit of Texas, we read: "It is of an animal about 15 hands in height, having somewhat the proportions of a western broncho, but with a very large head and with teeth greater than those of a modern dray horse, although very similar in pattern."[12] The mounted skeleton and the restoration of this species show the animal to have been so much like the modern horse that the skill of the expert is more needed for recognizing differences than similarities. From *Equus* to *Eohippus* and *Hyracotherium* this basic principle of comparison in search of resemblances and differences can be recognized, the limbs, feet and teeth receiving most attention. The paleontologist, Richard Owen, who named *Hyracotherium* did not recognize anything horse-like about it but considered it to have been a coney-like beast (as the name implies). Its (*Hyracotherium*) relation to the horse was not at that time suspected by Professor Owen, and was recognized by scientific men only when several of the intermediate stages between it and its modern descendant had been discovered.[13]

Another quotation from Lull illustrates the point as it applies at the bottom of the series; where likeness is relatively slight and unlikeness is relatively great. This has reference to the comparison between *Hyracotherium*, a European fossil, and *Eohippus* from North America. "These two genera are much alike, but the premolar teeth of *Hyracotherium*, especially the second one of the upper jaw, are more simple than in *Eohippus*, thus stamping the Old World

---

[12] *Organic Evolution*, by R. S. Lull, p. 619.
[13] *Evolution of the Horse*, by W. D. Matthews, Amer. Mus. of Nat. History Guide, Leaflet Series, No. 36, Sept., 1913.

type as the most primitive horse-like form known." [14]   The
kernel of the argument here is that the two genera are "much
alike." *Hyracotherium* is adjudged to be the most "primitive" "horse-like" form, on the ground of being "more simple" in various respects, particularly in the fact that the
second premolar tooth of the upper jaw bears the "stamp"
of relative simplicity. By turning to a fuller description of
the teeth we are informed wherein consists the greater simplicity of the *Hyracotherium* in contrast with the Eohippian
teeth. The molars of *Eohippus* "foreshadow" the "future
complication" of the true horse, while the hinder premolar
is becoming "molariform."

All these fossils can be ranged in a series chiefly on the
basis of a succession of complications in the molar and premolar teeth (their degree of "molariformity" after the type
of the modern horse); of a succession of changes in foot
and limb structure (reduction in the number of toes, and so
forth); and of a succession of sizes of the animals from about
that of a fox terrier (*Eohippus*) to that of the full-sized
horse. The making of this series does not necessarily imply
any conclusion concerning any derivational relation between
the members of the series. This is quite generally admitted
by believers as well as by disbelievers in the evolutionary
theory. The disagreement over such cases is due to the very
inadequate criteria heretofore applied in assessing the facts
as evidence favorable to the hypothesis that the members of
the series are derivationally connected. Writers on the
subject have expressed themselves in such a way as to con-
fuse their readers as to the rational difference between the
series as thoroughly legitimate and good classificatory ar-
rangements, and the inference of derivative connection between the members of the series.

A wording from Lull may be used to illustrate the point.
An illustration from this author should be especially instruc-

[14] Lull, p. 610.

tive because his language is much freer from unwarranted implications than is that of many another writer. "In *Merychippus,*" we read, "the milk teeth are short-crowned and have little or no cement and are thus reminiscent of its ancestry." [15]   Obviously, the short-crowned, slightly-cemented milk teeth of *Merychippus* are "reminiscent of its ancestry" if its ancestry had teeth thus characterized. But whether or not the ancestors had such teeth is exactly what we do not know, but which the facts in the case justify us in regarding as exceedingly probable. The short-crowned cementless milk teeth of *Merychippus* are suggestive rather than reminiscent of the creature's ancestry. They are not reminiscent in the sense of calling up memories of the ancestry, for what the ancestry was is the very thing we do not know but are trying to imagine on the basis of facts observed in this and other cases.

No matter how complete this or any other fossil series is as evidence on which to found a classification and arrangement, resemblance and difference between the members are the most basic facts we possess. Consequently, whatever conclusions may be drawn as to the origin and relation of these members must fall short of full demonstration. How far we are from tracing "every step in the evolution of the horse" (or of any other animal by the paleontological evidence) becomes obvious the moment we examine this wording critically. No naturalist contends that we are as certain of "every step in the evolution" of the teeth and feet of extinct horses as we are of the evolution of these structures in the individual life of horses now living. For many people, and among them no small number of scientists, the case is then closed; people, that is, for whom the origin and development of species must be demonstrated with the same certainty that the origin and development of individuals is demonstrated, if the hypothesis of evolutional origin is to

[15] *Ibid.,* p. 616.

have any standing. Undoubtedly a number of different elements go to the making of this attitude. From the standpoint of reason and logic the main elements are the failure to inquire seriously what the observed facts do signify if they do not signify evolution; and, growing immediately out of such inquiry, failure to appreciate the vast importance to the whole intellectual life of man of weighing observational evidence for determining the probable as contrasted with the *certain* truth which can be found therein.

We are now prepared to state in the briefest language possible the conclusions as to relationship and origination, justified by such facts as those of the horse-like fossils we have been considering: That the fossils once belonged to animals which resembled horses known to us by actual observation is probable, the degree of probability being very different for the different fossil species. As to the geologically more recent species, in which the resemblance to known horses is very close, the probability of these being actual horse remains is so great as to render negligible such uncertainty as necessarily inheres in the nature of the evidence. In the light of the evidence furnished by the fossils themselves and from many collateral sources, and in the further light of the knowledge processes involved in innumerable cases where the reasoning is similar, it is extremely probable that the animals represented by the fossils were related to one another by actual genesis. In other words, it is extremely probable that as species no less than as individuals they originated by evolution.

I hasten to make a few remarks forestalling two kinds of response to this statement. On the one hand I anticipate vigorous objection from paleontological experts. They are likely to say that such an outcome is so filled with qualification and skepticism as to rob it of intellectual satisfaction. Such scientists are likely to feel that if this sort of thing is the best that can be done, if nothing more certain can ever be attained from paleontological research, then such research has little allurement. My reply to this is that the question is not one of our likes and dislikes, but of what the truth is. What are the realities of nature and the realities of our minds as interpreters thereof? Such, as I see it, are the problems with which we have to deal. I do not believe it possible for any scientist or for that matter any other intelligent, educated person to examine for himself the facts, principles and conclusions we have been occupied with and come to a result as to the paleontological evidence of evolution essentially different from that contained in our statement.

The second kind of response to our statement which I would forestall, is that of those persons, by no means few in number nor devoid of influence, who rejoice at the least sign of discomfiture of evolutionists. To such persons I would earnestly commend attention to the first part of my remark to the other group: Not primarily our likes and dislikes but the realities of nature and man are what confront us. In this, the scientific expert and the most ordinary person are on common ground. It is the great problem of life which we are all compelled to do something toward solving for our individual selves. The measure of our success in this depends very largely upon whether we conceive the problem as it actually is in contrast with conceiving it as we would wish it to be or may erroneously believe it to be.

This whole discussion of evolution is an effort to resolve the contradictory theories of the origin of man and other living beings by examining the unquestioned facts bearing on the case with a view to finding which of the various theories have the greatest probability of truth. If opponents of the evolution theory would be faithful to the principles of their own mental life they cannot avoid explaining what the meaning is of the many close resemblances between the fossil remains which have been woven together to make the admittedly hypothetical horse series, if they do not mean that the members of the series are genetically related. Our results have led us to see the necessity of concluding that the members of the series are somehow derivatively related to one another if we conclude that the individual members of a given living species or genus, concerning the parentage and birth of which we are ignorant, are yet somehow derivatively related.

MAN'S MOST PROBABLE DIRECT ANCESTOR

Our critical general examination, now completed, of the nature of evidence for evolution furnished by the structure of animals living and extinct, has brought us to the place where we can examine the facts as evidence which have given such wide currency to the hypothesis that the human species originated from ancestors whose nearest living kindred are the anthropoid apes.

We must first reiterate what has been said several times, making the point more specific than heretofore: There is not the least likelihood that we shall ever know certainly from what particular species or even genus of prehuman animals man descended, or more truly, ascended. Vagueness on this point is constantly having unfortunate results, with the esoteric as well as with the exoteric. Such common expressions as those about some new discovery of *"the* missing link" between man and ape, and such undertakings as those of expeditions in search of *"the* ancestor of man," arouse interests and hopes, the unwarrantableness of which can only disappoint the credulous and encourage the incredulity and hostility of the skeptical. We have not the least chance of learning by direct observation from what source, when, or how, man originated, simply because the thing happened ages and ages ago. Common sense readily enough accepts the limitations on knowledge of many past events. It is well aware that it cannot know to-day any event which happened last year or ten years ago with the same directness and certainty that it could have known them by direct experience at the time they happened. Only when we become sicklied o'er with the pale cast of thought do we make ourselves believe we are as certain of things sensorily unexperienceable as we are of things which are thus experienceable. Nor have we any appreciable chance of learning second-hand, on the testimony of witnesses who did observe man's origin. Such witnesses left no record of what they saw even if they knew what they were seeing.

So long as it is admittedly impossible for any one, no matter how learned, to discover with certainty the parents of a given human individual by knowing his structure alone, just so long will it be impossible to discover with certainty the parent of the human species. Discovery of the probable ancestral species will be more difficult than would be discovery of an individual's parents on the sole basis of knowledge of its structure, in proportion as the origin of a species is more complex than the origin of an individual.

Despite this excessively skeptical attitude (as it is likely to appear at first sight to many evolutionists) we feel that the evidence justifies conclusions of the utmost importance, practical as well as theoretical, even though there is considerable disagreement among those most highly informed on the subject. After examination of what is written, and of my own first-hand information (very limited as to technicalities, though considerable as to generalities) the conclusion which seems to me most satisfactory on the whole is that reached by William K. Gregory. As to the evidence derived from the resemblances between existing man and existing anthropoids, we have: "(1) Comparative anatomical (including embryological) evidence alone has shown that man and the anthropoids have been derived from a primitive anthropoid stock and that man's nearest existing relatives are the chimpanzee and gorilla. (2) The chimpanzee and gorilla have retained, with only minor changes, the ancestral habits and habitus in brain, dentition, skull and limbs, while the forerunners of the Hominidae, through a profound change in function, lost the primitive anthropoid habitus, gave up arboreal frugivorous adaptations and early became terrestrial, bipedal and predatory, using crude flints to cut up and smash the varied food." [16]

Rewording the first of these paragraphs in conformity with the results of our study of the logical processes involved in reaching the conclusions, we have the following: Examination of the comparative anatomical (including embryological) evidence alone shows that the hypotheses that man and the anthropoids were derived from a primitive anthropoid stock and that man's nearest existing relatives are the chimpanzee and gorilla, are far more probably true than are any other hypotheses that have been proposed on the matters at issue. I have little doubt that this reworded sentence expresses more exactly what was really in the author's mind than does his own language. Nobody knows better than Gregory himself that the evidence referred to does not show for a certainty (as the wording implies) that man and the anthropoids have been derived from a primitive anthropoid stock.[17]

While it is highly probable that the chimpanzee-gorilla group is genuinely blood kindred to man, the evidence makes probable in almost equal degree that neither chimpanzee nor gorilla are in man's direct ancestral line. The anthropoids have reached their culmination in the gibbon, orang, chimpanzee and the gorilla. Discussing this topic, John M.

[16] "Studies on the Evolution of the Primates," by William K. Gregory, *Bull. Amer. Mus. of Nat. Hist.*, 1910, Vol. XXV, pp. 239-255.
[17] It appears to me that there are two practical advantages in guarding statements of this sort more carefully than most authors are wont to do. One of these is the avoidance of the charge of being dogmatic so often made against men of science by those who are not very sympathetic with science. The second is that such carefulness promotes attention to the

Tyler [18] says: "Every one of them approaches or resembles man in some respect more closely than does any other of them, and every one differs from him in certain important characteristics."

The practical question then becomes that of what conclusion the evidence warrants as to man's general as contrasted with his specific ancestry. This is in conformity with the logic of the situation which does not permit us to anticipate that we shall ever know from what particular anthropoid species man sprang. Turning to the actual evidence, we come back to our familiar realization of dependence on resemblance. Undoubtedly paleontology is giving us distinct help here. Southern Asia has yielded fossils derived from several species of primates including some anthropoids. These have been discovered particularly by the Geological Survey of India and have been studied with great care and skill, according to Gregory, by Dr. Guy E. Pilgrim.

Teeth are the most important objects among these fossils and certain resemblances of some of these to human teeth are striking indeed. Thus Gregory gives, on Pilgrim's determinations, a comparison between the breadth indices of all the lower cheek teeth of man and those of one of these creatures (Sivapithecus) as follows:

	Sivapithecus	Man
Third molar	93.7	91.6
Second molar	94.6	94.4

differences between different hypotheses touching the same matter, which in turn promotes appreciation of the common ground there is almost sure to be for such hypotheses. Scientific men not infrequently dwell upon their differences of opinion to an extent and with a vehemence that is entirely out of proportion to the importance of their differences as compared with the importance of their agreements. This is detrimental from the standpoint of science's rôle as a torchbearer for general public enlightenment. Perhaps at no time and on no question has there been greater need that all there is of solidarity in science shall be openly manifest than just now and on this very question of man's nature and origin.

[18] *The Coming of Man*, p. 38.

	Sivapithecus	Man
First molar	92.1	92.
Fourth premolar	116.5	112.7
Third premolar	110.1	111.6

No competent anatomist or paleontologist would make too much of such a resemblance as this, especially since it is merely quantitative. He would suspect that it is too close to be allowed face value as indicating general resemblance and real kindred. As a matter of fact the tooth and jaw characters do not on the whole bear out what is suggested by these measurements, though the premolars are said to approach the human type in fundamental pattern. The canines, however, are sharply apelike instead of manlike. Only after the comparison has been extended to all the parts and features available for examination can the best possible valuation of the resemblances and differences be reached.

Gregory's summing up from the studies by both Pilgrim and himself of these Indian fossils, may be taken as what is justifiable on the basis of the few parts of the creatures thus far discovered. He writes: "The ancestral chimpanzee-gorilla-man stock appears to be represented by the Upper Miocene genera *Sivapithecus* and *Dryopithecus* the former more closely allied to, or directly ancestral to, the Hominidæ, the latter to the chimpanzee and gorilla." Then follows a statement whose justification and significance come far more from the evidence as a whole than from that furnished by these Indian fossils alone. "Many of the differences that separate man from anthropoids of the *Sivapithecus* type are regressive changes, following the profound change in food habits above noted. Here belong the retraction of the face and dental arch, the reduction in size of the canines, the reduction of the jaw muscles, the loss of the prehensile character of the hallux. Many other differences are secondary adjustments in relative proportions connected with the change from the semi-gression to fully terrestrial bipedal progression." Concerning the relative structural resemblances between man, chimpanzee, gorilla and other primates, the labors of Arthur Keith have furnished important evidence. He tells us [19] that between 1890 and 1900 he made complete dissections of more than eighty animals extending the comparison to more than a thousand characters. This comparison brought out the fact that the number of points in common (resemblances) are greatest of all between man, gorilla, chimpanzee, and orang, and that there is a distinct falling off of resemblance on passing to the old world and still more to the new-world monkeys, especially when the Lemurs are reached. Could the comparison have been carried to any mammalian genera below the Lemurs, the falling off would be still more striking, bringing out the genus resemblance between *Homo* and the anthropoid genera still more sharply.[20]

MAN AND THE SOLIDARITY OF THE ANIMAL KINGDOM

As a purely observational matter we are bound to recognize that in structure man's resemblances to the higher primates, and especially to the chimpanzee-gorilla group, are closer than to any other living beings. Hence the conclusion, on the basis of resemblances as indicative of common origin among living beings, that man's genetic kinship to the chimpanzee-gorilla group is closer than to any other group.

[19] "Klaatch's Theory of the Descent of Man," *Nature*, Vol. 85, Feb. 16, 1911, p. 508.
[20] For the benefit of readers not versed in the practices and principles of zoölogical classification it should be said that the "common" characters entering into this discussion do not by any means include all the resemblances between the several organisms compared, but only such as are common in characterizing the different genera to which the organisms belong. The four-chambered heart is common to many other genera of mammals as well as to those here compared.

Does the fact that the definitive resemblances (hence, supposedly the genetic relation) between man and·other creatures diminish as we go down the scale, mean that they disappear entirely if we go down far enough? Not at all. The resemblances diminish only with respect to those attributes made use of in the comparison. When we draw other attributes into the comparison we find the scope of the resemblances broadening. The hordes of multicellular animals have nervous and muscular systems of some sort, as man has; the cellular constituents of both these systems are much alike everywhere. Even unicellular animals are by no means devoid of resemblance to man, many features in the structure of their cells resembling the cell structure of man. Finally all plants as well as all animals have certain likenesses to man, being composed of cells which have many things in common with the cells of the human organism.

The different emotional effects on us of recognizing resemblances between ourselves and all other living beings, and discovering scientifically that these resemblances are probably due to actual physical kinships, is great and important. The recognition of these resemblances is easier than is the discovery of their meaning, and hence, the former makes a more general appeal than the latter. For instance it would hardly be stretching the truth to say that poetry is rooted in such recognition. Would it be untrue to distinguish poetry from science by saying the first concerns itself chiefly with the likenesses of external objects and that the second concerns itself chiefly with their differences?

The distinguished surgeon, W. W. Keen, has presented his personal experiences on recognizing certain resemblances between man and brutes. "Not from the controversial side or from general arguments," we read, "but from a plain statement of a series of facts, many of them drawn from my personal experience as a surgeon and anatomist," would he exhibit evidence which "to my mind absolutely demonstrates

the solidarity of animal life, more especially in the vertebrates, such as fish, birds, other mammals and man, the
highest mammal." [21]

The specific instance relates to brain structure and involves the phenomenon of localization of motor centers in
the cerebral hemispheres. The incident goes back to a time
when knowledge in this field was meager as compared with
what it is now. He says: "In 1888, I reported my first
three cases of modern surgery of the brain. Attending the
meeting of the American Surgical Association in Washington, when I read this paper, was Sir David Ferrier of London. He had contributed very largely to this then wholly
new mapping of the brain centers which control motion. In
one case, I described how I had stimulated a certain small,
definite motor area in the brain of my patient by a battery,
and described the resulting movements of the arm at the
shoulder. Ferrier afterwards said to me, 'I could hardly
restrain myself from leaping to my feet, for this was the
very first demonstration on the human brain of the exact
identity of my own localization of this very center in animals.'" After giving a few other instances of his own
experience in this same field Keen writes: "Do not such
exact localizations of the brain centers in animals, as directly
applied to man, in hundreds, if not thousands of operations
by now, most closely ally man to animals?"

The other instance we will take from Keen hinges upon
the fact that if the vagus nerve be divided in a cat, several
results follow, among them being: (1) The pupil of the eye
on the same side diminishes from the normal large sized
pupil of the cat to the narrowness of a thread. (2) The
corresponding ear becomes very red from increased flow of
blood. The blood vessels become greatly dilated. (3) On
that side there is an increased sweating due to increased

[21] "Surgical and Anatomical Evidence of Evolution," by W. W. Keen,
Science, June 9, 1922, p. 603.

activity of the sweat glands which in turn results, partly at least, from the increased blood flow. (4) The temperature of the affected area is increased. Keen's incident reached back to the impression made upon him by a picture of a cat's face and eyes which he had first seen as a medical student in Dalton's textbook of physiology. In this picture one of the pupils was much smaller than the other consequent upon division of the vagus nerve on the side of the reduced pupil.

The narrative follows: "In 1863, during the Civil War, when I was assistant executive officer of a military hospital, one day a new patient approached my desk just as I was about to sign a letter. The moment I looked up at him I was struck with his appearance and instantly said to myself, 'Surely you are Dalton's cat.' 'Where were you wounded?' I quickly said. He pointed to his neck and I said to myself, 'His sympathetic nerve must have been cut.' Further observation showed the reddened ear, the increased temperature, the sweating and the greater flow of saliva, thus confirming in every particular the results of Brown-Sequard's experiments on animals. It is interesting to know that this was the very first case in surgical history in which division of the sympathetic nerve had ever been observed in man." Usually such an accident means severing the carotid artery and immediate death. Further experiments on this nerve in animals have "revealed a wholly new world of most important phenomena," all of these being just as true for man as for the other animals.

Keen is a convinced evolutionist, and his convictions rest largely on just such evidence as he gives here. Is his rational acceptance of the theory as potent with him as his emotional attitude, engendered by his recognizing the resemblances described? While he uses the term evolution in the title of his paper when he summarizes the meaning of his illustrations he does not use the word in a single instance. "Do not such exact localizations of the brain centers in animals as directly applied to man . . . most closely *ally man to animals?*" Further: Here, again, you perceive the *solidarity of the animal kingdom* in such identity of function that the thyroid gland of animals . . . performs precisely the same function as the human thyroid." (Italics are the present author's.)

Keen is apparently more convinced of the solidarity of the whole animal kingdom than he is of the relation of all animals by actual genesis. This feeling for "solidarity," is more to him than is his logical conviction of the truth of the evolution theory. "Do not so many such exact parallels between the human and the animal body strongly suggest a close interrelation of the two?" Undoubtedly they very strongly suggest such relation. But do they prove it? It would seem from Keen's language so far examined that he is dubious on this point. However, in the following we have his own answer: "Man's ascent from an animal of low intelligence seems to me to be absolutely proved by the many phenomena which reveal identical organs and physiological processes in the animal and the human body."

Keen's deductions from the evidence would be entirely acceptable to most present-day evolutionists. They would accept, as we do, his conclusion about the solidarity of the whole animal kingdom, man with the rest, but they would also accept his conclusion that man's ascent from a lower animal is "absolutely proved" by the evidence. Yet our discussion has shown conclusively that the evidence does not "prove absolutely" man's origin in this way. It proves only *that his origin thus is vastly more probable than is his origin in any other way that has ever been suggested.*

THE INFLUENCE OF MAN'S BELIEF IN HIS OWN EVOLUTIONARY ORIGIN ON HIS SELF-RESPECT AND CONDUCT

This discussion of the evolution theory in its application to man must end in a brief examination of the effect the theory tends to have on man's view of himself. How does it influence him rationally and emotionally? Does it enable him to understand his own life more, or less, truly, and to order it more, or less, wisely than do the other theories which it would supplant? If man should become entirely convinced that he is blood-kin to the whole living world, is part and parcel of nature, will this make him think better or worse of himself than if he should become convinced, as he has so long believed more or less positively that he originated in a different way, and stands in a different relation to the natural order? Would the final establishment of the hypothesis that he originated from ancestors which were not man but something much his inferior, make his self-respect more genuine and potent? Or would it commit him for all time to the spiritual slough of cynicism and pessimism relative to mankind generally, which has been such a blight on the neo-Darwinian view of human life?

In the present stage of our enterprise our answer to this query can be only an expression of personal conviction. An adequate presentation of the grounds of the conviction must be reserved for future presentation. This conviction may be summed up as follows: From the doctrine of organic evolution comes to us the fullest revelation attainable of man's moral nature, no less than of his physical nature. Faith in kindred by descent, that is, by evolution, of all mankind, known directly through sense-experience and indirectly through emotional response plus rational inference, is the substance out of which has been woven the entire fabric of civilized life. The conception of the brotherhood of the human species will become potent for human conduct only through recognizing that such unity is rooted just as truly in the physical as in the spiritual nature of man, and is validated by his reason no less certainly than by his affection. The culminating human usefulness of the doctrine of organic evolution lies in its revelation that the totality of relations among all the members of the human species which conditions the highest good of them all, called the moral law, is natural law, and must be so understood and practiced to accomplish the greatest benefits of which that law is capable.

From the doctrine of universal evolution comes the fullest revelation of man's religious nature. The narrower, intenser unity of man is but a segment in the all-embracing unity which is the matrix and source of all our understanding. From such gradually verified conceptions as the web of life, solidarity of the animal kingdom, and the limitlessness of natural bodies dynamically related into a true universe, arise all our strength and faith as well as our understanding, regardless of whether our reason conceives and our language names that unity as infinite nature, or as the living God.

From these combined sources come the perception that science is not religion, and religion not science, but that each is the complement and fulfillment of the other. Religion is the common magma of all emotional life as science is of all rational life. Religion is the individual's mighty reservoir of spiritual impulse and energy upon which all wisdom for personal and social life must freely draw in order that it may attain its greatest scope and efficacy and richness.

The supreme desideratum for man in this era is that he should understand the evolution theory to the end not merely of believing it but of living it. For man to live evolution means that so long as he is truly living he must be in some measure truly developing.

CHAPTER 5

SUCCESS AND FAILURE IN ANIMAL ACTIVITY

SOURCES, TRUSTWORTHINESS, AND ORGANIZATION OF DATA

THE task of getting before us enough data on activities in the animal world to serve as a basis for broad conclusions relative to the meaning of these activities for human life is basic for the standpoint of this book. It is therefore important that the source of the data and the methods of securing them should be placed before the reader at the outset.

The material appertains largely to animals living their lives in their own way under natural conditions. Students of animal psychology have for the most part regarded data of this kind with little favor. Recognizing the impossibility of getting evidence for analyzing such aspects of the animal mind as they were interested in without themselves controlling the activities of the animals, these investigators have largely restricted their efforts to laboratory experimentation. Furthermore, so fragmentary and lacking in critical spirit is much of what is told by out-of-door naturalists as to the doings of animals that it has appeared little of value could come from field studies.

Nevertheless, if one is more interested in the way animals solve their own problems than in the way he may solve his problems of their psychology, his only recourse is to do the best he can toward learning what the creatures do in the state of nature. This calls for study of them in nature by any means possible, whether by watching them with no interference whatever on the watcher's part; by such interference to a limited extent; or by carefully ex-

64

amining their "works" when they are not around. The life-problems of animals must be solved, with insignificant exceptions, as nature imposes them; otherwise the conclusions drawn by the investigator as to their problem-solving abilities and methods are deductively rather than inductively arrived at, and subject to all the dangers of the deductive procedure.

The question of the trustworthiness of the factual data is crucial. Here as in connection with the raw material of all scientific research two questions must be satisfactorily answered: Were the observations themselves accurate and adequate? Are the facts used as bases for generalizations thoroughly typical? With these touch-stones of the trustworthiness of data in mind the reader must judge for himself whether the factual underpinning we are about to lay is strong enough to carry the superstructure to be erected upon it.

The question of who made and reported the original observations is particularly important. A respectable fraction of the matters of fact presented is of my own gathering. Rather extensive personal observations have been made through many years on the doings in nature of a number of widely separated animal groups. Beavers, one species of woodpecker, and a few species of ants, have received especial attention.

But such a wide range of data is needed that great dependence must be placed on the work of other observers. The most careful discrimination as to what is and what is not trustworthy is essential. The interpretation placed upon animal activities is liable to be influenced by what the reporter knows or believes concerning human activities. Observers who are genuinely fond of animals, who are strongly sympathetic with them, tend to overhumanize the activities, to put them in too favorable a light. Observers who are emotionally negative or positively hostile to animals tend to underestimate such man-likeness as their activities have. Observers who are emotionally neutral toward animals but look upon them from an extreme mechanistic standpoint tend to unduly mechanize their activities, thus making too little of the organism's share in its own behavior.

The reported material in this field is fragmentary and chaotic. It has never been critically gathered nor critically studied, because there has been no organizing principle to direct observation and reflection. Such an organizing principle is operative when we study the activities of any organism with regard to the contribution made by those activities to the welfare of the organism. When we ask, not only how does the organism respond to a given stimulus or set of stimuli, but how does this response affect the welfare of the organism, we are making more adequate and fruitful application of the experimental method than when its use is directed wholly to the discovery and not at all to the interpretation of facts.

Much laboratory research has been devoted to animal behavior by professional psychologists. The purpose of this research has been primarily the interpretation of "the animal mind." Such research might be expected to produce the very kind of knowledge we are deficient in. But however much researches of this kind have enlarged our information and enriched our understanding of certain aspects of animal mentality they are able to do but little toward such a testing of activity as we are calling for.

The crucial thing about such activity is out of reach of direct laboratory research. Animal activities are so intimately tied up with innumerable other processes presented by the general system of nature that it is impossible to isolate any animal from its natural setting (as in its very essence the laboratory method aims to do) without breaking in upon the original system to such an extent that the activities under the new and simplified conditions cannot possibly be an exact duplication of what they would be under the original conditions. Think of the question of what the individual sparrows or mice or bears of any given area might do during a season so excessively dry as to seriously reduce their normal food supply. Any set experiment which duplicated such a situation would lose its character and value as an experiment, becoming as complicated and difficult to cope with in detail as the original.

To have any value for interpreting a given animal activity formal experimentation must be planned and executed with reference to questions defined on the basis of knowledge as broad and accurate as the natural conditions under which it occurs will admit. Experimentation can have no other legitimate aim, so far as concerns the general problem here before us, than to get more light on special details than studies in nature can obtain.

In so far as the acts of animals fall short of perfection, and are therefore judged to be maladapted, this judgment of maladaptation must be made with reference to animal lives under natural conditions. The struggle which we believe to have contributed so largely to making the animal world what it now is has already occurred, and in nature, not in laboratories. Animals under domestication, or in confinement in zoölogical parks and experimental laboratories, cannot exhibit much of the perfection or the imperfection of their abilities to act, nor can they teach us much about how they came by these abilities. It makes a crucial difference to an animal whether it is running wild in nature depending on itself alone for water, food, mates, and avoidance of enemies, or is shut up in a safe cage with no responsibility whatever for its necessities, these being furnished it by a bountiful Providence. Students whose experiences with animals are limited to those which live under these man-made conditions are incapable of treating either their maladaptive or their well-adaptive actions with full adequacy.

We have drawn as extensively from the zoölogical realm as has seemed necessary to provide a background for an adequate description of human conduct. This man-centered enterprise is approached in a way that appears strange and hostile to man as contrasted with the approaches of generally accredited students of human life. The human anatomist and embryologist draws freely upon any portion of the animal kingdom that will facilitate his description and understanding of such an infinitely complex part of adult man as his brain. Without this freedom of range as to material for research, and the confident acceptance of the evolutional idea of true homology between the human brain and the brains of all other vertebrates, no such fullness of knowledge of man's brain as we now have could ever have been reached. The comparative method possesses even wider applicability and importance for gaining knowledge of man's activities. Whereas no human neurologist would pretend to see a strict homology between the parts of the human brain and the parts of the brain of ants or wasps, no human psychologist would hesitate to regard the reflexive and instinctive activities of man and these invertebrate animals as strictly comparable in their basic natures. Animals are more broadly and in a sense more closely akin in their activities than in the chief structural bases of these activities. The food and mate-getting instinctive activities of insects and humans are more alike than are the mechanisms of the two groups by which the activities are performed. We are no less dependent on comparative psychobiological studies on brute and human animals in nature for sound conclusions relative to the origin and nature of these activities, than on comparative morphological studies for sound conclusions relative to the origin and nature of structure.

The fact that on the activity side of animal life we have no "record of the rocks" coming to us from the past is a sore deprivation to students of comparative activity. This makes it all the more imperative that such data as are available should be assiduously collected and critically treated. The extensive deductive studies relative to the probable size of the brains of various classes of extinct vertebrates, based on actual studies of the cranial capacities of the fossil skulls, are genuinely instructive. But they can give no satisfactorily detailed pictures of the lives of the individual creatures. How defective must necessarily be any imaged picture we can make of the performances of a *Diplodocus* as compared with what the real performances must have been! This is one of the animals in which much of the total work done was neurally presided over by an enlarged lumbar section of the spinal cord instead of by the brain, to judge from the size of the neural canal in this region as compared with the size of the portion of that canal represented by the brain case. Researches into the life activities of such reptiles as those modern Australian lizards which depend largely on the hind limbs for locomotion would help toward picturing the activities of *Diplodocus*. Manifestly we are forever precluded from knowledge of what the daily lives of these creatures of a long by-gone age must have been.

These reflections bring forcefully home to us the importance of any trustworthy bits of knowledge that can be secured relative to the activities of extinct animals from observations on objective results of their activities. "Fossil tracks" are perhaps the most common sources of knowledge of this kind, and considerable has been learned from this source about the modes of life of some animals. Another source of raw material for deductive knowledge of the activities of extinct animals is the remains of food either from the digestive canals of the animals or from their excrements. These enable investigators to infer something as to the nutritional activities involved.

Material remains of extinct activities, as they might be called, which contribute most directly to psychobiological knowledge, are those that show any sort of constructional ability on the part of the animals concerned. Every bit of man's handiwork that has been gathered into the great art and science collections of civilized countries which is unaccompanied by written records made at the time the objects themselves were made, must be recognized as evidence of this sort. The crude stone implements, and the prehistoric wall-paintings assigned to times thousands of years in the past, are as strictly evidence of extinct activity as is a fossil-worm tube or wasp's nest.

THE CRITERION OF SUCCESS IN ANIMAL ACTIVITY

Since Darwin's time all students of living nature have recognized the enormous mortality that occurs over and above what death from old age entails. So general is this phenomenon that some zoölogists and botanists have doubted whether there is any such death. It rarely happens that an organism dies from an inherent lack of ability to live longer. It does not die; it is killed. Vast numbers of individuals of nearly all species fall victim to external destroying agencies before, often long before, old age comes upon them. Countless millions of seeds and eggs and also of the very young of both plants and animals, are destroyed every year by inimical forces of inorganic nature and by parasites and other kinds of organic depredators, in ways against which the victims have not the slightest recourse.

This great victimized world is immobile and helpless; it is a static world so far as its fate is concerned. Thus do we become accustomed to look upon it. A large part of the directly observable evidence of destruction among adult higher animals, and of our information about defects that contribute to the destruction, is morphological. This aspect of life, no matter how complicated and perfect it may be, is inert, passive, static. From all this we have been habituated to associate the great mortality in living nature chiefly with the static aspects of organisms. An unexpressed, semiconscious contra-theory appears to have grown up to the effect that if an organism is highly active there is no room for question about the quality of the action. The old notion of a sort of divine inerrancy of "instinct" and the tendency in animal biology to think of animal adaptation in morphological terms have conspired to shield all those activities of animal organisms commonly classed as instinctive, from rigorously scientific study as to their significance and effectiveness for the organisms performing them. Recent physiology has done much to correct the staticism of morphology and to do away with what might be called the theological conception of instinct. The next step in the study of animal activities is to subject to scientific examination the question of how far the activities attain the ends at which they are unmistakably aimed.

Every naturalist whose attitude toward the realm he studies is permeated with feeling as well as guided by reason must of necessity find it more pleasant to dwell on the successes than on the failures among living beings, especially among those belonging to the higher orders. We are better satisfied with the sleek, well-shaped, vigorous dog or horse, than with rough-haired, scrawny, or mutilated individuals. Nobody really likes down-and-outers. When we speak of the beauties, the wonders, the harmonies, of animate nature we mean that those aspects of the great scheme of things which impress us in these emotional ways are the successes of nature.

It cannot escape the notice of anybody who observes

animals that some individuals of any species or variety are much finer, much more pleasing to look at and to be interested in, than others. It does not require very extensive zoölogical knowledge to discover that much of this kind of difference among individuals is connected with different degrees of success in the activities characteristic of the organisms. The "lean and lank" or "scrawny" condition of certain individuals is seen to be due to the failure of the creatures' food-procuring or food-using activities. We are apt to attribute conditions of the sort indicated to shortage of food and let the case go at that. We are apt to charge the whole responsibility to the environmental side of life. But a moment's reflection will convince us that this way of disposing of the matter is inadequate. The fact that an organism has the ability at all to seek for food means some ability to meet special conditions. In a special case of food scarcity what happens to a creature is essentially a matter of how far he can go by virtue of his seeking ability. In this very matter of the extension of the food-procuring and food-using activities is found one of the most important factors in the development of the higher animals from the lower, and in making man the most successful of all creatures.

The term "maladaptation" is convenient as a name for all kinds and degrees of falling short of completeness in any type of structure and of success in any kind of action. The nature of our undertaking will require us to examine the maladaptive side of activity somewhat more extensively and closely than the well-adaptive side. Works on the natural history of animals are very inadequate in dealing with this general subject, and especially with unsuccessful activities.

ACTIVITIES CLASSIFIED AS LIFE-OR-DEATH AND
LIFE-FULFILLING

After all is made that possibly can be made of the lives
of creatures long since dead and gone, our main reliance for
the task in hand must be the actually observed performances
of living creatures. The task before us is to examine as
critically as possible typical activities of animals, from the
smallest, simplest creatures known to us up to and including
man at his best, with a view to learning all we can about the
effectiveness of such activities for conserving and promoting
the lives of the creatures.

When the whole round of animal activities is viewed with
reference to the welfare of the animals performing them,
three groups, or categories stand out with boldness. No
animal ever fails to reveal his awareness of the absolute
necessity for food, using the term to include every class of
materials which must be taken from external nature in
order that the organism may continue to live in health and
strength. The unqualified self-centeredness of this category
of needs and activities is almost as striking as are the needs
and activities themselves. That no living thing can meet
an animal's food needs as long as it is living, is an impres-
sively ego-centric fact. Nothing alive is useful for this purpose to any of us until it is dead.

How different in kind is another group of needs with its
corresponding activities! The mate, no less imperatively
needed than food by all highly developed animal organisms,
must be as fully alive as the needy individual itself. The
activities the rôle of which is to satisfy these needs cannot
possibly be ego-centric in the sense in which the food-securing activities must be. In mating the aim is as positively
other-conserving as it is other-destroying in food-getting.

The third group of needs and corresponding activities is
less sharply delimited than are the other two, but no less

real and imperative. The fact that health, and life itself, are subject to countless inimical external agencies escapes the attention of nobody, even members of the most assiduously "safety first" communities. When it comes to those ages of human life and those places of its habitation wherein not much has yet been done by man to secure himself against these agencies, dangers beset him so thickly on every side that the need for activities in behalf of safety, and so the activities themselves, are as much in evidence as are those of the other two groups.

It is not contended that all the needs and activities of brute, much less of human, animals are included in these three groups. Since successful life at any level is conditioned on the fulfillment of these three groups of needs, the degree of success of activities relative to these groups will be a true measure, so far, of the efficiency of all organic activity. These three groups of activities are, from the standpoints of the species and of the individual, life-sustaining activities. Unless they are successfully performed, nature puts a check, abrupt and unmistakable, upon the life-adventure of individual and species.

There is another large group of activities which may be designated as life-fulfilling. As responses to stimulatory agencies these are as inevitable, as normal, as natural as are responses to agencies which answer to the organism's life-or-death needs, but they do not contribute anything to such needs. Light reaching my eyes from a wayside stone is as stimulatory as is light coming from a loaf of bread; and the light from neither source tells me anything about the nature of either object. In order, therefore, to fulfill my responsive nature I am as much bound to respond to the useless as to the useful agency.

From this universal but undiscriminating character of responsiveness it comes about that the life-fulfilling activities have great importance in organisms in which they are as numerous and varied as they are in man. They engage us in detail in the companion volume of this general enterprise; so far as this book is concerned we shall consider human activities chosen from the same life-sustaining groups of activities as have furnished the material for the examination of brute activities, and shall classify them under the same general kinds of successful and unsuccessful activities.

CLASSES OF MALADAPTIVE ACTIVITY

The character of the maladaptive activities found by us in this study only confirms and extends results previously reached by other investigators.[1] Thoughtful students of animal activities sum up their conclusions in some such phrase as, "All instinctive activity is wasteful." Although this is too terse to be unqualifiedly true, it contains unescapable truth. The wastefulness and otherwise maladaptiveness of instinctive activities result in part from the ever-present liability of organisms to overdo, i.e., to perform a useful, or at least a harmless, act more times than are necessary to yield the best results for the organism itself. This may be designated as the tendency to excessiveness. This excessiveness may be wasteful of the animal's energy and time, and may even work positive harm. The woodpecker, equipped to store

[1] The maladaptivity of animals in what they do has received relatively little special attention by experimentalists. We are acquainted with the work of no one who has approached the subject from the side of the experimental control of animal activity who seems to have come so near conceiving the problem as it is conceived by us as does the psychopathologist, G. V. Hamilton. His important book, *An Introduction to Objective Psychopathology* (1925), to which R. M. Yerkes contributes a significant foreword, escaped us until our book was nearly through the press. It would otherwise have received more attention. This author's thought appears to run parallel with ours in several particulars, most notably, perhaps, in recognizing the large part played by imperfect adaptation in the doings of animals, brute and human, and in perceiving the transcendent importance of reason, especially human reason, as a corrective of the imperfection.

nuts in holes which he has pecked in trees, pecks far more holes than he ever fills, and fills far more than he or his fellows ever empty. If a woodpecker's time and his acorns are worth anything to him (and they certainly are if his life is worth anything to him) this excessiveness of activity is wasteful and may be positively harmful.

The organism tends not only to excessiveness but also to misdirection of otherwise advantageous activities. The woodpecker who stores pebbles instead of acorns has plainly chosen the wrong objects for his activity; judged as a food-storing enterprise this undertaking is a failure, however neatly the pebbles are fitted into the holes.

So vast in quantity is the material available for such an undertaking that the use of more than a small fraction of it is out of the question. Practically the problem is one of making such selections from the data as will be most widely illustrative of the basic phenomena and most cogent and convincing as to the general conclusions reached. As should be expected the two great zoölogical subdivisions of arthropods and vertebrates have furnished a large majority of the instances used. Even from these subdivisions selection has had to be restricted. Entire major divisions, as for instance that of fishes among vertebrates, have been requisitioned but little, though innumerable data are here available.

CHAPTER 6

SUCCESSFUL ANIMAL ACTIVITY

OUR central requirement in the criterion of success will be attainment of welfare—welfare of the individual creature performing the act, and welfare of the group of which the individual is a member. The mere bringing to a successful conclusion of a specific set of activities, as those involved in a piece of construction or in the accomplishment of a journey, does not constitute success as we shall use the term. The final test of successful animal action is not found in any material product or immediate accomplishment but in the administration of that action to the life of the animal, individual and group. Were a food-storing rat or squirrel to lay up enough grain or nuts to make an ample food supply for a long winter, this of itself could not be accounted full success. Such could only be ascribed to the accomplishment when the stores had actually done their part in preserving the animal the whole winter through. Should hard rains or some marauding enemy destroy the stores before they had been eaten by their owner, the storage work would fall short of real success. It would have to be regarded as defective in not providing adequately against such destroying agencies. No matter what else may be included in welfare, the continuance of existence in the individual and in the species, and the continuance of some measure of functional efficiency, is basal. When life terminates in an organism, or comes so near it as to render the organism utterly helpless, the term welfare can hardly be said to have any meaning as applied to that organism.

There are many activities which, though typically promotive of welfare, become positively subversive under some conditions, as when carried beyond a certain quantitative optimum. Eating, no matter how good the food or how much needed, may be carried to excess by any organism.

Many kinds of activity other than those indispensable to the mere continuance of physical existence in health, efficiency and comfort are highly promotive of welfare in man and in many animals below man. We have to recognize spiritual welfare, welfare that is psychical in the broadest sense, as well as physical welfare. The idea of welfare can be extended without ambiguity to a great range of activities, covering some of life that is physical and some that is spiritual or psychical, by defining welfare as being nearly synonymous with the common expression: "fullness of life."

In examining the activities of animals for the purpose of ascertaining their successfulness it will be convenient and sufficiently accurate to recognize these activities as occurring at three levels of complexity.

AT THE LEVEL OF REFLEX ACTION

At this level the action is an immediate and often direct response to a stimulus. It is relatively much more important in the lowly animal orders, as in the cœlenterates and molluscs. The direct though slow contraction of the tentacles of sea-anemones and hydroids has been seen by most persons who have had experience at the seaside. The prompt closure of the open shells of the living clam when the mantle edge is touched is also familiar. The closure of the clam's shell is a less direct response than is the contraction of the anemone's tentacles, for the stimulus must be transmitted from the mantle to the muscle of the shell hinge. The stimulus is applied to one organ and the response is in another some distance away, whereas in the case of contraction of the tentacle, response and stimulation pertain to the same organ. The lightning speed with which the tube-dwelling annelid worms disappear into their tubes upon the slightest contact of their tentacles with foreign bodies, is well known to frequenters of the seashore. In these animals the action, always regarded as reflex, is executed by the body muscles as well as by the tentacles, though the stimulus is applied to the tentacles only.

In all these cases there is no ground for doubting the general usefulness of the actions to the creatures, nor can there be any doubt about the successfulness of each specific act in most instances. If the mussel's shell and the annelid's tube are real protections of the creatures against enemies, or against desiccation when the animals are left high and dry every day by the outgoing tide; and if the closures are perfect, as they usually are, there seems nothing to be said against the completeness of the success of the actions which accomplish them. On the whole it is beyond question that a great range of reflex activities in animals are successful even as judged by our rather exacting test of success. The importance of such success is particularly striking in those animals in which this type of action constitutes the whole repertoire of activities upon which their lives depend.

While it is true that in all higher creatures other types of action play a far more dominating part, the reflexes are still indispensable. Except for the constantly successful performance of a great number of reflex actions there could be no successful life; in the entire absence of such reflexes there could be no life in us at all. The major portion of the digestive, respiratory, circulatory and reproductive functions, upon which continuance of life in the individual and the species is absolutely dependent, is accomplished by activities of this sort.

AT THE LEVEL OF INSTINCTIVE ACTION

The second type of activity which our examination will recognize we shall call instinctive. For the purpose of this discussion, we need not be concerned with the question debated by modern psychologists as to what instinct is, or whether there is any such thing. We are in need of a descriptive term for a kind of activity of animal organisms which is unmistakable throughout a great part of its range. Those actions which are common to all the individual organisms of the same natural kind or sex of that kind, the performance of which implicates many parts or the whole of the individual, and which do not have to be learned, we shall characterize as instinctive.

In no other classes of animals does instinctive action come to quite as clear expression as in the insects and spiders. As a first illustration we will describe the nest-building operations of the trap-door spider. Since I have watched this operation being performed by very young individuals it is worth while to describe it somewhat fully. These spiders, representative of several species inhabiting a large area of southwestern United States and adjacent Mexico, make their nest by digging a cylindrical hole in the ground, lining it with a thin layer of web-material, and closing the entrance with a lid attached by a hinge to the edge of the orifice. The nicety of fit and ease and efficiency of action of' this "trap-door" elicit the admiration of all who examine the structure. The lid, which is composed chiefly of hard sun-dried dirt reënforced by web-material and especially by an inside covering of this material, is beveled at its margin all around, and fits so perfectly a corresponding bevel inside the rim of the hole as to make the closure almost water-tight. At least, the closure excludes absolutely any wasps or other small creatures that might try to enter the nest through the doorway. The bore of the full-sized nest of the California species with which I am familiar is an inch or more in diameter, and the depth is four to seven inches.

The young spiders, though essentially the same in structure as the adults, are very small, not more than two or three millimeters in length. Yet these young, relatively minute spiders construct a miniature nest exactly on the pattern of, and almost as perfect as, the adults' nest, though they have never seen the adults perform the task nor had an opportunity to examine a completed nest.

Enough details will be given to enable the reader to appreciate something of the elaborateness, orderliness, and exactness of the activities involved. The baby spider begins by making a hole in the moist clayey ground, the mouth of which is sharp edged and almost a perfect circle. The diameter is just enough to permit the animal to go freely in and out, about three millimeters. The depth of the hole at this stage is sufficient to permit the animal to enter and hide himself completely in it. So far the hole seems to be made more by pushing the body into the ground than by excavating. Lid-making soon begins and is prosecuted in the following way: A minute projection is made at some point on the edge of the hole's mouth, by the combined use of the two front pairs of the spider's appendages. To this projection additions are made by particles or pellets brought from within the hole, probably from the bottom, deepening of the hole being thus combined with constructing the lid. Following every deposition and fixation of a load of earth by the anterior appendages, which implies that the animal comes to the place of deposit head-end up, a descent into the tunnel and a reversal of ends are made. Then follows a backing-up to the mouth of the tunnel, a placing of the tip of the abdomen against the edge of the lid-to-be, and a moving of the tip over the surface. This performance is undoubtedly accompanied by a discharge of web-material from the web-secreting gland which is located in this part of the body.

The two acts of bringing earth from the depths, the animal being head-end uppermost, and depositing it on the expanding lid; and of discharging web-material on the earth, alternate with perfect regularity until the lid mass has become broad enough to completely close the orifice of the tunnel. But a mere cumulation of materials, clay and web-substance, would not make the lid. Obviously there must be some genuine fashioning of materials. This modeling of raw materials into the nicely fitting, freely working trap-door is the really astonishing part of the whole operation. Each deposition of clay is immediately followed by a shaping operation, this being done chiefly by the same body members by which the earth was brought to the lid and put in place. By this means the lid is given its proper circular outline and thickness. After the lid has become broad enough to reach nearly across the orifice it is pulled down from time to time with sufficient force to do considerable toward beveling its own and the mouth's edges for producing that nice fit which is so conspicuous a feature of the completed product. Following each trial closure the lid is pushed open again for further construction work.

Two of my most vivid memory pictures of the operation, the whole of which I watched with such thrills of expectancy and surprise as to make me almost dubious at times about the trustworthiness of my eyes, must be specially mentioned. One of these pictures is of the little animal's abdominal tip being rubbed back and forth around the circumference of the nearly completed lid. A house-painter's brush or a plasterer's trowel could hardly work with more efficacy. The other special performance, even more startling than the first because less regularly done, consisted in pulling down the nearly finished lid, finding where the closure crack was widest, and then promptly pushing up the lid and refashioning it at the defective spot. It seems almost incredible that this last-mentioned act could be instinctive, yet such it must have been if judged by the characteristics of such actions as given above. It is certain that these spiders had no chance to learn the process they went through or even to do it by sheer imitation, for immediately upon hatching they had been taken from the parental nest into the laboratory and placed by themselves in a large dish containing moist earth.

This illustration of instinctive action presents evidence that the process was not learned but that the ability for it must have been obtained by inheritance from the creatures' ancestors, and that the ability is probably a common possession of all normal individuals of this species of spider. This particular observation was limited to members of only one brood. But since there were some dozens of these; since most of them were at work in the same way; and since observations on activities of other species have shown this commonness of ability, we are safe in presuming that all normal trap-door spiders, whether young or old, can construct the same kind of nests about equally well, and without having to be taught to do it. That nest construction by these spiders is a success in a majority of cases is certain. Were this not so the species would presumably have become extinct long ago.

There are innumerable other activities in the insect world and in many other animal classes, which are as unmistakably instinctive as is the nest-building by the trap-door spider, and as unmistakably successful. One other very striking form of such activity among bees and wasps is found in the wide range of cases in which the mother makes a nest solely for the young, deposits in it not only her egg or eggs but also food for the young, then leaves the whole accomplishment to its fate, either completely abandoning it or, in some cases, dying. In such a scheme there can be no possibility of the young mother's acquiring the building art from her parent either by direct imitation or by formal learning, since she never sees her mother; just as, in turn, her offspring will never see her.

It is difficult if not impossible to find such elaborate and clear-cut instances of purely instinctive activity among any

of the vertebrate classes as these noticed among the higher
arthropods. Especially among the higher vertebrates, the
activities are modified from the hard-and-fast hereditary and
mechanical type, in the direction of what we call intelligent
action. That the ancient type of action still predominates
even among the highest vertebrates below man there can be
no doubt. Among the lower vertebrates, fishes, amphibians
and reptiles, activity is almost wholly instinctive, but it
rarely attains to such elaboration and nicety of detail as it
does among the best of the arthropods. The lower vertebrates, notably the great piscine tribe, must be looked upon
as less well off from the standpoint of mentality than the
higher arthropods, being the inferiors of their arthropodian
kindred in perfection of instinctive activity but not yet having attained more than the earliest stages of modification in
the direction of intelligent activity. The real significance
of the lower vertebrates, more particularly the amphibians,
may be said to lie in the developmental possibilities, both
physical and mental, which their type of organization gives
them.

Two unmistakable examples of instinctive activity among
vertebrates which are almost as "pure" as any to be found
among arthropods are furnished, one by fishes and one by
birds.

The fish example is furnished by the Grunion (*Leuresthes
tenuis*) from the coast of California. It has been long
known that at its breeding time in March and April this
species comes in vast numbers onto sandy shores at high
tide. Only recently has the full meaning of this performance
been worked out. Thanks to the investigations of Mr. Will
F. Thompson we now have a fairly complete picture of what
happens during the exciting night runs of these fishes.[1] Fer-

---

[1] *The Spawning of the Grunion (Leuresthes tenuis)*, California Fish
and Game Commission, Fish Bull. No. 5, 1919, pp. 1-29.

tilization of the eggs is accomplished as the commingled females and males are thrown upon the beach by the waves. The females become partly buried, tail downward in the sand, where the eggs are "planted" with a shallow cover of sand over them. The planting ground being near the upper limit of wave action at the full-moon high tide of a given month, remains undisturbed by further wave action until the next run of high tides, approximately two weeks later. During this period the embryos develop to the hatching stage within the tough egg membranes. When the next high tide comes the encased embryos are washed out of the sand, and the wetted membranes so softened that the little fishes are enabled to escape into the water and be carried by the retreating waves into the sea.

Certain points of similarity between this and such reproductive procedure among bees and wasps as was referred to above are obvious. Perhaps the most notable of these is that the mother fish, like the mother wasp, goes through a definite and rather complex set of activities in depositing her eggs, the chief significance of which has reference to the welfare of the young yet to be, she herself taking no further part in the business, even to the extent of being present to see what goes on. As a consequence, with the fish as with the wasps, there is no chance for the young to learn from their mothers what to do when they in turn are to become mothers. In the one species as in the other the ability to perform the acts essential to the next generation is inborn, instinctive. With the fish as with the insects there is no evidence that any of the new-born females are devoid of this peculiar ability. All alike inherit it, thus furnishing another evidence that it is instinctive within the limits of our definition of that term.

The single illustration of what appears to be purely instinctive activity among birds is taken from an observation of my own on the crowing of roosters. Having moved several years ago to a home isolated by some two miles from the nearest human habitation, it was decided to raise a few chickens for the family larder. To this end a dozen or more recently hatched incubator chicks were secured from a dealer some ten miles away. As these youngsters developed, healthy and strong, to the stage in which the sex differences gradually came to view, I was on the lookout to learn what would happen as to the crowing ability of the young cocks, the assumption being that they had not, since the first few days of their lives outside the eggshells, had a chance to hear, much less to see, a rooster crow. One day while I happened to be near the cage in which the flock were confined, I saw one of the most developmentally advanced roosters stretch himself up in true rooster fashion and deliver a clarion blast as typical and well rounded as ever issued from the most learned and best experienced of his kind.[2]

While it is impossible to assert that this rooster's crowing mechanism had not been influenced to some extent through eyes and ears during the few days of its extra-ovate life while it was still in its original chicken-yard environment, this much seems certain: Immature as that mechanism certainly was at that early period it is impossible to conceive that the series of acts constituting a completed crow was learned and remembered in any such meaning as we ordinarily attach to those words. The mechanism must have been potentially and not actually capable of perform-

[2] It is certain that young roosters do not all begin their crowing with any such perfection of the act as that here described. In the ordinary chicken-yard conditions, the youngsters often begin with quite remarkable noises and only become real crowers by a course of practicing. The discrepancy between this and the performance in the instance described may be due to the fact that when a young rooster is constantly surrounded by crowing adults his crowing ability is stimulated into action earlier, by imitation, and so begins before the mechanism is mature enough to enable the first effort to be as perfect as it might be if it were brought into action only at a later time, as might have been the case in the instance described. It is barely possible that my individual practiced a few times before I heard him; but I do not think so, as I was near, and on the look-out, pretty constantly.

ing the acts. The tiny cock-chick was no more able to imitate his grown-up companions or to act on the basis of learning from them in the matter of crowing than in the matter of doing or being anything else that makes the full-grown rooster different from the rooster just out of the shell. Even granting all that might possibly be attributed to external crow-inducing influence upon the just-hatched rooster, by far the major part of the performance actually witnessed must be attributed to heredity, that is, specifically, to instinct.

The act of crowing involves much more than uttering a particular form of vocal sound. There is the characteristic up-stretching of legs and body and the characteristic forward movement of the head and crooking of the neck, to say nothing of the movements of the beak and other parts more directly concerned in producing and emitting the sound. The activity viewed as a unitary whole belongs so unmistakably to the physical organization of the creature that at best there is little room in the small mental part of it for anything else than what is instinctive. How far the notes and modulations of the crow were exact reproductions of those of his ancestors, it is impossible to say. Quite likely they were different in these respects, for it is known concerning various birds that whereas they possess large instinctive ability to produce vocal sounds, the particular form which these sounds take on, the particular notes and songs they actually produce, is dependent on what sounds, as songs of other birds, they hear. The song of the noisy mocking bird for example is made very largely of imitations of noises occurring around him.

There is no room for doubt that much of the activity of the higher vertebrates is instinctive even though considerable modification occurs in the direction of activity which we call intelligent. Nor is there any doubt that to a considerable extent these modifications are due to imitation of the old by the young, and to the actual teaching of the young by the parents and other grown-ups of the species.

AT THE LEVEL OF INTELLIGENT ACTION

The third level or type of action we shall call intelligent action. Here, as in the discussion of instinctive action, we are much more concerned with a particular type of action performed by some but not all organisms, than with a definition of an abstract principle called intelligence or intellect which some organisms are supposed to possess. *Whenever an organism receives a stimulus and has an impulse to act, but withholds the act pending a decision as to whether the act would be likely to procure the welfare of the organism, and finally acts according to the decision reached, we shall call such an act intelligent.*

OF LOW TYPE

A familiar illustration is seen in the method by which the house cat catches its prey. This can be observed to particular advantage when a cat is laying for a ground-burrowing rodent which ventures to emerge from its burrow. In order to succeed the cat must select a position not so near the hole as to scare the occupant when it comes to the hole's mouth, but also not so far away as to be beyond the cat's ability for an effective spring. A rather nice measuring of distance is here required. The cat holds a crouching position during the period of "watchful waiting." The tension under which a number of muscles are held while the belly side of the body is lowered nearly to the ground, and the position taken by all four limbs in maintaining this body posture while preparing for the impending jump, involve a series of significant psychobiological adjustments. The cat usually has to execute repeated starts and stops, according to the behavior of the victim. The instant eyes or ears of the watcher detect the slightest evidence that the prey is about to emerge, the readiness to spring is redoubled; but despite this renewed preparation to spring, the actual spring is withheld long enough to enable the cat to make sure whether or not the prey has emerged far enough to give the greatest chance for a successful trial. Stimulus and impulsion to action and organismal readiness therefor, but also a withholding of the full act till the greatest probability of its success is assured, are all well exemplified; as is both success and failure of action. Any one who has observed hunting cats must have seen them triumphantly running away with the dead victim dangling from their mouths. The observer must also have seen the well-calculated spring miss its goal, and the cat go more leisurely away with a certain manner that may easily be imagined to have in it something of disappointment or disgust.

The question of when a particular act can be counted a success arises here. If the would-be victim of the cat is actually captured and killed, is the operation entitled to be declared successful? Not necessarily, according to our criterion of success. Suppose that some hostile dog chances along just in time to be attracted by the cat's spring or the victim's cry, and plunges for the cat with as deadly intent as the cat sprang for the gopher, with the result that neither the cat herself nor her kittens benefit in the least degree by her "kill." Or suppose that serious injury or even death comes to the cat from this canine raid. The cat's characteristic hunting activity has no other meaning than the securing of food for herself or her young. That activity is composed of a whole series of acts in a sense distinct, yet all so related to the whole as to admit of being accounted successful only if the whole series succeeds.

Although the type of activity presented by the cat's hunting operations meets our test of intelligence, the level of the

type is too low to serve as a basis for such examination of
successful activity as we wish to make. The intelligence illustrated is of a decidedly simple order. The welfare sought,
satisfaction of the need for food, is positive and imperative.
The kind of food (fresh meat) is strictly accordant with all
of cat experience. The benefit sought is for the immediate
future, the consumption of the prey to be at once and complete. No recognizable question of psychical welfare ob-
trudes itself into the case. The only point in the whole
activity at which appears guidance of action involving inhi-
bition of impulse anticipatory of a more favorable chance
of attaining the ends sought is in the delay of the leap
until the prospective victim is sufficiently advanced in coming out of its hole.

OF HIGH TYPE

Just as it is impossible to understand the animal brain
without including in the study of it examples from the
whole range of the type, the human brain at its highest
development not excluded, so is it impossible to understand
animal intelligence without including in the study of it
examples from the whole range of the type, human intelligence not excluded. Where shall we go among mankind
for such illustrations except to such as not only bear all
the marks we have indicated of such activity, but which
were performed sufficiently long ago to enable us to see
unmistakably that they contributed to human welfare in
exceptional measure? High-level intelligent activity is illustrated by the discovery of America by Christopher Colum-
bus, Copernicus' achievement in astronomy, Galileo's in
physics, Harvey's in physiology, and Lavoisier's in chemistry. But on the whole some one of the achievements of
Louis Pasteur will perhaps serve us best as an illustration

to be closely examined. Let us take his work on the diseases of silkworms.

The life and labors of this great Frenchman are now so fully told that a general knowledge of what he did for the silk industry can be assumed. During the first half of the nineteenth century sericulture was one of the most important industries of southern France. By the middle of the century a disease of the silkworm had grown to such an extent, despite efforts to check it by some of the ablest statesmen and scientists of the time, as to almost ruin the industry not only in France but in other parts of the world. This caused great loss and suffering among those dependent on sericulture for a livelihood. Finally in 1865 when Pasteur was bringing to a triumphant conclusion his researches on spontaneous generation, on the diseases of wine, and on vinegar, an appeal was made to him to undertake an exhaustive research for the cause and a cure of the blight on the silk industry. To this appeal Pasteur yielded after much hesitation, due to the fact that he knew very little about insects or any other branch of zoölogy and had, as he said, "never touched a silkworm." The researches occupied much of his time and those of several assistants for about six years. The whole story is told by Pasteur himself in his *Études sur les maladies des vers à soie.*

We will restrict our examination to so much of the case as illustrates intelligent activity, centering the examination around the elements which constitute the chief marks of such activity. These marks are: the fact that the activities are in an essential part muscular; that activities of the particular class are known to promote welfare; and that decision as to performance of the specific acts is made on the basis of their probable welfare-production. In this case the welfare sought was the relief from distress of the people suffering from loss of the silk industry, by learning enough about the disease to make its control possible. That this rather than a desire to carry out a purely scientific research was the ruling motive with Pasteur we may definitely learn from his own words. In the preface to his *Studies on Silkworm Diseases* he wrote, "Nothing is more agreeable to a man who has made science his career than to increase the number of discoveries, but his cup of joy is full when the result of his observations is put to immediate practical use." [3] Many other statements of like purport might be quoted from his writings.

The mark of intelligence which we have listed as second, that of muscular activities of certain kinds inseparably connected with brain activities, is obvious in this case. All research in natural science is a sort of sublimated manual labor. No scientist ever advanced real knowledge of nature without using his hands or other body members along with his brain and sense organs. The most cursory glance at the descriptions of these silkworm studies shows that the truth of this general statement is exemplified in the special case before us. Sorting over grubs and chrysalids and adults as part of the work of observing which were diseased and which were not; dissecting many individuals preparatory to searching with the microscope for the "corpuscles" which were the particular telltales of the disease; grinding animals in a mortar with a bit of water to get pulp for examination; arranging eggs to protect them from contagion—the "intense work" during this period frequently mentioned in biographies of Pasteur was by no means a figure of speech, even from the purely physical standpoint.

The third attribute of intelligence, the making of decisions and choices as to what particular actions shall be performed under particular conditions, is clearly displayed in this illustration. The whole matter is involved in the most distinctive thing about the methods of natural science, namely, experi-

[3] Vallery-Radot, *The Life of Pasteur*, p. 150.

mentation. In a letter which Dumas wrote to Pasteur in connection with the work of Lavoisier, we read:"The art of experimentation leads from the first to the last link of the chain, without hesitation and without a blank, making successive use of Reason which suggests an alternative, and of Experience, which decides on it, until, starting from a faint glimmer, the full blaze of light is reached." [4] Choosing between two or more alternative possibilities, then acting in accordance with the choice—these two things lie very close to the heart, not only of scientific research, but of all intelligent living. The making of decisions as to how and when to act is cardinal in all scientific research. Consider as a typical instance of such decision-making the observation made early in the studies that eggs from healthy worms and moths might develop into diseased worms, while on the other hand, eggs from diseased worms and moths might produce healthy worms. "Is it," we find Pasteur asking, "that among the eggs of a very much diseased male and female there may be some sound ones? or are some eggs less infected and able to produce grubs which will return to health during culture?" "I do not know," is his answer at the outset, "which of these two explanations is the better, and there may be reason in both." Three alternatives, you see, necessarily indicating as many variations in the course of action to be pursued for ascertaining in which direction the truth lay. When it was finally discovered that a second disease, named by Pasteur "flacherie," was involved, as well as pebrine, the researches had revealed enough of the truth to make control of the disease possible.

Concerning the welfare attained by this six-year period of activity we will let Stephen Paget tell.[5] In his brief enumeration of the achievements of Pasteur we read with reference to this one: "He had been the very saving of the

[4] *Ibid.*, p. 122.
[5] *Pasteur and after Pasteur*, p. 54.

silk trade. It is only a few weeks ago, at Le Nuy, near St. Raphael, that I went over a silkworm nursery, and found his methods in use, as in 1870, so in 1914. *Flacherie*, I was told, has disappeared: *pebrine* is detected in good time. Of late years, in the south of France, horticulture has become a far more important industry than sericulture. . . . But the exportation of seed (silkworm eggs) goes on: and that seed is tested by Pasteur's methods."

Although it would be impossible to locate the welfare element in every scientific discovery as positively as it is located in this particular case of Pasteur's, we are of opinion that any genuine discovery in natural science examined closely enough and after the lapse of sufficient time will be found to be definitely promotive of human welfare in some of its forms and hence can be shown to possess this as well as the other marks of intelligent activity. Unless a reputed discovery can be shown sooner or later to have this mark it does not properly belong to the category of intelligent activity. Final judgments concerning the lives of nations are pretty sure to rest upon their kind and grade of culture and this is found upon analysis to depend more upon the achievements in literature, art, science, philosophy and religion than on purely physical developments and the accumulation of material wealth.

SYSTEMATIC STUDY OF SUCCESSFUL ACTIVITY IN SUBHUMAN ANIMALS

Having presented illustrations of intelligent action at low and high levels we shall now bring forward evidence that the success of the lives of various animals below man results to some extent from activities of the grade we are characterizing as intelligent. The ability to act with some degree of intelligence is very wide-spread in the animal world. There are numberless instances reported by hundreds of observers wherein it is contended that creatures of diverse rank in the zoölogical scale have shown intelligence. Although these descriptions of intelligence are rarely based on so clear-cut a criterion of what constitutes intelligence as we have adopted, close examination of specific instances finds recognizable actions of the kind we are regarding as intelligent among lower animals. The widely reputed intelligent action of certain species of ants affords instances of true intelligence and also of overestimating the degree of intelligence manifested in them.

Even naturalists of excellent reputation have interpreted so erroneously and written in such humanized language concerning what they have seen some of these animals do as to give wide currency to the notion that ants in general are far more intelligent than they really are. Here is an example: "Observe the little ants of our fields and paths, and see how they work. Watch how they dig their tunnels and cover them in, like so many railway engineers. . . . See how they stop every now and then to study out their plans; how they consider all obstacles and avoid them; how they use every leaf and stick and straw to make a wall or a roof for their galleries. . . . Then they watch the state of the weather very carefully. If the sun is warm, and it will do the eggs good to be in the upper galleries, every little ant begins tugging them along to put them in a warm place."

Something of the way human sentiment is imported into such narration as this is illustrated by a passage in Thoreau's account of the battle he witnessed between two races of ants. Concerning the effect upon him of what he saw, he says: "I was myself excited somewhat as if they had been men. The more you think of it, the less the difference. . . . I felt for the rest of the day as if I had had my feelings excited and harrowed by witnessing the struggle, the ferocity, and carnage of a human battle before my door."

We now know for a certainty that such interpretations of

the doings of ants is largely erroneous. So little similarity
is there between the fighting of ants and the "ferocity and
carnage of a human battle" that there is no occasion for
being thrown into such a state of mind as Thoreau experienced from being an eye-witness of fighting of this sort.
It may be true that the "more you think about it" in Thoreau's sense of thinking, "the less the difference" between
ants and men; but it certainly is not true that the more you
know about it the less the difference. No critical present-day
student of animal behavior believes for a moment that any
species of ants "stop every now and then to study their
plans." Nor do they "watch the state of the weather" very
carefully, or even very carelessly in any human sense.

That a residuum of true intelligent activity among ants is
left after the dross of humanization is completely driven off
seems almost certain in some cases. We will take a case
reported by Thomas Belt in his *Naturalist in Nicaragua*.
The species concerned was one of the leaf-cutting ants,
genus Occodoma, though Atta is, I believe, the name now
used. The observation was on colonies which raided Belt's
own garden so it had a double reason for being thorough:
it was made by an able naturalist bent on getting scientific
knowledge and saving his own property.

Having discovered the nest a short distance outside the
garden, and having tried unsuccessfully several methods of
heading off the raiders, he finally routed them by pouring
carbolic acid mixed with water down their burrows. "The
effect was all that I could have wished, the marauding parties
were at once all drawn off my garden to meet the new danger
at home. . . . Next day I found them busily employed
bringing up the ant-food from the old burrows, and carrying it to a new one a few yards distant." It was in connection with their moving that Belt says: "I first noticed a
wonderful instance of their reasoning powers." Between
the old burrows and the new one was a steep slope. Instead

of descending this with their burdens, they cast them down on the top of the slope, whence they rolled down to the bottom, where another relay of laborers picked them up and carried them to the new burrow. It was amusing to watch the ants hurrying out with bundles of food, dropping them over the slope, and rushing back immediately for more. They also brought out great numbers of dead ants which the fumes of carbolic acid had killed." Even this much of the operation justified, I should say, Belt's conclusion that the ants acted rationally: they met an unusual situation promptly and in a genuinely advantageous manner. It seems as though they must have decided between the alternative possibilities of action, and then carried out the decision effectively. The rest of the story confirms this view.

"A few days afterward," the narrative continues, "when I visited the locality again, I found both the old burrows and the new one entirely deserted, and I thought they had died off; but subsequent events convinced me that the survivors had only moved to a greater distance. It was fully twelve months before my garden was again invaded. . . . I followed them to their nest, and found it about two hundred yards from the one of the year before. I poured down the burrows, as before, several buckets of water and carbolic acid. . . . The ants, as before, were at once withdrawn from my garden; and two days afterwards, on visiting the place, I found all the survivors at work on one track that led directly to the old nest of the year before, where they were busily employed making fresh excavations. . . . It was a wholesale and entire migration." Then, after a few sentences giving further details, comes the concluding statement: "I do not doubt that some of the leading minds in this formicarium recollected the nest of the year before, and directed the migration to it."[6]

[6] *The Naturalist in Nicaragua*, 2nd ed., pp. 75-78.

Despite many gaps in this, we do not believe any interpretation of the case can be given that will accord as well with the facts presented as the one taken for granted by the author himself, that it was a "display of reasoning powers." Expressed in closer conformity with our conception, it was a manifestation of genuine intelligence even though of low order and mingled with much purely reflex and instinctive activity.

This view is made the more justifiable by other observations on ants of this same species and of different species. One other observation on the same species made by the same observer is worth noticing. A certain nest was so situated that the ants had to cross a tramway to reach the trees which they particularly liked. For a while they trailed over the rails and many were crushed to death by the wheels of the passing trams. Finally they set to work and tunneled under the rails, thus making the crossing safe. One day when the trams were not running, Belt stopped up the tunnels with rocks. "But although great numbers carrying leaves were thus cut off from the nest, they would not cross the rails, but set to work making tunnels underneath them."

We might go on indefinitely winnowing chaff from writings which attribute all sorts of mental excellence to many kinds of animals, finding considerable wheat in the form of evidence of genuine intelligence. We will take time for a few other studies in order to secure to the higher animals the proportionally greater attention to which their supremacy in this matter undoubtedly entitles them. The first of these will pertain to bears, the second to beavers. These two animals are chosen not because they are entirely unique in the amount of "fact and fancy" woven about them in the literature of animal life, but because they stand near the top of the list in this respect and each presents in a rather striking way certain traits of mentality that are especially important for us.

It is the opinion of some naturalists of wide experience with wild mammals that bears are among the most intelligent of all animals. Of all bears the North American Grizzly appears to be allowed first place in this regard; according to Hornaday's intelligence tests, this species is "the most keen-minded species of all bears." [7] The single bear case chosen as our illustration is one described by Wright.[8] Wright and his hunter companions tried to capture this bear in the Bitter Root mountains. The specimen being a particularly large one, they first tried to take it alive by means of a log pen and a steel trap so devised as to hold the animal without seriously injuring it. The bear eluded these efforts. The next plan was to kill him with two spring guns. The hunters were particularly confident of success by this means in that the cache of elk-meat which the grizzly was nightly visiting was so situated as to restrict his possible approaches to the meat. "The next morning when we went out to examine our trap we found written in footprints on the dirt as wonderful a record of animal sagacity as I have ever seen. The bear had come as usual for his evening meal. He had come down from his covert, circled the two cedars where our steel trap still waited for him, crossed the creek, and climbed to where the lower string (of the spring gun) was stretched across his path. But though he had come up to it he had not touched it. On the contrary his track showed that he had turned to his left, followed the string to the barrier of fallen trees, had found himself unable to get around it there, had turned and followed it to the rocks, had found himself blocked there also, and retraced his steps to the creek. He had then circled the rocky point, had climbed to the flat above, and had tried to reach the cache from the other side. But here he had again encountered the suspicious string. Once more he followed it down to the timber,

[7] *The Minds and Manners of Wild Animals*, p. 128.
[8] *The Grizzly Bear*, by H. M. Wright, 1909.

turned and made his way along the rocks, and then the wily old fellow had climbed out on the rock point, and making his way from ledge to ledge, had arrived safely between the two strings, eaten his meal in comfort, and gone out the way he came. We never got that bear." [9]

We see no reason for questioning the essential accuracy of the narrative here given. Nor do we see that any causal explanation fits the facts as well as the one assigned by the author, that of intelligence; and, we may add, intelligence in the sense in which we are using the term. There were surely two phases of the welfare of the bear himself in view. He needed food and he needed to avoid danger to himself while in pursuit of it. He went through a rather extensive set of actions to accomplish his twofold needs, and he several times found himself in situations where he chose between alternative possibilities of action.

Of all the lower animals there is no other species known to us whose industrial activities so much resemble those of the human species as do those of the beaver. The kinds of work done by beavers may be treated under four heads, namely, the construction of dwellings, the building of dams, the felling and disposing of timber, and the digging of canals.

Our immediate aim is to ascertain how well the operations actually serve the ends to which they appertain. The work done possesses a very high degree of general usefulness, of adaptiveness. Due attention to the most highly elaborated beaver creation taken each by itself and in its completed form, finds these to be truly wonderful in their exhibition of what, were they the handiwork of man, we should not hesitate to ascribe to conscious foresight in planning, and manual skill in executing. Subhuman animal accomplishment seems here to reach its climax. Consider first the general usefulness of each of the four categories of accomplishment indicated above.

[9] P. 141.

The house proper of the beaver is the family residence almost exactly as the human house is the family residence. It is where the children are born and reared and where parents and youngsters sleep, eat, and pass much of their time. In the typical beaver habitat the winter season is long and severe. As a result the dwelling is very important as a protection against snow and ice. This aspect of the protectiveness of the beaver house we humans can appreciate quite readily. Its protection against enemies we modern men can not so readily appreciate, since it is not ourselves but our remote ancestors whose experiences corresponded to those of the beaver in this respect. Bears, wolves, mountain lions, and coyotes are mortal enemies of beavers. The house proper and other structures often associated with it play as large a part in saving the family from destruction by these enemies as from killing temperatures.

The dams are used for impounding the waters of streams, to secure a depth of water into which the beavers can dive beyond the reach of their chief enemies, and in which they can move about freely. Of these aquatic activities the most characteristic is that of towing portions of trees and shrubs, for food and for the construction of dams and houses. By storing green timber with the bark on at the bottom of the reservoirs in autumn, a winter supply of food is assured, which is security against the two deadliest natural foes of the beaver, frost and marauding carnivores. The value of the artificially produced ponds as water supplies in times of drought is undoubtedly considerable. The similarity to man's water supplies in arid and semiarid countries is obvious.

The canals are transportation waterways, and as such are of high usefulness in the general economic and social life of the animals. They enable the animals to swim from one place to another where this mode of travel would be otherwise impossible. Usually they lead from the body of water where the dwelling is located toward the trees and shrubs which are the beavers' source of raw material for food and timber. In other words, the canals greatly facilitate the transportation of these materials from the place where they grow to that where they are used. Some good observers have regarded these structures as the highest expression of beaver engineering.

Lumbering is the chief source of food supplies and of material for houses and dams. Although beavers feed on grass and other succulent vegetation, and on roots, still the great staple is bark, the bark of trees and shrubs, fresh and green or as nearly so as possible. This being the case there is no way of getting a sufficient quantity except by felling the timber. The bark of a tree of moderate size once prostrate on the ground or in a pond is available for beaver use. But actually to consume all the bark by gnawing it off where the tree fell would be greatly to expose the animals, old and young, to their deadly carnivorous enemies. The places of greatest safety for the beaver are the depths of its home body of water, its dwelling house, or the burrow or passageway leading to it. The creature is a submarine under conditions of perpetual war so far as safety is concerned. The material must be transported as soon as possible to some safe base, the bark there to be gnawed off from the sticks, the sticks later to be used in construction and repair. Even trees of small size are too large and awkward to be transported and dealt with whole. They must be cut up into manageable pieces. The branches must be trimmed and the body and all limbs of considerable length must be reduced to pieces that can be readily dragged along the ground or floated in the water and, frequently, carried into the houses.

Given beavers living under present conditions, lumbering of such character as we actually see among them is indispensable to their existence. The activity as a whole is useful, is adaptive, in a vital sense. To assess the value of this adaptiveness accurately we must examine some of the operations and their fruits. For this we will take the dwelling and the dam, and the relation between the two.

It is probable that the primordial element in this combination of things was the burrow in the bank of a stream or pond of considerable depth of water. The animal was a bank burrower before it was a house builder; various facts indicate that both burrowing and house building are more ancient habits than dam building. The habit of damming up streams probably came into being for the purpose of producing depth of water sufficient to make the house proper, plus the underground, underwater passageway by which it is reached, practicable and safe. House, passageway and dam are normally intimately and remarkably related. The house is typically so placed at the water's edge on an island or on a mainland bank that its floor is only a few inches above the water level. One end of the passageway is in the pond at considerable depth; the other end is in the floor of the house. As a consequence the passage must slope up to the house, and the water level of the pond cannot change much without seriously interfering with the household life of the beaver family. An important element in the beaver's problem of dam construction and maintenance is therefore that of keeping the water level of the pond as nearly constant as possible. On this point Morgan writes: "From the uniform relation found to subsist between the level of the floor and of the pond, it is evident that the beavers regulate the discharge of the surplus water through their dams with a view to the maintenance, as near as possible, of a uniform level of the pond. Any great variation in this respect would either flood their habitations or expose their entrances; and therefore the maintenance of their dam becomes a matter of constant supervision and perpetual labor." [10] This constant

[10] L. H. Morgan, *The American Beaver and His Work*, p. 146.

supervision and labor consist in repairing leaks in the dams to keep the water up to the proper level, and making openings in the dam at times of high water to keep the water down to the proper level.

The remarkable adaptiveness displayed in connection with dwellings does not end with this production and maintenance of a proper relation between house and dam. The construction of the entrance passages themselves, is, according to Morgan's account, quite as notable. He writes: "The entrances to a beaver lodge, of which there are usually two, and sometimes more, are the most remarkable parts of the structure. They are made with great skill, and in the most artistic manner." [11] After stating that the difference between the two passages is such as to indicate that one is a mere entrance for the animals while the other is the "wood entrance," by which the wood cuttings used for food are brought into the house, Morgan gives a detailed description of the passageway. "Both entrances were rudely arched over with a roof of interlocked sticks filled in with mud intermixed with vegetable fiber, and were extended to the bottom of the pond and trench. . . . At the places where they were constructed through the floor they were finished with neatness and precision; the upper parts and sides forming an arch more or less regular, while the bottom and floor edges were formed with firm and compact earth, in which small sticks were embedded. It is difficult to realize the artistic appearance of some of these entrances without actual inspection." [12]

This account should be coupled with the statements by Morgan and others that the earthen floor of a well-made house is so hard and resistant to water that it remains dry and solid although it stands typically only a few inches above the water level. Obviously a prime object, if object they

[11] P. 144.
[12] Ibid.

consciously have, in the construction of floor and passage-
ways is to make the walls and surfaces both strong and as
nearly as possible impervious to water.

The wall of the house presents some features of special
interest in connection with the problem of adaptation. Sticks
and poles of wood are the main materials entering into the
composition of full-sized beaver houses. Mud containing
great quantities of vegetable fiber plays a large part in many
houses. Morgan and other observers affirm that in some
localities the exterior surface of the walls is given a coat of
mud by the beavers at the approach of winter. This increases not only the warmth of the dwelling but, through
the freezing of the mud, the strength of the walls against the
depredations of carnivorous animals which, under the hunger
stress of winter, often try to reach the beaver families by
house-breaking.

Although a few authors deny that the animals avail themselves of this means of protection, the earlier affirmations of
it were verified by so many recent observers that there no
longer seems any doubt about it. Thus both Enos A. Mills [13]
and A. R. Dugmore [14] give accounts of such procedure with
so much particularity in both description and illustration,
that the statements of Morgan and others must be accepted.

Because of the remarkable resemblance of the construc-
tions by beavers to some of those by men all sorts of ex-
travagant estimates of the intelligence of the creatures have
been made. Thus we have from Samuel Hearne, writing in
1785: "There cannot be a greater imposition, or indeed a
grosser insult on common understanding, than the wish to
make us believe the stories of some of the works ascribed to
the beaver." But: "To deny that the beaver is possessed
of a very considerable degree of sagacity would be as absurd in me as it is in these authors who think they cannot

[13] *In Beaver World*, 1923.
[14] *The Romance of the Beaver*, 1914.

allow them too much. I shall willingly grant them their full share." As an example of the sort of thing Hearne was aiming his irony at, he mentions the yarn that beavers "drive stakes as thick as a man's leg into the ground three or four feet deep" and then "wattle these stakes with twigs." Such stories are not necessarily, indeed not usually, deliberate falsifications, nor are they pure fiction; they usually result from bad observation coupled with bad general information and bad use of the imagination. They do not appertain to any particular people or cultural state, though unquestionably they become less general and less glaring with the advance of culture.

My own observations on the work of beavers lead me to conclude, as numerous other observers have concluded, that as a matter of fact the creature's activities are no more intelligent than are those of numerous other mammalian species. Various members of the wolf and bear families, for instance, are probably somewhat superior to beavers in this respect; and beyond question any of the monkeys, to say nothing of the anthropoids, are greatly their superiors.

The most significant thing about beaver work is the illustration it affords of the extent to which instinctive activity can come to resemble rational and even intelligent activity.

It is now beyond question that the creatures which come nearest to man in ability to act intelligently are the anthropoid apes, the same creatures which, as everybody knows, most resemble man in structure. Any doubt concerning the degree of intelligence of these creatures is due to the meagerness of our knowledge of them in the most crucial situations of their wonted careers in their native wilds. Such situations are the final test of intelligent action. So difficultly accessible to civilized man are the regions inhabited by the anthropoids that the observations on their habits in nature are very few and fragmentary as compared with those on many other groups of animals. We are dependent for what is known about the activities of man's closest of kin among the lower orders on studies of individuals taken by force from their natural environments and held in captivity.

But thanks to the efforts of several people who have lately interested themselves in the activities of these creatures considerable has already been done to improve our knowledge of them. The investigations of Köhler and Yerkes are outstanding for the chimpanzees and orangs; as are the amateur, but none the less important, experiences of Miss Cunningham with the gorillas.

So abundant, varied, and convincing is the evidence of manlike psychical attributes of chimpanzees presented in *The Mentality of Apes*, by Wolfgang Köhler, and so simply and entertainingly is the story told, that we will assume all readers particularly interested in this aspect of our general subject will acquaint themselves with this book. We will restrict our presentation to one of the most telling instances of human-like activity. We take the widely quoted instance of stick-splicing for a purpose by the chimpanzee, Sultan.[15] The ape had acquired facility in using a stick to get food which was beyond the reach of his hand thrust through the bars of his cage. The situation created for Sultan by the experimenter was this: Food (a banana) was placed outside the ape's cage, too far away to be reached with one stick but not too far to be reached with two sticks spliced together. Two separate pieces of bamboo, which thus spliced would be long enough to reach the fruit, were placed in his cage. Such pieces, one sufficiently smaller than the next to let its end be slipped a little way into the bore of the other, were placed within easy reach of the ape. Question: Would Sultan's intelligence be sufficient to enable him so to combine the several detached elements in the situation as to secure the coveted food?

[15] *Op. cit.*, pp. 130 ff.

The situation and the problem stated in this way seem to have been too much for the ape. He made no real progress toward getting the food. But a little later two other elements came into the situation through which the problem was solved. These elements were the animal's playfulness after experimenter and animal had wearied of the formal experiment, and mere fortunate accident. From this point the story can best be told in the words of the keeper and the experimenter: "Sultan first of all squats indifferently on the box, which has been left a little back from the railings; then he gets up, picks up the two sticks, sits down again on the box and plays carelessly with them. While doing this, it happens that he finds himself holding one rod in either hand in such a way that they lie in a straight line; he pushes the thinner one a little way into the opening of the thicker, jumps up and is already on the run towards the railings, to which he has up to now half turned his back, and begins to draw a banana toward him with the double stick. I call the master: meanwhile, one of the animal's rods has fallen out of the other, as he has pushed one of them only a little way into the other; whereupon he connects them again."

The key to the problem once in Sultan's hands, by these partly playful, partly accidental and partly intelligent activities, was used regularly and varied in several advantageous ways. A noteworthy thing about the ape's success in solving this problem was the evidence of satisfaction shown by him, not merely in getting the food but in the achievement itself: "The proceeding seems to please him immensely; he is very lively, pulls all the fruit, one after the other, towards the railings without taking time to eat it, and when I disconnect the double stick, he puts it together again at once and draws any distant objects whatever to the bars." A modification of this experiment in which intelligence shows distinctly, consisted in putting three instead of two sticks at the ape's disposal, two of them being nearly the same size, and larger than the third. Köhler emphasizes the statement that Sultan never tried to join the two larger sticks. Good observation coupled with judgment seem unmistakable here.

Concerning the manipulative difficulties encountered in using the double-length stick, we are told: "The long tool sometimes gets into his way . . . by its farther end getting caught between the railings, when being moved obliquely, so the animal quickly separates it into its parts, and finishes the task with one tube only."

When the fruit was placed beyond the reach of the double-length stick, but not beyond a triple-length one, and the three pieces were at hand, the solution of the problem proceeded as follows: "He puts them (the two larger pieces) opposite to each other for a moment, not touching, and looks at the two openings, but puts one aside directly (without trying it) and picks up the third thinner one; the two wide tubes having openings of the same size. The solution follows suddenly: Sultan fishes with a double-stick, consisting of the thinner one and one of the bigger ones, holding, as usual, the end of the smaller one in his hand. All of a sudden he pulls the double-stick in, turns it round, so that the thin end is before his eyes and the other towering up in the air behind him, seizes the third tube with his left hand, and introduces the tip of the double-stick into its opening. With the triple pole he reaches the objective easily; and when the long implement proves a hindrance in pulling the objective to him, it is disconnected as before."

But even with this convincing evidence of intelligence of the chimpanzee before us it yet seems that the gorilla at its best may rank next to man in mental ability. The ground for hesitancy in accepting this statement is in part the limited number of cases which the evidence contains, there being as a matter of fact only one such, that of the young

"John Gorilla," kept and trained by Major Rupert Penny and his relative, Miss Alyse Cunningham, of London.[16]

The statements concerning this animal most important for us are those detailing the activities involved in food-taking. After mentioning the surprising fact "that the only thing he stuck to was milk," Miss Cunningham says: "I found that he preferred to choose his own food, so I used to prepare for him several kinds, such as bananas, oranges, apples, grapes, raisins, currants, dates, and any small fruits in season, such as raspberries or strawberries, all of which he liked to have warmed.

"These displays I placed on a high shelf in the kitchen, where he could get them with difficulty. I think that he thought himself very clever when he stole anything. He never would eat anything stale. He never cared much for nuts of any other kind than baked peanuts, save walnuts. I found that nuts gave him dreadful spells of indigestion. With cocoanuts he was very funny. He knew that they had to be broken, and he would try to break them on the floor. When he found he couldn't manage that, he would bring the nut to one of us and try to make us understand what he wished. If we gave him a hammer he would try to use it on the nut, and on not being able to manage that, he would give back to us both the hammer and the cocoanut. . . . He always liked nibbling twigs, and to eat green buds of trees. He did not care to eat a great deal, but he especially liked to drink water out of a tumbler. He was the least greedy of all the animals I have ever seen. He never would snatch anything and always ate very slowly. He always drank a lot of water, which he would get for himself whenever he wanted it by turning on a tap. Strange to say, he always turned off the water when he had finished drinking."

[16] The data concerning this gorilla are taken from the account given by Miss Cunningham to Dr. Hornaday and published by him in *The Minds and Manners of Wild Animals*, pp. 95-99.

Despite the brevity and defectiveness of this narrative, it seems to us there is evidence here of real choosing and other forms of guidance of the food-taking activity in accordance with the nutritional interests of the organism. Some of these interests were peculiar to the conditions of life under which John found himself as contrasted with those he would have lived under had it been his lot to live in the same environment and in the same way that all his ancestors before him had lived. Surely his taste for baked peanuts could not have been part of his hereditary equipment. His desire to "choose his own food" seems significant in this direction. His mental make-up appears to have enabled him so to modify his instinctive food-taking activities that he was able to live in health, comfort, and efficiency under conditions very different from those to which nature and heredity would have consigned him.

The justification and full significance of this conclusion depend partly on facts not yet presented. When John came into Major Penny's possession he was seriously ill, and was in a "rickety" condition, weighing only 82 pounds. He was bought in a London department store where the atmospheric temperature was 85°F. and where his nights were spent in "solitude and terror." December, 1918, was the date of his transfer from this state of wretchedness to his healthy and comfortable new home, which seems to have been entirely agreeable to him. One of the consequences of this transfer was that by March, 1921, he weighed 112 pounds, and was in "robust health and buoyant spirits." In view of the great improvement thus indicated in John's physical and mental life, it seems to us justifiable to make the hypothesis (though a simpler one would be possible) that the changes which he adopted in certain of his feeding activities were due to some extent to his memory of the distressful consequences of his earlier mode of life, and to some extent to prerecognition of how such consequences might be avoided. Should later in-

vestigations of gorilla life prove this hypothesis correct, it
would place this species considerably higher in the scale
of psychical development, so far as nutritional matters are
concerned, than, as the evidence now stands, either the
orang or the chimpanzee has reached. As to the chimpanzee particularly, Köhler has presented evidence of very
limited ability to act at a given time with reference to its
welfare at a future time. "As a matter of fact," we read,
"one never saw them deliberately settle on the successful
manner of choice with an eye to the future; on the contrary,
the animals were carried away by their immediate interest
in the goal before them (food), and if now and then a glance
settled for a moment on the objects they had to choose from,
this seemed to occur only because something chanced to
strike them; not intentionally in order to turn the lucky
method of choice to future use." [17]

With such evidence as these cases furnish of ability on
the part of subhuman beings to do things as human beings
do them, it would seem there is no longer any more reason
for doubting the mental and spiritual unity of brute and
human animals than there is for doubting their morphological and physiological unity. Some of the most urgent
needs of psychobiology at the present moment are comparative researches on anthropoids and very young human
children. It is gratifying to note such well-supported and
well-directed effort as that now being instituted at Yale
University for anthropoid studies and that in progress at
several places for studies on young children.

PERSONALITY AS AN ELEMENT IN GROUP SUCCESS

Our examination of the animal world has shown us that
activity on the plane of intelligence is broadly and securely
established in large portions of that world. Our knowledge

[17] P. 284.

of the biological fact of individual variation indicates that any evidence of tendencies toward improvement in intelligent action would be found as a variant in personalities. No two individual plants or animals in all the world are quite alike. This fact of difference between individuals is a securely founded biological principle, well recognized as basic to all true organic development. Man's knowledge of himself convinces him that all human beings differ from one another more or less, not only in body but in mind even more than in body.

This fact of spiritual difference among individuals is an absolutely indispensable factor in man's cultural development. All forward movements in human culture are initiated by individuals who differ in their capacity for activity at all levels from other individuals. The most essential factor in any forward movement in human culture is some attribute or group of attributes which make the individual possessing them to some extent unlike all other individuals. This is only a way of giving greater definiteness and precision to the common pronouncement that all progress in civilization is due initially to personalities of outstanding spiritual attributes.

The question now arises: Are there among the higher sub-human animals a few personalities which by reason of endowments distinctly superior to those of the rank and file are able to come to the front at times of stress and danger as savers of their individual lives and of the lives of their kindred? Are we to suppose the "safety-first" ability shown by the grizzly bear reported by Mr. Wright was a common possession of all grizzlies? Or was the particular individual especially endowed? Are we to suppose that the labor-saving device resorted to by Belt's ant colony, or the life-saving device of those that tunneled under the tram rails, were manifestations of abilities possessed in equal degree by all the individual ants? Or is it more probable that some, perhaps a very few, individuals were responsible in the first instance for the new and better ways of acting? Were the rank and file of ants saved by outstanding personalities of their groups?

If these questions are answered in the affirmative, we must recognize here one of the prime means of success in animal activities. This means is twofold, involving on the one hand the possession by certain individuals of exceptional powers; and on the other hand the ability of the rank and file of the species to profit by these unusual abilities of the outstanding individuals. It is easy to see that observations on which to base positive answers to such questions might be somewhat rare. They require more continuous studies on animals in their native wilds than can be made without special training and effort.

As to domestic animals there is no difficulty in recognizing the mere fact of more or less unique personality. This is especially so with reference to the dog and the horse. Such personality is too obvious here to escape notice of any one except those so unfortunate as to be deprived of all companionship with them. Most of the domesticated species have been so long subject to the shielding and modifying influence of man that one can never feel quite certain about the natural developmental significance of the attributes exhibited. We want evidence from species unmodified by man, and undoubtedly a good deal of such evidence exists. One source of it is the behavior of wild animals held captive for experimental studies. The records of such behavior contain many references to individual differences in response, temperament and ability to learn. These are all symptomatic of a measure of special personal "gifts."

Perhaps the most important source of evidence under this head are the experiences of trainers of wild animals for exhibition and similar purposes. From conversation with Mr. W. E. Winston, who has had great experience in training Cal-

ifornia sea lions for exhibition, we learn that the first thing
to be done when young animals come fresh to the training
school, is to get a general acquaintance with them to determine what chance there is of their being made into good
performers. Some individuals, according to this trainer,
soon show themselves to be hopeless and are discarded, while
others can be trained to varying degrees of excellence and
with varying amounts of effort and patience on the trainer's
part. A variety of elements such as shyness, irritability,
degree of activity, enter into the final determination.

Hornaday [18] has some apposite remarks on this subject.
The species which have some zoölogical park training are
named in the order of importance: "Elephants, bears, apes,
hippopotomi, rhinoceroses, giraffes, bison, musk-ox, wild
sheep, goats and deer, African antelopes, wild swine, and
wild horses, asses, and zebras. Of large birds the most conspicuous candidates for training in park life are the os-
triches, emus, cassowaries, cranes, pelicans, swans, egrets,
and herons, geese, ducks, pheasants, macaws and cockatoos,
curassows, eagles and vultures. Among the reptiles the best
trained are the giant tortoises, the pythons, boas, alligators,
crocodiles, iguanas, and gopher snakes."

All these animals, rather common in zoölogical gardens,
undergo some education toward becoming peaceful, toward
not attacking or fearing their keepers, toward doing as they
are told about going here or there, toward accepting the
food that is provided for them, and finally, as to some of
the species, toward "showing off" a little when commanded
for the benefit of visitors. "Every wild animal species,"
says Hornaday, "contains the same range of bright and dull
individuals that are found in the various races of men.
Naturally the animal trainer selects for training only those
animals that are of amiable disposition, that mentally are
alert, responsive, and possessed of good memories. The

[18] *The Minds and Manners of Wild Animals,* p. 206 et seq.

worst mistakes they make are in taking on and forcing ill-natured and irritable animals that hate training and performing. . . . While nearly every wild animal can be taught a few simple tricks, the dull mind soon reaches its constitutional limit. Even among the great apes the conditions are quite the same." Some of the attributes mentioned by Mr. Winston and by Mr. Hornaday come under the head of temperament, rather than of reason, in the nomenclature of human mentality; it is quite conceivable that some temperamental elements, which would be inimical to the training aimed at, might be combined with specially high ability to reason. It may be that the "amiable disposition" spoken of by Hornaday for doing such "stunts" and other acts as would please keepers and visitors of zoölogical parks might mark a rather inferior grade of reasoning ability of the animals.

Much more could be drawn from other sources which would tend to show that the whole animal world, but especially the higher levels of it, presents the phenomenon of personality much as does the human world. Animals with the same instinctive and reflex equipment differ in ability to use that equipment for successful adaptive activity. Animals, like humans, differ greatly in their ability to meet the problems of life. It is justifiable to suppose on such evidence as we have that, as with the human world, so with the animal, security of existence and assurance of progress of the individuals of the whole group are largely dependent upon the ability of these individuals to profit by the achievements of certain personalities of very special and hence very rare adaptive departures from the average of their kind.

CHAPTER 7

MALADAPTIVE ACTIVITY RESULTING IN WASTE OF TIME AND ENERGY

IN the activities of every species as it exists in nature there is sufficient measure of success to enable it to exist. While life and activity are not synonomous terms, an organism as well as its activity being essential to life, the organism is dead and not alive as soon as its activities cease wholly. This proof of a degree of success in activity is by no means proof that the degree of success is the highest possible degree. This is particularly clear as to individuals. The life processes may run on for several years so smoothly as to constitute what is regarded as success for that individual. Then some critical situation may arise, some havoc-working occurrence in external nature, some miscalculated undertaking of the individual himself, which tests the adaptive capacity of the organism to the limit. Though the test may be withstood in the sense that the organism does not succumb utterly, the degree of success which might have been achieved without the impairment may be seriously lessened.

The elements which enter into the life of any creature, especially of a human being living under a high state of culture, are too diverse to make possible a mathematically exact estimate of the degree of success of an individual life as dependent on the activities of that life. But there is a great range within which such success is measurable; elements which tend to interfere with it are recognizable and controllable, and therefore within the scope of activities which are determinative of success.

If a bird builds its nest where snakes or cats may get at and destroy its young, when by the exercise of foresight it might have built it out of reach of such dangers; if a human mother feeds her infant milk that endangers its health from being defective as food, when by the exercise of foresight she might have avoided this danger, both bird and human are acting unsuccessfully or maladaptively.

Our present task is the presentation of facts showing, as far as possible in a comparatively brief space, the extent to which maladaptive activity does occur in both the brute and the human animal worlds.

Viewing these activities with reference to the ways in which they are disadvantageous to the organisms concerned, we find they fall into four subdivisions. Activities which result in waste of time or energy or both; activities which result in waste of materials needed by the creatures; activities which result in injury to the close-of-kin of the individuals performing the acts; finally, activities which result in injury to the acting individuals themselves. Although this classification rests on indubitably observable facts, and hence is far from arbitrary, it is used here merely to facilitate our discussion. We may therefore take more liberties with it than we could were our purpose to give it the greatest possible measure of scientific accuracy and logical consistency. The subdivisions may cross one another in the actual application of the system. Waste of materials, in the second subdivision, may be injurious to close-of-kin and to the individuals themselves. In the course of our presentation we turn this plasticity of the scheme to our advantage without impairing its scientific integrity.

There is little doubt that maladaptive activity of the first mentioned kind occurs in all the animal groups, but there is less detailed information here than in any of the other of our four classes of such activities. Precise data as to when expenditure of energy and time passes the limit of usefulness are wanting, especially for the animal groups below man. This class would be omitted from the present treatment were

it not for the need of a class in which to place those activities
often characterized as lost motion in lower animals and in
children. Loosely as this phrase is ordinarily used, it is somewhat discriminating, for it distinguishes between movements
lost through error of judgment or inadequate knowledge, and
those lost by mere error-upon-trial. Examples of this latter
may be seen by anybody anywhere among brute animals.
Mark Twain's account of the performances of ants is good
natural history even though it sacrifices scrupulous truth
here and there to the requirements of spicy writing. We
read: [1] "During many summers, now, I have watched him
when I ought to have been in better business, and I have
not yet come across a living ant that seemed to have any
more sense than a dead one. . . . I admit his industry of
course; he is the hardest working creature in the world . . .
but his leatherheadedness is the point I make against him.
He goes out foraging, he makes a capture, and then what
does he do? Go home? No,—he goes anywhere but home.
He doesn't know where home is. His home may be only
three feet away,—no matter, he can't find it. He makes
his capture, as I have said; it is generally something which
can be of no use to himself or anybody else; it is usually
seven times bigger than it ought to be; he hunts out the
awkwardest place to take hold of it; he lifts it bodily into
the air by main force, and starts; not toward home, but in
the opposite direction; not calmly and wisely, but with a
frantic haste which is wasteful of his strength; he fetches
up against a pebble, and instead of going around it, he climbs
over it backwards dragging his booty after him, tumbles
down on the other side, jumps up in a passion, kicks the
dust off his clothes, moistens his hands, grabs his property
viciously, yanks it this way, then that, shoves it ahead of
him a moment, turns tail and lugs it after him a moment, gets
madder, then presently hoists it into the air and goes tearing

[1] *Tramp Abroad,* Chap. XXII, and quoted by L. O. Howard in *The
Insect Book,* p. 41.

away in an entirely new direction; comes to a weed; it never occurs to him to go around it, he must climb it . . . which is as bright a thing to do as it would be for me to carry a sack of flour from Heidelberg to Paris by way of Strasburg steeple."

This is only a literary man's way of saying what a scientist makes shorter work of, at least as a summary of his conclusions. Thus we have from Albrecht Bethe as a final conclusion to his extensive researches on the mentality of ants and bees: [2] "They learn nothing, but act mechanically in whatever they do, their complicated reflexes being set off by simple physical stimuli." Bethe finds no evidence of any "psychical quality"; but with this conclusion we are not here concerned.

My own notes on the work of the black harvester ant (*Messor andrei?*) of southern California add some quantitative definiteness to Twain's story. The loads being carried by thirty-nine individuals of this species headed for home on the same path were examined in the early morning of July 13, 1920. Of these loads thirteen were grass seeds containing meats, six were filaree seeds containing meats, and twenty were classed in my notes as rubbish, most of them being unidentifiable fragments of vegetation, though four were empty shells of the seed of the ice plant, and of an atroplex. Of these thirty-nine loads at least one-half were useless. They contained no food, so far as I could see; and as this species harvests for no other purpose, all the effort bestowed upon these good-for-nothing items was lost motion. The regular course of things would be for the objects to be carried into the colony burrows, allowed to remain there for a time, as are seeds while being shelled, then brought out and thrown on the dump as are the empty seedshells.

[2] Albrecht Bethe, *Arch. f. d. Ges. Phys.*, Vol. LXX, No. 15, p. 100, Jan., 1899. Also a review of same by Caswell Grave, *Amer. Nat.*, Vol. XXXII, pp. 437-439.

It might be unjustifiable to conclude from one instance like this that a half of all the work of harvesting done by these ants is lost motion. My guess is, however, that when all activities performed in connection with the business are taken into the account the figure is under rather than over the truth. I am of opinion that fuller quantitative studies of ant harvesting would discover that the per cent of useless material gathered is correlated with the per cent of such material there is in the area over which the harvesting extends.

Another type of lost motion in ant harvesting is illustrated by the following: On September 27, 1919, a black harvester belonging to a colony on the grounds of the Scripps Institution at La Jolla, California, was seen carrying an atroplex seed toward the colony nest. When first noticed the ant was about forty feet from its destination. Several serious obstructions in the path had to be overcome before the nest was reached, and a full quarter of an hour was consumed in accomplishing the distance. Of the obstacles in the path, two were the spreading branches of the plant, Atroplex, which produced the kind of seed the ant was carrying. Both these plants along the path and another at the very mouth of the nest holes were laden with seeds, many of which had already fallen to the ground. The ant had carried a seed more than forty feet, at two points along the way laboring through the branches of plants which had strewn the ground with seeds of the same kind as the one it was carrying, while a third plant had dropped an abundance of the same seeds at the very door of its home. Enough energy had been expended to transport a load of food forty feet at least; essentially the same load of entirely similar food could have been secured by the expenditure of only a minute fraction of the energy. Any open-minded watcher of the activities of these ants can see just as much of this sort of thing as he cares to take time for.

This class of maladaptive activities affords a convenient pigeon-hole for the reception of activities which, though in themselves unavailing, cannot be adjudged entirely useless. They are due to inadequate knowledge or erroneous judgment, but they contribute to the rectification of this inadequacy or error. They may constitute a quantitative offset to qualitative defectiveness in action.

A man following an obscure trail comes to some point at which he is uncertain which way to go. Several trials may be necessary before he is sure he is on the right course. Considerable time and strength may be consumed in this way; such loss is apt to be charged to the lost motion account. In a sense, both the effort and the time are lost. But the circumstances were such as to make the trials indispensable, and their outcome was success, the right course having been found at last. Although excessive activity in such a case may be in itself injurious, its final usefulness is undoubted. The chance of some measure of loss or injury is deliberately risked for the advantage of final success.

The assessment of human activities on this basis is obviously a very difficult, delicate and important matter which cannot be attempted here. The proneness of children to spend too much energy and time in play is generally recognized among experts in child health. This recognition is not in essential conflict with the universal recognition that play is highly useful in a variety of ways. The only question is as to when and where it ceases to be useful and becomes neutral or harmful. This problem needs more study than it has had.

Many primitive people care so much for their games and ceremonies, and spend so much time and substance on them, as to impair seriously their economic welfare. One of the main objections made by agents and teachers responsible for Indians on the reservations controlled by the United States Government to the keeping up of the native dances and other

ceremonials is economic. The performances are recognized
as serious obstacles to that measure of industry essential to
the economic and social well-being of the people concerned.
This matter is discussed at some length in the section on
maladaptive activities among low-cultured peoples. An illustrative example may be given here from my own experiences among the Navajo Indians in the fall of 1920. The
annual Indian fair at the San Juan Agency was held while I
was on the reservation. A trip of 120 miles through the
heart of the Navajo country impressed me with the Indians'
interest in the event. The entire population, men, women,
and children, were en route for San Juan.

Hardly ever have I seen a more novel and significant exhibition. Rugs, as any one acquainted with Navajo industry
would expect, were the outstanding feature of the fair, but
raw wool from the flocks, and corn, squashes, melons from
the land, entered considerably into the exhibition. On the
basis of the evidence assembled, the Navajo appeared to be
one group of American Indians well on the road to industrial
development and economic independence. While on the
whole a conclusion to this effect is probably justifiable, the
testimony of one of the traders, confirmed by that of Government agents, teachers, and physicians, was rather shocking
from this standpoint. "This is called an 'Indian fair,'" said
the trader, "but really it is nothing of the sort so far as
getting it up is concerned. The Indians don't care a d——
about these exhibits. The whites have all sorts of trouble
to get the Indians to bring their rugs, corn, squashes, etc.
The only way we can induce them to come is to promise
them a good *hibushai* [medicine men's ceremonial with much
dancing] and races. It is the big ceremonial hogan and the
race track out on the mesa and not the fair here in town
that brings the Indians."

There is abundant evidence that the American Indians,
like all other backward peoples, are far more responsive to

various stimuli which bring immediate satisfaction than they are to any considerations of future advantages. Improvidence, either from overindulgence in immediately gratifying activities or from inactivity, is put down as a universal characteristic of primitive people.

CHAPTER 8

MALADAPTIVE ACTIVITY RESULTING IN WASTE OF USEFUL
MATERIALS

AMONG INSECTS

LOST motion is not necessarily harmful. Our other three classes of excessive activity all result in harm to the animals. The kind of harm to be examined next we have spoken of as waste of useful material. The studies of the Peckhams [1] on the habits of solitary wasps furnish the first illustrations. The authors tell of watching a wasp of the genus *Cerceris*, hunting bees. "Of two victims which were procured with great trouble one was abandoned on the threshold, and the other was dropped half way in—neither served as food for larvæ." Since the wasps themselves are nectar and honey feeders and never eat the prey they capture, if the bees were not used by the larvæ they were not used at all. In another case, the female has the habit of storing her nest with spiders (Epeira) which have been killed or paralyzed by stinging, preparatory to depositing her eggs on the prey. The nest is then closed and left to its fate. The wasp pays no more attention to it. The little ones when hatched have to look out for themselves except as to such provision as the parent has made for them before the eggs are laid. When a store of spiders is laid up, but no eggs deposited in connection with them, the work done and the material stored is a dead loss. "A second nest gave us fourteen specimens of *Epeira juriperi*, including many varieties of this variable species. There was no egg, although the nest had been closed. This was

[1] *The Instincts and Habits of Solitary Wasps,* by George W. Peckham and Elizabeth G. Peckham, Wisconsin Geological and Natural History Survey, Bull. No. 2, Science Series No. 1, 1898, p. 245.

the finest looking and best conditioned lot of spiders that we had seen."

This wastefulness of the solitary wasps has been amply verified by other naturalists. One of those who has given particular attention to the point is Phil Rau. From his observations [2] we have the following: "In 1912 we were watching a Pelopeous mother industriously filling her cell with spiders. While she was out foraging we borrowed four fine fresh spiders from another new nest near by and with the forceps carefully inserted them into her cell. Upon her return she was at once aware of the intrusion and set about carrying out the foreign spiders with much indignant buzzing. Nor did she stop at this, but carried out and threw away three of her own hard-earned prey as well, before her indignation had cooled sufficiently to permit her to continue her work." A majority of his experiments produced similar results, the placing of spiders in the nest by the experimenter resulting in most instances in the throwing away by the wasps not only of the donated specimens, but of those of her own collecting as well. Rau's general conclusions from these experiments are significant. "The detailed examination of many hundreds of completed nests shows that 'in normal, free life these wasps commit blunders or follow disastrous whims in a large proportion of their cells; sealing them stark empty or with only a fraction of the food necessary for the young one, or providing abundant supplies and omitting the egg, or other blunders which would defeat the whole purpose of the wonderful instinct of nest-building." That sealing nests "stark empty" and "providing abundant supplies and omitting the egg" result in waste of material is obvious.

Many illustrations of waste of material could be drawn from every group of insects; we will restrict ourselves to the ants, selecting examples which illustrate forms of wasteful-

[2] "The Ability of the Mud-dauber to Recognize her own Prey (Hymen)." *The Journal of Animal Behavior*, Vol. V, 1915, pp. 240-249.

ness differing from those already shown. The harvester ant of Texas (*Pogonomyrmex molefaciens*) was reported many years ago to practice agriculture in a small way. It was stated that the ants sow the seeds of "ant-rice," plants of the genus *Aristeda,* around their dwellings, cultivate the crop, harvest it when ripe, and garner it into their granaries. This story which has long passed muster as evidence of ant intelligence, Wheeler [3] tells us, "even the Texan schoolboy has come to regard as a joke." Four years of nearly continuous observation on this species enabled Wheeler to discover the truth about their habits which probably gave rise to the fiction. Examining the nests during the cold winter months (while the fiery sting of the ants is subdued by the low temperature): "The seeds, which the ants have garnered in many of their chambers will often be found to have sprouted. Sometimes the chambers are literally stuffed with dense wads of seedling grasses and other plants. On sunny days the ant may often be seen removing these seeds when they have sprouted too far to be fit for food and carrying them to the refuse heap, which is always at the periphery of the crater of cleared earthern disk. Here the seeds, thus rejected as inedible, often take root and in the spring form an arc or a complete circle of growing plants around the nest."

Since the seeds of "ant-rice" are one of the favorite articles of food of the ants it happens that sometimes the plants of these circular growth areas near the dwellings are composed largely of this species. The "ant-rice" plants growing around the colonies therefore are not to be taken as evidence of the intelligence of the ants, but on the contrary of their unintelligence, of their doing work which though generally useful turns out in particular applications to be harmful. Storing food in such a manner that it spoils falls into the class of maladaptive activities upon the ma-

[3] *Ants,* p. 286.

terials requisite to life which fail in one way or another to make these materials serve their ends. These ants store food for their future use, and some of these stores are lost by spoiling. The storing activity fails of its purpose, more or less: the stored material is a loss, to a considerable extent.

AMONG BIRDS

Further examples of waste of materials through activities that are imperfectly adapted are found among birds. The most conspicuous examples are connected with food habits. The habit of the California Woodpeckers (*Melanerpes formicivorus bairdi*) of pecking great numbers of small pits in oak, pine and other trees, and placing acorns in these, usually one in each pit, has been often described. For a long time there was some uncertainty as to whether the acorns were stored in order that the birds might feed on the "worms" contained in the nuts, or on the acorn meats themselves, or whether any use at all was made of the nuts by the birds which garnered them. Studies on the crop contents of the birds show that the meats of acorns are used as food by the woodpeckers, thus making it almost certain that the stored acorns are so used.

Studies of my own [4] confirmed the view previously held as to the usefulness as food of both grubs and acorn meats of the stored nuts. Although I was unable to catch the birds in the act of feeding off the stores, the circumstantial evidence that both grubs and meats are extensively eaten left no doubt of the importance of the harvesting and storing activity in the economic life of the species. In carrying on the study the question, "How effectively is the work done?" was as constantly before me as was the query, "Is the work useful at all?" Positive proof has been furnished by other

[4] "Acorn-storing by the California Woodpeckers," *The Condor*, Vol. XXIII, Jan., 1921, pp. 3-14.

observers, that at times pebbles instead of acorns are placed in the holes, and that on quite an extensive scale. Consideration of all the facts convinced me that the birds simply fail to discriminate between pebbles and acorns and consequently store up quantities of material for food which has not the slightest value as food.

Admittedly some forcing is required to bring such a case under the heading "waste of material." "Waste of energy" might seem a more appropriate class for it. Yet the situation can easily be viewed in such a way as to make "waste of material" appear a not inappropriate term. Imagine the stores of a particular group of the woodpeckers composed half of acorns and half of stones. The proportions are approximately this in the specimen illustrating the error contained in the Museum of Vertebrate Zoölogy at the University of California. Imagine further the winter in preparation for which the storing was done to be an uncommonly severe one as to food demands by the birds. In such a situation the entire store might not be any too much to meet the needs, even if the whole were available for food. What, in such a case, might be the consequences were the birds to find upon going to their granaries for food that half of the bins were filled with pebbles instead of the acorns? An appeal for bread responded to with stones, sure enough! And the irony of it, were woodpeckers only endowed with the sense of irony, would be that the hungry birds themselves had provided the stones.

Evidence of the inefficiency of the work of the woodpeckers is not limited to such gross mistakes as that of storing pebbles in place of acorns. Concerning the use of the holes drilled and the acorns stored, the evidence secured led me to formulate conclusions thus: "As to hole drilling: While the holes are made expressly for the reception of acorns, many holes are probably made which are never used, holes are made at seasons of the year when there are no acorns to store, and large numbers of perfectly serviceable holes seem to be abandoned even in localities where both birds and acorns are abundant, and new holes are being made. As to the storing business itself: "While this is of distinct service to the food necessities of the wood-peckers . . . large quantities are sometimes stored, the use of which is so long delayed that the acorns become wholly or largely unfit for food, and this in places where the bird population seems normal. Finally, acorns are sometimes stored in such fashion as to make them easy prey for ma-rauding rodents, when with some definite foresight and a little more work such exposure could easily be avoided." [5]

Observations made since the article quoted from was written have confirmed the loss of acorns through spoiling and through being placed where the birds could not get them.

Morton E. Peck [6] writes of the habits of another sub-species of the same woodpecker, (*M. f. albeolus*) observed by him in British Honduras. "These extremely industrious birds not only store acorns in the same manner as the Cali-fornia woodpecker, but also deposit them in great quanti-ties in hollow trees and similar places. I have seen a hollow pine tree with a cavity six to eight inches in diameter filled for a distance of nearly twenty feet with acorns dropped into a good-sized hole at that distance above the ground. Acorn-filled trees of this sort I found not uncommon. Some-times an opening at the bottom showed the earlier acorns deposited, completely decayed and crumbling to dust. They must have been there for several years, and probably were not brought by the same birds that completed the accumula-tion. . . . In these cases, it would be utterly impossible for the birds ever to make use of the acorns in any way, yet they go on generation after generation laboriously gathering

[5] P. 14.
[6] "On the Acorn-storing Habit of Certain Woodpeckers," *The Condor*, Vol. XXIII, July, 1921, p. 131

them. Furthermore, in an even, tropical climate like that
of British Honduras, where there can be but little variation
in food supply from season to season, it is difficult to see
how, under any circumstances, such a habit could be of any
great advantage; but even granting that it is so in some
cases where the accumulation is accessible, these instances
show how an overdeveloped instinct may lead to actions not
only useless but highly absurd."

This case illustrates "waste of material," since portions of
the acorns stored in hollow trees were "completely decayed
and crumbling to dust," and many of those in the house
timbers were out of reach of the birds. If the climatic and
productive conditions of Honduras are such as to make un-
necessary food storage to tide over periods of scarcity, the
whole quantity of stored-up acorns would be useless so far
as the food supply of the particular birds was concerned,
and the performance would be nothing worse than absurd.
But the supposition that the birds' welfare is wholly independent of what they do with acorns or any other article
on which they depend for food involves all sorts of difficulties. Absence of winter snows, enabling the birds to get
the nuts where they fall from the trees all the year round,
might be supposed to make collection and storage unneces-
sary, but this involves the further supposition that the quantity of acorns is so much in excess of the demands that the
collections made and rendered useless would be no drain on
the supply left on the ground. The knowledge we have of
acorn production does not warrant the supposition that in
any particular locality where acorns are known to be produced, the crop is always at its maximum. We know for a
certainty as to many acorn-producing regions that the crop
varies greatly from year to year and from locality to locality.
I am of the opinion that full knowledge of acorn production,
and of acorn consumption by any animal in any part of the
world, would forbid the assumption that the animals could,

without endangering their own welfare, destroy or render useless large quantities of the nuts, even though a stationary bird population were assumed. Such a supposition about population is not permissible in the light of facts. Few biological principles are better established than that increase of population tends to keep up with food supply where food and feeders are of as high grade as are oak trees and woodpeckers, other conditions remaining the same. If acorns are a dietetically adequate food for Honduras woodpeckers, or for any other animal, acorn production will never be so in excess of the needs of the animals that acorn waste could be devoid of injurious possibilities to the animal species responsible for the waste. Acorn excess would promptly be taken up by woodpecker excess, or excess of such other animals as may depend wholly or in part upon acorns for food. So close woven is the "web of nature" that complete independence of any one element for a given locality can never be assumed without considerable positive evidence.

Various explanations of the origin of maladaptation in food-storing by woodpeckers have been offered. Peck suggests that the Honduras subspecies of woodpecker is derived from a more northern form, and that its storing habit is due to the survival of an ancestral instinct, useful in the higher latitudes but useless in the tropics. Whether this suggestion is justifiable in this particular case does not particularly concern us, for it is certain that there are thousands of animal activities which can be better explained on the hypothesis of such survival than on any other. The question raised here of the probable injuriousness to animals resulting from the persistence of activities long after the conditions have passed away which made these activities useful to their ancestors is a general and important one.

This explanation of woodpecker maladaptation by Peck may be compared with Henshaw's explanation of a similar situation in the activities of the California woodpecker.[7] "In searching for the motives underlying the storing habit of the California woodpecker we should not lose sight of the fact that the several acts in the process, the boring of the holes, the search for the acorns, the carrying them to the holes and the filling them in, bear no resemblance to work in the ordinary sense of the term, but is play. I have seen the birds storing acorns many times, and always when thus engaged they fill the air with their joyous cries and constantly play tag with each other as they fly back and forth. When thus engaged they might not inaptly be likened to a group of children at play.

"In further illustration of the play habit of this woodpecker it is to be noted that its bill, as in the case of others of its tribe, is wonderfully well adapted to digging into wood, and it is as natural for the bird in its idle moments to dig just for the fun of it as it is for a boy to whistle or the proverbial Yankee to whittle a stick.[8]

Interesting and suggestive as these explanations are, they have no bearing on the question of the establishment of the fact of maladaptiveness in the complicated activity of acorn-storing by woodpeckers. If a given activity of an animal species is really harmful to the animals obviously the bald fact is not palliated by its mode of origin. It is maladaptive however it came into being, and consequently is subject to that general remedial process which is the very essence of organic evolution. Henshaw remarks: "While I do not doubt that the acorn-storing habit is based on more or less definite interest to provide food for future use, the faulty methods employed and the imperfect results obtained show that as yet the birds have only imperfectly learned their

[7] "The Storage of Acorns by the California Woodpecker," by H. W. Henshaw, *The Condor*, Vol. XXIII, July-August, 1921, pp. 109-118.
[8] P. 111.

lesson." [9] One of the most crucial of all questions for the improvement of animal activity might be stated thus: What is the evolutionary way by which the birds "learn their lesson" more perfectly?

Assuming that a measure of wastefulness, of maladaptiveness, in food habits, is proved for woodpeckers of this group, we should not be justified in supposing without more evidence that something of the sort is universal or even widespread among birds. This instance makes one curious to know whether it stands entirely alone. Have all other birds "learned their lesson" so well that food gathering and using are carried on entirely without waste or loss? Are these woodpeckers the only birds thus imperfectly adapted in their economic affairs?

Henshaw calls attention to the fact that the food storing custom prevails among birds to a very slight extent. There is ground for surprise at this, in view of the manifest advantage of the practice and the fact that it is so highly developed among insects, animals which are usually regarded as ranking far below birds in the evolutional scale. However, there are a few other birds which practice the art, and the question of the effectiveness with which it is done by these is important for us. At least one other woodpecker, the Red-head (*Melanerpes erythrocephalus*), has acquired the storing habit in some localities but not in others. That the individuals of a species living in some places perform so complex an activity as collecting and storing nuts, while individuals of the same species living elsewhere do not, raises a question as to the hereditariness of the habit. That the stored nuts are used as food by the Red-heads is definitely known, according to the account. The activity is adaptive with these as with the California woodpecker. The imperfection of the adaptation in the one case as in the other is indicated by the following observation quoted by Hen-

[9] P. 111.

shaw: "Miss Pellow further states that she noticed the board along the ridgepole of her house was curling up, and on investigation it was found that under this board for a distance of from 8 to 10 feet from the eaves were decayed and half-decayed acorns to a depth of at least 1 inch, and a friend of hers had the same experience."[10] Such observations indicate that the Red-headed woodpecker has not "learned its lesson" any better than its far-western relative.

Among North American birds, the only species besides these woodpeckers that practice anything like food storing for their own future use, are the Blue Jay (*Cyanocitta cristata*) and some of the Shrikes. The jay gathers and stores nuts of various kinds. All observers of the bird from Alexander Wilson to the present day testify to this. My own early life in the "oak openings" country of Wisconsin, made me familiar with the fall activities of the bird in collecting acorns and inserting them into all sorts of crannies in trees, fence posts, fence rails, deserted buildings, etc.

That the habit is adaptive in its fundamental nature appears to be taken for granted by many ornithologists. "The Blue Jay . . . lays up large stores of acorns and beech mast for food in winter, when insects cannot be procured in sufficient abundance."[11] Nevertheless the question of how far the stores are utilized is raised by many persons, laymen as well as ornithologists. The opinion expressed by a farmer neighbor of mine in Wisconsin was: "The fools never go near the acorns they hide away." While so sweeping an ascription of foolishness to the birds is probably unwarranted, there appears to be some ground for it. Mark Twain's famous "Baker's Blue Jay Story" in *Tramps Abroad*, is endorsed by at least one competent student of

[10] P. 113.
[11] Baird, Brewer, and Ridgway, *A History of North American Birds*, Vol. II, p. 275.

birds as "good ornithology in so far as it reports the way a jay acts." [12]

While such nut-storing as is done by blue jays must be accounted as wasteful and hence imperfectly adapted, there are certain indirect results from this activity which might be considered to contribute to the general welfare of the species, though hardly of the individual birds concerned. From W. B. Barrows we have this: "Undoubtedly the Blue-jay is an important factor in reforesting burnt or cut-over lands, since it is continually planting acorns, nuts and seeds of various kinds." This results from the fact that "it gets a large part of its food from the ground and also buries or hides there any surplus that it may have." [13] The same idea is expressed by other ornithologists.

An interesting question is raised by animal activities of this sort. Imagine a seed-eating animal, a blue jay, for example, that does not limit itself merely to satisfying its needs by eating what it finds *in situ,* but moves the materials about for any purpose whatever. There can be no doubt about such activities. Seeds thus moved and left permanently, sprout and grow into plants which produce more seeds, these in turn serving as food for other animals of the same and different species. How are we to estimate the usefulness of activities when the use is of this general sort? Obviously this question faces us directly toward that endless maze of phenomena aptly called the web of nature: the maze so baffling to everybody but so fascinating to the philosophical naturalist.

It seems clear enough that if the blue jays collect more acorns than they can eat, and store or hide them away and never return to them, those acorns are a dead loss to those birds, it matters not at all whether the nuts are put where the birds could not get them if they tried to; or where they

---

[12] E. H. Forbush in *Nature Lovers' Library,* Vol. II, p. 218.
[13] *Michigan Bird Life,* p. 414.

would be stolen by rats, squirrels, or other thieves; or where they would soon rot; or again where they would, in the course of years, grow into acorn-producing trees. Such nut-storing as is done by blue jays must be accounted as wasteful and hence imperfectly adapted, even though some of it may be immediately useful in supplying food for the birds themselves, and some of it remotely useful in supplying food for their descendants.

The only other North American birds known to store food are the shrikes. Several species and subspecies of the genus (*Lanius*) to which these belong occur in different parts of the continent. All are primarily carnivorous, and their practice of impaling prey on thorns, sharp sticks and barbs of fence wires is widely known. The significance of the practice has been much speculated upon. A few writers have contended that the birds get pleasure from seeing the death struggles of their victims. But in addition to the improbability of this explanation, deducible from our general knowledge of bird psychology, there are trustworthy observations showing that the habit is useful. While the shrike has become a carnivore so far as the structure of its beak is concerned, the structure of the foot is less like that of typical birds of prey. Both capturing and holding prey must be done chiefly with the beak. As the prey is often too large to be swallowed whole, it must be torn to pieces before being eaten. The thorns and barbs upon which victims are impaled are a substitute for claws at meal time.

This is best shown by experiments tried by Dr. Sylvester D. Judd with a captive loggerhead shrike. When a dead mouse was offered the bird, which was in a cage containing no impaling place, it was seized and dragged about for several minutes, the effort being made "to wedge it into first one and then another corner of the cage." Finding these efforts unavailing the bird then tried to impale the mouse on the blunt broken end of a branch that had been placed in the cage for a perch. This too proved unsuccessful. Next the bird tried to hold the mouse with its feet and tear it to pieces, but the feet were too weak. At this juncture the experimenter himself took a hand by driving a nail in such a way that the projecting point was in plain sight and easy reach of the bird. "Immediately the Shrike impaled the prey, fixing it firmly, and then fell to tearing and eating ravenously."[14] This experiment was varied in several ways, always with much the same result.

These experimental observations, corroborating field observations by several ornithologists, show conclusively that the prey-impaling habit of the shrike has a basis of direct utility. Accepting it as proved that the impaling practice is useful and hence adaptive, is there evidence of imperfection in the adaptation such that loss of material results? Most writers agree that prey is hung up in excess of the bird's immediate needs. However the view that the storing bird itself or other individuals may later be the beneficiary of the surplus seems to be rather prevalent among ornithologists. A statement by Dr. Judd in another publication[15] is quite typical. "It is well known that the shrike kills and hangs up in his shambles more than he can utilize. But this apparently wanton slaughter may often be the salvation of many a shrike whose hunt over snow-covered fields has yielded no returns." On the other hand, some of the most specific evidence we have is opposed to this interpretation. Mr. E. A. Schwarz of the U. S. Department of Agriculture made observations on the loggerhead shrike in Duval County, Texas. Schwarz records that during an excessively dry period in the spring no insects were impaled as far as he could discover. In late May a copious rain brought myriads of tumble bugs (scarabids of the

[14] *Birds of a Maryland Farm,* quoted from *Nature Lovers' Library,* Vol. III, p. 100.
[15] *The Food of Shrikes,* Bull. 9, Division Biological Survey, U. S. Dept. of Agriculture, 1898.

genus Cathon). These were greatly relished by the shrikes, and "large numbers of specimens could now be seen impaled every day." Why this excess impaling when the insects impaled were so abundant as to make a fresh supply available all the time, while there was little or no impaling when the supply of insects was short, if the future needs of the birds were the purpose of the excessiveness?

If the stored insects had been preserved in some way, as are those stored by solitary wasps, so that a supply would be on hand after the present abundance had become a thing of the past, the purpose of the oversupply would seem fairly clear. But insects hung up in such ways with no provision against decomposition or desiccation could last for a short time only. In view of the facts presented, the conclusion reached by Schwarz appears unescapable. He says:—"Most of the impaled specimens are never eaten by the birds, and remain for many weeks on the thorns. It would seem that the bird has acquired the habit of impaling insects without having the intention of eating them." This conclusion is in harmony with much evidence from other sources although I have found no record of other observations quite so specific and detailed. Henshaw [16] speaking of the storing method of the shrike says the habit is "more often than not unavailing, since the bird more often than not fails to profit by its foresight in any way, either forgetting all about its stores, or perhaps, wandering too far away to make it worth while to return to them." But this author does not believe the habit is very frequently practiced.

Another interpretation of the excessiveness of the shrike's impaling habit is well expressed by F. E. L. Beal. [17] Referring to the habit of the California shrike particularly,

[16] *Condor*, p. 112.
[17] *Birds of California in Relation to the Fruit Industry*, Bull. 30, Biological Survey, U. S. Dept. of Agriculture, 1907.

Beal writes: "Various more or less plausible explanations of this habit have been offered, but the simplest and most natural seems to be that much of the time the bird hunts simply for the pleasure and excitement of the chase, and as prey is often captured when hunger has already been satisfied it is stored for future use. It is the same instinct and lust for slaughter that prompts man to kill game that he cannot use." Though Beal speaks of the storage being for future use, he says in another sentence "nine-tenths of this stored food is wasted so far as the shrike is concerned." This view connects the storing habit of the shrike with play or instinct, and agrees with Henshaw's conclusions concerning acorn-storing by the California woodpecker.

Critical examination of the impaling and storing activities of shrikes from the standpoint of adaptation shows that, while the activities are useful and so adaptive, the adaptation is far from perfect, the activities often resulting in waste if not in actual loss of the food materials depended upon by the birds.

We have now examined the food habits of the three groups of North American birds which are known to store their food to some extent, this examination having in view the question of the adaptiveness of the storing methods used. The conclusion reached for each group is that the storing is unquestionably useful in its fundamental nature, but that the adaptation is distinctly imperfect as judged by the effectiveness with which the end served by the habit is actually attained. This imperfection consists in a measure of waste and loss of the food materials for the procuring and handling of which the activities are fundamentally performed. These three groups of birds include only a small fraction of all the species of birds which inhabit North America. To have proved a degree of maladaptation in the food activities of these groups is very far from proving anything of the sort for North American birds generally; we must extend our examination to other groups which practice other methods in securing their sustenance.

It is generally recognized that the vast majority of birds make no material provision for their own future needs either of food or of protection against the exigencies of weather. They live from hand to mouth. That this is connected with their great power of movement is obvious. The freedom of bird activity, freedom through its swiftness, ease, and grace, has attracted the attention and aroused the imagination of many people in many lands. There are numerous aspects to the question of how the unique power of locomotion with which birds are favored has affected the means by which the creatures solve, and through their evolutional history have solved, their food problem. Our purpose now restricts us to that aspect which includes the question of whether the great facility of bird activity manifests itself with the least possible waste of food materials, in so far as the activity is concerned with securing food.

As one observes the common land birds, finches, warblers, vireos, flycatchers, thrushes, wrens, larks, hawks; also the water and shore birds, gulls, terns, cormorants, pelicans, ducks, sandpipers, willets, and curlews, he must be impressed with the amount of time they devote to searching for food. Many of these birds appear busy in this way almost without respite. I do not know of any serious efforts to ascertain how many hours of the twenty-four any bird under typical conditions spends in hunting something to eat, though knowledge of this sort would be essential to a real science of bird economics.

Some ornithologists go so far as to believe that practically all bird activity, except that connected with sex, is determined by the compelling requirement of food. Grinnell brings out with clearness and force the idea that the food requirements of birds really drive the creatures to the limits of their powers in this direction. "The more I reflect upon the observed actions of birds, and of animals generally, the more I am confirmed in the conviction that there is no such thing as wasted effort." Grinnell's contention here is that, given bird activity guided as it actually is guided, none of it performed in procuring food can be spared. To such an extent are most birds driven by necessity in securing enough food by the hand-to-mouth fashion of their wonted lives that there appears little chance for waste or even for laying up anything for future use.

If we consider that it is impossible for birds to supply their food needs in any other way than by the wasteful methods they actually use, we must admit that all their food-getting activity is indispensable to their welfare. But if the problem of animal need and possible natural supply for such need be viewed more broadly, so as to include a better guidance of activity on the part of the animals concerned, it appears that both effort and material are wasted, if compared with the effort and material which would be necessary to meet these same needs if more effectively directed.

It would seem that food necessities drive birds so hard that those who waste food, or waste energy in collecting food, would be rigidly eliminated. That great wastefulness occurs is plainly established by many competent observers, with regard to many different groups of birds. Barrows makes the statement that the shrike often follows flocks of tree-sparrows or juncos and kills many more than it needs for food, more or less independently of its impaling habit. The same author [18] says the blue jay "frequently attacks ripening apples and pears, pecking holes in the sides of the largest and ripest fruits and injuring a much greater number than it can possibly use."

For the first illustration of this wastefulness of food take

[18] *Michigan Bird Life*, p. 414.

the case of the Carolina Parrakeet (*Conurus Carolinensis*) a bird formerly very abundant in the southern United States, but now nearly if not quite extinct. In an article by E. M. Hasbrouck,[19] the author quotes Audubon as seeing an immense flock enter the orchard of a fruit grower and in a few hours strip it completely of its fruit: "The birds working in regular manner from tree to tree, and failing so far as he could observe to make use of any of the spoils as food." Butler says [20] "Often they seemed to destroy in a spirit of mischief. They would tear off apples and other fruits, and after taking a bite throw them to the ground, and so continue. They tore off the heads from wheat stalks, and seemed to delight in throwing them away." [21] Several other writers give similar testimony as to the destructiveness of these birds.

This case of the parrakeet by no means stands alone. Crows and blackbirds attack growing corn and spoil many ears by tearing open the husks and eating only a portion of the milky kernels; house sparrows in Europe are said to beat much more grain out of the ripe unharvested ears than they eat; wild geese invade the grain fields of the interior valleys of California in early spring, and do much more damage by tramping down the tender shoots than they do by feeding on them; rose starlings in Europe injure apples on the trees by pecking into more of them than they fully consume. The information we possess on the subject seems sufficient to serve as a basis for a generalization concerning

[19] "The Carolina Paroquet (*Conurus Carolinensis*)," *The Auk*, 1891, Vol. VIII, p. 369.

[20] "Notes on the Range and Habits of the Carolina Parrakeet," *The Auk*, 1892, Vol. IX, p. 49.

[21] There is one point of difference between the observations of Audubon and Butler. While Audubon could not see that the fruit destroyed was used for food at all, Butler notes that to the extent of "a bite" apples, etc., were utilized; the depredations of the birds were never just pure wantonness. It was only that what they ate was but a small fraction of what they destroyed.

the adaptiveness of birds' activities related to food, which may be stated thus: All birds, being physically and mentally constructed as they are, must tend to excess in their various nutrimental activities whenever they find themselves in the presence of food materials in excess of their immediate needs and ability to consume.

In most of the instances of wastefulness just mentioned, the phenomenon is connected with crops cultivated by man for his own use. Orchards and fields of ripening wheat and Indian corn and of fresh-bladed grain are quantity productions of human industry. The birds concerned find themselves, thanks to human skill and energy, in the midst of an abundance of food material the like of which neither they nor their ancestors have heretofore known. This superabundance means food material in excess of the birds' needs, which provides stimuli to collecting and feeding in excess of these needs. In the absence of any well-developed mode of inhibiting or directing the responses corresponding to these stimuli, the excessive activities observed take place. The quantity of nutrimental activity of the avian type is dependent not alone upon the quantity of need and of power to act, but also upon the quantity of stimuli, upon which food taking depends. Manifestations of the tendency in cases where the excess of food material is due to human agency would be special cases of this general tendency. We should expect that similar excessiveness of food production in nature, if such ever occurs, would be attended by similar excessiveness in nutrimental activities by the birds affected. That this expectation is realized there can be no question, I think. The woodpecker, the blue jays, and the shrikes illustrate the principle for birds that have the storing habit. The tendency to excessiveness is more obvious in the few birds that store than in those that consume their food directly, only because the evidence is more easily obtained.

There is a Turkish proverb, we are told by Herman and Owen,[22] which says that the "Rose Starling kills ninety-nine grasshoppers before it eats one." Grasshoppers are a kind of food material for many birds which, by their enormous fertility, produce a condition in nature quite comparable so far as abundance is concerned to that produced under human culture by fruit orchards and grain fields. Stating the proverb in conformity with our knowledge of the psychic life of birds it would read: at times of excessive abundance of grasshoppers, for every hopper that the Rose Starling eats it kills ninety-nine which it does not eat.

[22] *Birds Useful and Birds Harmful,* by Otto Herman and J. A. Owen, p. 99.

CHAPTER 9

THIS wastefulness of food materials under conditions of over-abundant supply is not limited to Birds. Every one familiar with domestic animals will recall the way such animals go about the utilization of their food when they come suddenly into a situation where it is abundant. Indelibly stamped into my memory are the experiences of my youth on a Wisconsin farm in "watching cattle." My task was to ward off cattle raids upon unfenced or poorly fenced fields of grain. If a herd of cattle gained access to a field of grown-up corn, the damage would often be very great in a short time, not so much from what was actually eaten, as from what was broken down, trampled into the ground, and half-eaten.

Were a herd of cattle turned into a field of half-grown corn and deprived of any source of food except the corn they would eat it up clean before they would starve to death. But this they would do in a highly wasteful fashion, judged by human standards. Not the slightest effort would be made to restrict feeding at the outset to a portion of the field in order to allow the plants of the remaining portion to grow larger and thus produce more food. Under such conditions, animals often waste food through what is characterized as "sheer wantonness." What farmer has not been made furious by seeing some cow or ox get loose in a well-tended growing crop of some kind, plunge into it with head and horns, go jumping and kicking through it, hardly stopping to eat a mouthful? The presence of a specially rich supply of a favorite food seems to act as a stimulant of the play impulse of animals. While this need not necessarily result in wastefulness to the animals themselves it is ever liable to do so.

Wastefulness of material occurs in a type of activity in which carnivorous animals, who ordinarily kill only for food, kill without regard to their needs and to the great detriment of their natural food supply. It is well known that once a dog gets the "sheep-killing habit" it is almost impossible to break him of it, and that his killing may have little or nothing to do with his need for food.[1] The loss of sheep in the United States from this cause in 1913 was 107,760 head.

Concerning the operations of these dogs Wilson tells us: "Sheep-killing dogs work both singly and in groups, but usually in twos or threes. They do not limit their attacks to the flocks of the immediate vicinity in which they are kept, but travel for miles in all directions, spreading destruction in the flocks with which they come in contact. . . . Some dogs simply kill one or two in a flock while others continue the attack until all the sheep are either destroyed or crippled. In many cases in which large numbers are killed, they are neither bitten nor wounded but simply chased until they die from exhaustion." This last statement shows clearly that something more than need for food or even "taste for blood" is involved. "After a dog has once formed the habit of killing sheep it seemingly becomes a mania with him and he is seldom if ever broken of it. He not only destroys sheep himself but he leads other dogs to the work. No consideration should be given such dogs. They should be killed as soon as their habits are known."

That this sort of thing is not restricted to domesticated carnivores is proved by experiences of cattle raisers with wolves on the great ranges of the Rocky Mountain states.

[1] Farmer's Bulletin 935, U. S. Department of Agriculture, *The Sheep-Killing Dog*, by J. F. Wilson.

A dramatic story is that of the Custer Wolf of South Dakota. It is told in the *Weekly News Letter* of the United States Department of Agriculture for January 26, 1921, under the title, "Widely Famous Custer Wolf Hits the Long, Long Trail." "When he killed for food, he took only the choicest animals, but sometimes he killed for the mere sake of killing. Often he wounded cattle, breaking their legs, biting off their tails, mutilating them in unspeakable ways."

Attention may be called at this point to the fact that dogs and wolves cache their food to some extent and return to it for later meals; that is, they make some provision for future needs. It may be said that such instances of excessive killing are really provision for the future. This explanation and implied justification of wastefulness involves a fallacy. If a dog kills a dozen sheep or a wolf eight steers in one night, and if neither this dog and this wolf nor any of their kind are able ever to use more than a minute fraction of the kills, all that is fit for use but is not used is waste, and the activities which produced it are imperfectly adapted. In so far as the killings really met the needs of the animals or of their kind, the acts were adaptive; but in so far as they exceeded those needs they fell short of being perfectly adaptive.

In the case of the California lion (*Felis hippolestes olympus* Merriam) we have unquestionable information of wastefulness in sheep killing from which even the possible excuse of providing for the future through caching or any other means is excluded. These animals are so destructive to sheep, especially while the flocks are in the mountains during the summer, that the State Fish and Game Commissioners have for several years employed a state lion hunter to kill them.

The facts to be presented are taken from an article,[2] the

[2] *The black bear in relation to stock,* by Jay Bruce, California Fish and Game Com. Bull., Vol. IX, Jan., 1923, p. 16.

purpose of which is to exonerate the bear from the common
charge of sheep-killing, and show that the real culprit is
the lion.[8]

Practically no sheep-killing is done by the bears in this
region, the lion being the offender in almost all cases. "The
lion seeks out the bedding grounds of the sheep during the
night and slays several sheep in a few minutes, or he lies
in the brush on the range and kills sheep during the day,
in either case eating only the liver and part of the hams,
leaving the balance to decay." Then the bear gets his
chance as a scavenger. As evidence that the lion makes no
use of his "kills" after the first meal, we have this: "A lion
travels a definite beat over about one hundred square miles,
usually making his rounds every four or five days; when
the summer sheep range in its beat at any place, the lion
may kill several sheep within a few minutes some time during
the night, take one feed and then continue on around his
beat, make a kill or two at some other point and not return
to the range for several days." It appears that the lion feels
he must have perfectly warm, fresh meat at every meal.
That possibly ought not to be held against him as altogether
discreditable. But it is hard to see any justification whatever in his notion that he must have tastes out of several
sheep carcasses at one and the same meal.

Our examination of the question: "How far do those activities of animals below man, which are concerned with the
utilization of materials essential to the lives of those animals,
solve the problem in which such utilization is involved?"
has brought to light three things: Such activities do unquestionably meet the needs of the animals sufficiently to insure

[8] By way of evidence that Mr. Bruce knows whereof he speaks in
the story he tells, he informs us that he has traveled afoot as a hunter
more than 30,000 miles over the mountains of California, and has killed
42 bears, 155 mountain lions, and 200 bobcats.
Instances of how he has followed up clews in particular cases to prove
or disprove his surmises (hypotheses they would be with scientific investigators) are sufficient proof of his trustworthiness.

the completed life period of a considerable number of individuals of the species, and hence of the species itself.

The activities are performed in such fashion that extensive wastefulness often actually results and is always liable to result, this wastefulness being a large factor in preventing more than a small fraction of the potential number of individuals from living out the life period typical of the species.

This imperfection in the utilization of material results in making more severe the struggle of life.

Under our general discussion of successful animal activity an attempt was made to give enough of beaver activity to convince the most skeptical of its great usefulness to the animals. In regard to our general inquiry as to how successful animals are in utilizing the materials upon which their lives depend, in avoiding wastefulness of food and other material necessities, we are bound to ask whether even this wonderfully adaptive animal activity is perfect. Are the various things which beavers do so completely in accordance with every need to which they correspond that there is nothing more to be desired? Do the animals realize from their every performance as full satisfaction as the parent beavers do actually realize from a full meal off the bark of a fine poplar sapling brought into the house for the repast of themselves and their half-grown youngsters?

The facts I present first are taken from my own observations. The literature presents no observations made with the point in view of determining the degree of success or failure of beaver activity. My first opportunity for personal study of beaver activities was at Old Forge and Fulton Chain in the Adirondacks. It is an interesting question whether the Adirondacks do not now contain a larger beaver population than they ever contained before the white man injected himself into the situation. Rehabilitation of the beaver of New York was begun by rigid State protective legislation in 1895, the original population of the Adirondacks at that time having been estimated at five to ten individuals. In 1919 the Commission made an effort at a census of the Adirondack beaver population with the result that from 15,000 to 20,000 beavers were estimated to be then living in the area. It was estimated by the Forest Rangers of the Commission that there were 587 beaver dams, these resulting in the flooding of 8,681 acres of land by which $51,425 worth of merchantable timber had been killed.[4] So far as the present beaver population of the Adirondack Mountains is concerned, the region is virgin country. The streams, ponds and lakes are now everywhere clothed to their margins with vegetation consisting largely of trees and underbrush. Various authors writing of beavers and beaver countries as these originally existed in the Great Lakes and other portions of North America, tell of considerable areas at certain places along the stream courses which were devoid of timber and shrubbery owing to the cutting and flooding operations of the beavers. Whenever the beavers have been exterminated or greatly reduced in numbers, and the country has remained largely unoccupied by man, these treeless, shrubless areas have been reclothed with vegetation similar to that which was destroyed by the beavers. The Adirondack region has been a sharer in the widespread influence of varying beaver fortune. Consequently, in this very latest time when this region is reinhabited by beavers through the agency of man, the new population finds the country virgin, so far as the waterways and vegetation are concerned. This situation therefore presents an opportunity to judge beavers as to the intelligence shown in their use of their natural resources: whether their activities tend to the conservation of these or to their destruction.

[4] *State of New York Conservation Commission,* report for 1919; also *Beavers and the Adirondacks,* by Charles H. Willoughby, *The Conservationist,* Vol. III, No. 5, May, 1920.

On approaching the dam and pond on Hatchery Creek, I was struck by the narrow fringe of dead trees around the whole margin of the pond. ·The contrast of its gaunt brown death with the soft billowy green life everywhere else was striking indeed. The pictures of expanses of forests dead from fires or from smelter fumes, familiar to me in the far West, at once came before my mind. The first piece of beaver gnawing that we came upon was a great gash in the butt of a yellow birch tree which was growing very near the water and was leaning strongly toward it. The tree was fully twelve inches in diameter at the center of the cut, which extended more than halfway through. The surface of the cut was weather-stained, showing that the work had been done months ago. "What about this?" I asked my companion, a warm and decidedly apologetic friend of the beavers. "Why," I asked, "did the workers not finish their job after having done so much upon it?" Since this species of tree is their first choice for food and other uses, and since this particular tree would certainly have fallen all the way to the ground and partly into the pond, where it could easily be got at, there would seem to be every reason why the beavers should have carried the work to conclusion. The reply to my question was that once in a while beavers make mistakes or do foolish things "just as men do." Had my companion been as resourceful an apologist for beavers as some writers are, he might have suggested that an enemy frightened the workers away when the cut had reached this depth. But his knowledge of the fact that the modern Adirondack beavers have no enemies, either human or animal, of the frightening kind, might have restrained him from making this suggestion. Again, he might have guessed that this gash was made not with the intention of felling the tree, but for getting wood chips for food. But too many of the chips could be seen scattered about on the ground to permit much plausibility to this theory. Furthermore, the beaver's perference for bark rather than wood, and the abundant supply of the preferred article hereabout, were so well known to my friend as to deter him from offering this as an explanation for what the beavers had done, or rather failed to do.

My best opportunity to give special attention to the engineering skill displayed by the beavers was found at Bald Mountain Pond. The beaver colony here had been longer established and had done correspondingly more work. The dam was longer and higher, and many more trees had been felled. I went entirely around this pond, a mile and a half or two miles, and examined as carefully as possible in the hours at my disposal the beaver work of the entire circuit. Of the tree-felling operations observed, I will describe in detail one only. The essential features in this case were two yellow birch trees felled, the cutting on each having been partly done from the same old log and partly from the ground. The felled trees were about twelve inches and eight inches in diameter at the cut. The work done and its results were as follows. The gash in one tree made from the log had been carried about half through the trunk; that made from the ground, about a foot and a half lower down, reached about half through on the opposite side from the log-made gash. This disposition of the cuts would clearly tend to make the tree fall away from the log, as it actually did. The felled tree went flat to the ground, but directed at a wide angle away from the water and up the hill. Very few of the branches had been cut from this tree, and only a little bark had been gnawed from it, either from trunk or branches.

As to the smaller tree, the cut made from the log had been carried almost completely through the trunk, so as to result in the fall of the tree from this gash alone. A small cut had been made from the ground, on the side opposite the log-made gash made from the log, but it was not deep enough to figure in the downfall of the tree. This tree had likewise fallen away from the log, but a standing tree had intercepted the fall, and held the tree above the ground far out of reach of the beavers. They could not possibly make any use of its branches or its bark. All this work showed indubitable signs of age. Going on the usual supposition that timber cutting is mostly done in autumn, the inference would be that this was done some nine months before.

From the standpoint of effectiveness in activity relative to raw material wrought upon, consider what is before us in this case. Both the cut trees were yellow birch, the most useful species to the beavers in this locality. Examination of the trees and shrubs around Bald Mountain Pond discovered this species to be by no means abundant. Epecially was there a dearth of smaller birches, which are naturally most available for beaver use. Yet these two trees were wasted. The smaller one had lodged against a standing tree, and was so situated that it would be impossible for the beavers to bring it down by any other means than that of felling the tree which was holding it. This of course might sometime be done, but there was nothing whatever to suggest that it would be. Account must be taken of the fact that live bark is what the animals want, while this tree had already been felled some months at least. The chance that any use would be made of it was practically nil.

As to the tree that lay full length flat on the ground, almost no use had been made of it though it had lain there some months, within a few hundred feet at most of the single beaver house on this pond. Possibly it might still be utilized, as the bark and wood were not yet fully dead and dry. If we accept their customary food habits as evidence of their food preferences, we must conclude that beavers prefer fresh green bark to that which is well on the way to death and dryness. Putting the felling of this tree in the most favorable light, we still seem bound to decide that they made a bad job of it.

I do not by any means imply that this case is truly typical of the effectiveness of tree felling by beavers. Both from my reading and from observations, I do not question that probably much the larger proportion of all the wood-cutting done by them subserves the ends for which the cutting habit was evolved. What I would assert is that this instance is sufficiently illustrative of the kind of defectiveness to which this activity is subject, to prove conclusively that it has almost no likeness at all to engineering in the proper sense. The kind of human activity which it most resembles is that characteristic of the least intellectually developed men, of those who have made only the smallest beginning in scientific planning and guidance of their activity. Such activity as that of engineering by modern men represents the highest stage yet reached in the process of organic evolution toward improving the adaptiveness of such activities as that of beavers.

These two instances of beaver cutting drawn from my own observations, taken in connection with others which might be cited, convinced me that so far at least as concerns these modern Adirondack beavers, their work is wasteful, though its general importance to the animals is great and obvious. From a critical consideration of the accounts of other observers, I am sure this wastefulness is by no means limited to Adirondack beavers. Take for instance loss due to felled trees lodging against standing trees and thus made unavailable. This source of loss appears to be very considerable, and avoidance of it is a mere matter of chance so far as tree cutting in itself is concerned. Grinnell and Dixon [5] have pointed out one of the main "chances" which save the beavers from still greater loss from this source than

[5] *Fur-bearing Mammals of California.* (In preparation.)

actually does befall them. These authors call attention to the fairly obvious fact that the forest trees growing on the margin of a pond tend to be heavier branched on the side toward the pond for the simple reason that this side has more open space, more room for expansion and freedom to light, and consequently, when felled will be more likely to fall toward than away from the pond merely as a gravitational matter. From this "chance" alone seemingly all trees felled could be brought not only flat to the earth, but directed toward the water, were the beavers to restrict their cutting to marginal trees all the time. As a matter of fact, however, this is just what they do not do. They are much given to penetrating more or less into the woods after their material. Lack of systematic procedure, so characteristic of animal work generally, is very manifest here.

The most striking form of wastefulness which came to my attention was in connection with land-flooding consequent upon dam-building. The main charge against the beavers of the Adirondacks is that much timber is killed in this way. A considerable portion of the timber destroyed is a loss not only to human beings, but to the beavers themselves. The only locality in which I was able to look into this carefully was at Bald Mountain Pond. Of the dead trees standing in the water, something like a third were yellow birch, very few of which were too large for the beavers to cut. These had all been dead so long that some of them were well on the road to decay. They were wholly useless to the animals, even for dam construction. Since this species of tree is most favored by the beavers, and since it was by no means very abundant near the water, the loss to the beavers would be great.

From cursory observations at one other pond, and from photographs of, and statements about, dead timber in various other parts of the area there is little doubt that such loss to the beavers themselves is widespread. We have here exhibited a type of wastefulness in beaver work that can hardly be conspicuously operative in a region long occupied by the animals. In a region inhabited by beavers for centuries something like an equilibrium would be reached and maintained between the natural growth of timber and the destruction of it by the animals. A region of virgin forests for beavers, like that presented by the Adirondacks in this era of repeopling by them, would be a forest untouched in its resources of raw materials for beavers. The ability of the animals to conserve these resources judiciously would be severely tested. The yellow birches, dead and decaying, killed by the water raised by the beavers themselves, stood there in Bald Mountain Pond, somberly impressive testimony to the way in which animal activity, guided only by a lowly-developed intellect, can work to its own detriment, even to its own destruction.

It may be said that though the beavers work against their own interests in situations like this, the case is exceptional and can hardly have much significance for beavers in nature generally. There is evidence that something of the sort occurs in regions where man has never interfered. Thus Enos Mills told me in conversation that he had seen localities in Colorado where beavers had established themselves on streams or parts of streams not hitherto occupied by them; and that in such places dam-building has resulted in flooding and killing timber much as in the Adirondack region.[6]

From the standpoint of Adirondack beavers' own interests the loss of part of their food supply through their own

[6] Statements occur in the writings of various observers which strongly imply similar consequences. Thus Alexander Agassiz (*Notes on Beaver Dams*, Proc. Boston Soc. Nat. Hist., Vol. XIII, for 1869-1871, p. 104) tells us: "From talking with intelligent trappers who have hunted in the lands of the Hudson Bay Company, I learn that the works of the beavers are so extensive there in some localities, that they have played a not unimportant part in changing the whole aspect of large tracts of the country, and covering with water a great extent of country which

activities is insignificant as compared with the greater disaster they are bringing upon themselves. Their timber-killing is injurious to their human neighbors as well as to themselves; these neighbors, more appreciative of the meaning of such destructiveness than the beavers, will see to it that the destruction is reduced to a minimum. The State of New York will adopt some method of controlling this and other destructive activities of the beavers, despite the fact of its friendliness to the beavers as shown by the reintroduction and protection of the animals in this locality. Since there is no likelihood that the beavers will learn to control their destructive activities themselves, the only way open to the humans will be to limit the number of beavers, by killing off a certain number each year. This is only one instance of the deadly conflict that is absolutely unescapable for the whole animal world, when increase in numbers runs on unrestricted, side by side with insufficiently guided animal activity.

was once thickly wooded." Agassiz relates that in the country examined by him, on the south side of Lake Superior, dams were usually built where the elevation was not great so that the "flowage" produced shallow water over large areas relatively far back from the dam, covering the "bases of stumps of trees cut as well as of the bushes." That many of the trees and bushes thus flooded and killed would be of species useful to the beavers is almost certain.

CHAPTER 10

MALADAPTIVE ACTIVITY RESULTING IN INJURY TO KIND

ACCORDING to our general plan we take up next the question of how far animal activity is effective in those aspects of it upon which the welfare of kind is dependent.

Our treatment will assume on the basis of evidence previously presented that what all animals of the same species do relative to one another is on the whole contributory to the well-being of the animals. Our task is to consider what exceptions to this contribution to well-being are implied by the restrictive phrase "on the whole." Do animals of the same kind ever treat one another badly? Do they ever injure one another? There is abundant information on this point to be had relative to animals representative of the whole range of phyla. Injury due to waste of materials involves injury to kindred as well as injury to self. Even more widespread is injury to kind through the universal tendency to excessive reproduction.

AMONG ARTHROPODS

More direct and hence more easily recognizable forms of injury to kind are found in various cannibalistic activities. Beginning with arthropods, we find the following description of unmistakable death-dealing injury to kindred among spiders. "The infant mortality among these creatures (spiders) must be appalling. There is first their cannibalistic propensity to be reckoned with. Newly hatched spiders while still in the cocoon seldom attack each other, but as soon as ever each sets up for itself, no quarter is given. It often happens that numbers of a brood of sedentary spiders spin their first snares in close contiguity, and if food is scarce they eat one another without compunction. It is said that a few individuals of a brood may be reared to maturity on no other food than their sisters and brothers." [1]

Such cannibalism as that exhibited by young spiders raises a very nice question: Is it in reality a case of injury to kind? The answer to the question can be given only on the basis of more detailed information. An illuminating case in point is furnished by B. G. Wilder.[2] ". . . The young of *Epeira riparia* live together for many weeks in a confined space, and with no *food excepting one another*. That they do eat each other is certain; first, because in cocoons opened later in the season, the spiders were found to be fewer in number, but larger in size; and second, because they were seen to do it, even when out of the cocoon and supplied with other food (as blood) which they seemed to relish." "There never was any fighting, however; the smaller and weaker seemed to understand that for the good of the species (*pro bono publico*) they must be devoured by the larger and stronger, who performed their part 'doucement et sans cholera.' "[3] This absence of resistance on the part of the eaten and of pugnacity on the part of the eaters means, in all probability that the performance ran on after the young had escaped from the cocoons and had come into the presence of other sources of food, essentially as it had been running before the escape.

If a group (a family of brothers and sisters for example) of young animals, all essentially on an equal footing and all devoid of food, determine among themselves which ones shall serve as food for the others, can it be said that those which get the wrong side of the decision are injured by their mates?

---

[1] *Spiders,* by Cecil Warburton, 1912.
[2] *The Habits and Parasites of Epeira riparia, with a note on the Moulting of Nephila plumipes,* Proc. Amer. Assoc. Adv. Science, for 1873, Vol. XXII, p. 257.
[3] P. 260.

Can the question of wastefulness of kind properly apply in such a case? The supposed situation presents an emergency which has unquestionably occurred over and over again among the animals of many kinds, even among men at all levels of development. So long as the foodless condition prevails, and there is mutual agreement to this way of meeting the emergency, ascription of injury or of waste would be irrelevant. From the standpoint of the good of the group, injury and waste would result from failure to deal with the emergency thus. The cannibalistic mode of solving the dilemma might delay the death of the whole group, thereby increasing the chances that relief would come for a surviving fraction of the original number. The young spiders were seen to eat one another "even when out of the cocoon and supplied with *other food* (as blood) *which they seemed to relish*" (italics mine). So the charge of injury and waste holds good. Were a group of civilized men, who had found themselves in a like dilemma, to continue to eat one another even after having been supplied with other food, the judgment of mankind upon those who continued to nourish themselves thus would be quick and terrible.

This may be taken as an example of many statements occurring in writings on spiders. Their custom of dining upon one another is not, however, restricted to the young. Adults often prey upon weaker members of their own species.[4] "It is a common occurrence for the female to destroy the male of its own species, which is smaller and weaker."[5] However, we are told by Warburton[6] that the frequent mention of this habit as universal among spiders is not correct, it being restricted principally to one family, the Epeiridæ.

[4] *The Spider Book,* by J. H. Comstock.
[5] P. 185.
[6] Cambridge Natural History, Vol. IV, p. 380.

Nor is cannibalism the only form of fatal injury that insects inflict upon their own kind, in such a way as to preclude the ascriptions to it of usefulness to either individual or species. Lindsay [7] expresses the view that in such cases as those of the periodical massacre of neuters by wasps and of drones by bees we are unable "to explain the *object or cause* of such dire waste of life." [8]

We are unable to give a full causal explanation of such facts. We can see in them another of nature's ways of controlling the numbers of organic beings. This, falling short of a complete explanation, yet makes the situation as a whole more intelligible. But dire waste of life still has to be recognized, for if numbers of neuter wasps and drone bees are produced beyond what is needed and can be supported, and so must be killed off, the whole business is more than merely futile. It constitutes a real falling short of perfect adaptation.

A very different sort of "injury to kind" among insects is that of inadequate provision of parents for their young. Blowflies are known to mistake flowers which smell like carrion for the real thing, deposit their eggs thereon, and so cause the death of their young by failing to provide them with food. [9]

Mud-daubing and other wasps not infrequently fail to provision the cells in which their eggs are deposited with adequate food for the prospective larvæ. Thus: "The detailed examination of many hundreds of completed nests (of *Pelopeus cæmentarium*) shows that in normal, free life these wasps commit blunders or follow disastrous whim in a large proportion of cells; sealing them stark empty or with only a fraction of the food necessary for the young one, or providing abundant supplies and omitting the egg,

[7] *Mind in the Lower Animals*, by W. Lauder Lindsay.
[8] Vol. I, p. 150.
[9] Romanes, *Mental Evolution in Animals*, p. 167; Schneider, *Der thierische Wille*, p. 268.

or other blunders which would defeat the whole purpose of the wonderful instinct of nest-building." [10]

Truly wonderful and effective as are the many ways in which insects provide automatically for the welfare of their young, miscarriages like those just mentioned could be given almost indefinitely. All such complex types of instinctive activity as that before us involve many reflexes and instinct-impulses concatenated with one another to make what have been called instinct cycles. The constituents of these cycles are related to one another in regular order, and the tendency is strong for the whole series to be run through once a start is made, regardless of whether each step or link is really needed or not for a given situation. Because of the stereotyped character of these cycles they might be called instinct routines. An example from the solitary wasps studied by Fabre illustrates one of these cycles. One of the ground diggers of the genus Sphex had completed its hole, placed in it a large locustid (an ephippiger) upon which she had laid her egg in the usual way, and gone through all the preliminaries to sealing up the hole. At this point Fabre interfered by putting the wasp to one side, carefully withdrawing the ephippiger from the hole and taking it away. He then released the wasp which had been watching him rob her nest. She returned to the hole at once, entered and explored it as usual, came out and resumed her work at the point where it had been interrupted, and continued until the hole was sealed with the ordinary elaboration. The fact that the nest contained neither egg nor prey, and that she knew it so far as by her means of acquiring knowledge she knew anything, was no deterrent to her going through the regular routine of sealing up and concealing her nest.

The relevancy of this case as illustrating the complicated instinctive routine referred to above is manifest. Fabre's

[10] Phil Rau, "The Ability of the Mud-dauber to Recognize Her Own Prey (Hymen)," *Journ. of Animal Behavior*, Vol. V, 1915, pp. 240-249.

statement of the matter is worth quoting: "The various instinctive actions of insects are then necessarily connected; since one thing has been done, such another must inevitably follow to complete the first, or prepare the way for the next, and the two acts are so necessarily linked that the first must cause the second, even when by some chance this last has become not only superfluous but sometimes contrary to the creature's interest. . . . In the normal state of things the Sphex hunts her prey, lays an egg, and closes the hole. The prey has been caught, the egg laid, and now comes the closing of the burrow, and the insect closes it without reflecting at all or guessing the fruitlessness of her labor." [11]

This section on injuries which insects do to their own kind we conclude with a description of a form of injury which, though not direct and positive, yet involves such palpable failure to do a good turn, as to amount to real injury. I refer to the failure to impart information under circumstances which make the lack of it actually or potentially harmful. While watching some harvester ants at work one late autumn day in New Mexico, I noticed a single individual exploring the exhausted flower head of some plant of the composite order, the name of which I did not know. From the fact that the ants were "harvesting" both ray petals and seeds of the plant, it seemed clear that the ant had climbed to the summit of the plant and was exploring the head for such things as it was accustomed to get from this source. Having failed to find either petals or seeds (the single head on the plant was absolutely empty), the ant started down the plant stem. At about the same time that she began her downward journey, I noticed another ant, almost certainly of the same colony, starting to climb the same plant. Would the ant descending empty-handed inform the ascending individual of the state of affairs at the top of the plant? As the two were traveling on the same side of the plant stalk and

[11] Quoted in Kellogg, *American Insects*, pp. 645-647.

consequently must pass each other within easy touching distance, my human feeling welled up and I thought to myself of course the down-going individual will inform the up-going one of the uselessness of her continuing. What happened was exactly what our knowledge of the ways of ants would lead us to expect. The two passed without taking the slightest notice of each other, so far as I could see. At any rate ant number two went on to the flower head and discovered for herself the fruitlessness of her journey.

Here we have an example of injury that is exceedingly widespread not only among insects but among all animals. It amounts to the negative of most of the benefits which come to animals from their ability to communicate with one another. This ability in arthopods does not go much beyond the mere recognition of one another, especially as between individuals of opposite sex. The odor-olfactive mode of communication among the hymenopters and the sound-auditive mode among many orthoptera are well known. The highly socialized insects, the honey bees especially, perform acts which can hardly be interpreted without supposing they respond to sounds produced by their companions.[12] Communication on this level is very different from that which gives information about some object or event which is wholly distinct from the communicating organisms. To be able to respond to a stimulus and to be able to know something about the source of the stimulus, are very different matters, as the most elementary psychology teaches us.

AMONG LOWER VERTEBRATES

Passing now to injury to kind among vertebrates, we notice a few instances among the lower orders, the wholly aquatic fishes and the semiaquatic amphibians. For fishes

---

[12] "Sind die Bienen Reflexmachinen?" H. von Buttel-Reepen, *Biolog.* *Centralb.*, V. XX, Feb., 1900, pp. 97-109.

none will serve our purpose better than the well-known sticklebacks. These remarkably prolific, voracious, and active little fishes have been much studied. What is known about their mode of life contains much of interest for our general thesis that an animal's activities may be highly adaptive on the whole, but may fall far short of perfect adaptation at particular points. The shortcomings in this way which result in harm to kindred are numerous. The habit of the males, of selecting each his small territory and defending it with great ardor and efficiency against all intruders is clearly adaptive. "I have occasionally known three or four parts of the tub taken possession of by as many little tyrants, who guard their territories with the strictest vigilance, the slightest invasion bringing on invariable battle. As may be expected they usually fight best on their own ground, and the invader is generally repelled; but when the contrary occurs the victor adds the defeated party's possession to his own." [13] So far the charge of injury could hardly be made with justice. It certainly could not were the offending fish poacher aiming to gain possession of the area held by his antagonist. But according to the same observer the fighting methods of these fishes are far from harmless. "I have seen one of them," he writes, "during a battle absolutely rip his opponent quite open, so that he sank to the bottom and died." [14]

The pugnacity of these fishes is not restricted to defense of home and family. Couch relates of another species, the ten-spined stickleback, that "it is a fearless and ferocious little fish, instantly reconciled to captivity, and attacking with fury any prior inhabitant of the vessel in which it is placed. It will frequently seize a fellow prisoner by the gill, the tail or a fin, and retain its grip with the firmness of a

[13] *A History of the Fishes of the British Islands,* by Jonathan Couch, Vol. I, p. 172, 1877.
[14] *Ibid.,* p. 173.

bull-dog." [15] Another observer is quoted by Couch to the effect that under some conditions this same species devours its own eggs "with the greatest voracity," this despite the fact that one of the notable habit characteristics of the species is the great care over its eggs and young, exercised typically by the male.

Nor does the pugnacity of the male stickleback spend itself on the rivals of its own sex. Different observers tell how, under some circumstances, they are severe with females as with males. Thus Romanes [16] speaking of nest-building and courting by the ten-spined species kept in captivity by Ransom, writes: "When he first courts the female, if she, not being ready, does not soon respond, he seems quickly to lose his temper, and, attacking her with great apparent fury, drives her to seek shelter in some crevice or dark corner."

Many more examples could be drawn from fishes of injury to kind due to excessive or ill-guided activities of the sexual and nutritional instincts. But our purpose will be better served by taking the next example from the amphibians, the vertebrate class next above the fishes.

Several very instructive studies on the mating activities of frogs and toads have lately been published, which contain matter bearing on the subject now occupying us. The instance selected is from Banta.[17] This study was made on the frog population of a single pond in the breeding season, the number of individuals involved being from 150 to 250 during the three years over which the observations extended.

The male's way of recognizing the female is so imperfect that the efforts to find her fail very frequently until the test of actual contact is made, and even then it is uncertain

[15] P. 178.
[16] Animal Intelligence, 1883, p. 243.
[17] "Sex Recognition and the Mating Behavior of the Wood Frog, Rana Sylvatica," by Arthur M. Banta, Biological Bulletin, 1914, Vol. XXVI, pp. 171-183.

whether the act performed shall be successful, when tested by the criterion of fructifying the female. Spent and much weakened females and even dead females are shown by Banta to be readily seized by the males. This uncertain recognition of the females is compensated for by a much greater amount of moving about on the part of the males in search of the females than would be otherwise necessary. "At the height of the chorus the frogs present a picture of remarkable activity for amphibians, the males swimming about and each attempting to mate with any frog or small moving object it encounters. Any individual which moves within a radius of several feet of another male is likely to be tested by him." [18]

The indeterminateness and great vigor of the efforts put forth by the males result at times in serious injury to the females. "In the height of the pairing season there is usually to be seen one or more cases of more than one male clasping a female. Such multiple copulation is fraught with danger to the female as well as to the more successful males. There is a constantly recurring struggle on the part of the rival males for possession of the female. Unless the female is able to leave and remain beneath the surface these struggles are certain to attract other males which also attempt to get possession of the female. The result is a struggling, writhing mass of males holding on to the female and to the males already clasping the female. Each male strives to get into a more favorable position and (incidentally) to push off the other males. In one mass the female was lying on one side with the head under water and was apparently dead, while five males were holding to her and to one another in various positions and several other males were making occasional efforts to fasten hold on the bunch." [19]

That some salamanders as well as some frogs eat their

[18] P. 173.   [19] Pp. 176-177.

own eggs and young is certain. The following is from a study by myself.[20] "During the breeding period their own eggs and young form an important food staple, particularly, as it seems, for the old males. One often sees one of these fellows taxing his ingenuity and mouth capacity to the uttermost in an effort to get a large egg mass whole into his stomach; and his efforts are frequently successful. I have also seen such males pulling to pieces the jelly of bunches in which the embryos were well developed, apparently for the purpose of extracting the little ones. I must, however, admit that I have never found young larvæ freed from the jelly in the stomach of an adult." [21]

I will give but a single example of injury to kind among reptiles, selecting this because it illustrates the tendency for the food-taking impulse to go wrong as judged by its legitimate use. It is from R. L. Ditmars.[22] We read: "A cage containing a number of water snakes can be set in a turmoil by simply rubbing a frog or a fish across the bottom. The hungry reptiles, catching the scent of the prey, dart wildly about in every direction, biting at each other's bodies in their excited search for the food."

AMONG BIRDS

Passing now to instances among birds, the often cited case of swallows and house-martins deserting their young may be noticed first. Darwin's footnote on this subject [23] is worth quoting. "This latter careful observer (Mr. Blackwall) examined, late in the autumn, during two years, thirty-six nests; he found that twenty contained young dead birds,

[20] "The Life-history and Habits of the Pacific Coast Newt (*Diemyctylus torosus Esch.*)," by William E. Ritter, *Proc. Calif. Acad. Science*, Jan. 18, 1897, Vol. I, No. 2, pp. 73-114.
[21] P. 84.
[22] *The Reptile Book*, p. 253.
[23] *The Descent of Man*, Vol. I, p. 80.

five contained eggs on the point of being hatched, and three
eggs not nearly hatched. Many birds not yet old enough
for a prolonged flight are likewise deserted and left behind. . . ."

Other instances are well known in which the eggs and
young of birds are destroyed through the habits of the
birds themselves,[24] the course of things being different in
different species. The so-called parasitic birds furnish
instructive examples. The best known of these are the cow-
birds (genus *Molothrus*) and the cuckoos (genus *Coccy-
gus*). The "parasitism" consists in the fact that the breeding birds place their eggs in the nest of other species. By
this means the tasks of incubating the eggs and rearing the
young are imposed upon the "host" bird. The instance
most instructive for the present discussion is that of the
Argentine cow-bird, *Molothrus bonariensis,* studied by W.
H. Hudson.[25] Summing up his results under the heading
"Mistakes and Imperfections of the Procreant Instinct,"
Hudson says: "The Cow-birds . . . frequently waste their
eggs by dropping them on the ground. They also occasionally lay in old forsaken nests. This I have often observed
and to make sure, I took several old nests and placed them
in trees and bushes, and found that eggs were laid in them.
They also lay in nests where incubation has actually begun.
When this happens the Cow-bird's egg is lost if incubation
is far advanced. . . . Several females often lay in one
nest so that the number of eggs in it frequently makes incubation impossible. . . . Cow-birds, male and female, destroy many of the eggs in the nests they visit, by pecking
holes in the shells, breaking, devouring, and stealing them
. . . In some nests found full of parasitical eggs every egg
has holes pecked in the shell, for the bird destroys indis-
criminately eggs of its own and of other species." [26]

[24] *Mind in the Lower Animals,* by W. Lauder Lindsay, Vol. II, p. 64.
[25] *Birds of La Plata,* ed. of 1920, Vol. I.
[26] Pp. 74-76.

Of all the instances of parasitism in the cuckoo tribe, that displayed by the European species seems to have reached the highest state of development. Some of the performances connected with it are certainly remarkable from the standpoint of adaptation. An important fact is that parasitism proper is restricted to the eggs and young. The adult birds are not themselves parasitic. The high degree of effectiveness of the egg-and-young parasitism is accompanied by a correspondingly high degree of effectiveness in the activities of the adults in selecting their hosts and placing their eggs. The birds usually place one egg only in each foster nest. The reason for this is that the relatively small size of the nests chosen makes it impossible for the young of both host and parasite to grow up in it. Almost as soon as the egg is hatched, the young cuckoo proceeds to empty the nest of whatever happens to be in it other than itself. Although usually only one cuckoo egg is placed in the same foster nest, occasionally two are, either inadvertently by the same individual, or by different individuals. When this occurs, after the rightful young occupants have been ejected by the two foreigners, these proceed to test their ejecting ability upon each other, and the less able goes the way of the unfortunate natives.

Another aspect of the fatality to nestlings resulting from cuckoo parasitism is mentioned by Frank Finn.[27] Loss of the young of the foster species is due not alone to the cuckoo, but to the "duped" (using Hudson's term) parents themselves. Finn writes: "The foster-parents do not concern themselves about this fratricidal behaviour in their nursery, but assiduously feed their changeling and leave the rightful heirs to die." This apparently results from the inability of the foster parents to distinguish their own young from the cuckoos.

Still another phase of nestling birds which involves the

[27] *Bird Behavior,* p. 188.

problem of adjustment is that of the age and hence the state of development of the different individuals of the same cradle. Since all the eggs of a clutch are usually the product of one and the same female, and since they are never all laid at one time, but at considerable intervals, the chance is obviously present for the young to be hatched at different times, and so to be of different stages of development. The common way of meeting this is for the parents to put off beginning to sit until the full number of eggs is produced. By this means, and then by sticking to the job until the slower hatching young are out, the discrepancies of age and size are overcome as a rule. But, says Finn, "birds may make a mistake or get impatient, and go off with a partial brood, leaving tardy or insufficiently incubated hatchlings to perish in the shell." [28]   In the event that a nest full of young is kept together, some members of which are much more developed than the others, the smaller, weaker ones are apt to fare badly at the hands of their nest fellows. Finn mentions an experience of his own with a brood of canaries in which the last member hatched was fatally crushed by the other three older and larger ones. The same author refers to a brood of young barn-owls, of unequal age and size, which when shut up in a room together, though furnished with plenty of meat, yet killed and ate the smallest member of the family. Owls are carnivorous animals, and this fact would make intrafamily cannibalism more likely among these than among purely fruit-eating birds.

Despite the innumerable ways in which the propagative operations of birds exhibit safety devices for eggs and young, these measures fall far short of perfection. The shortcomings are so obvious in many cases that, seen through human eyes, they are characterized as senseless or silly. Illustrations of this are easily recognized by anybody who has a chance to study breeding birds. Safety measures carried

[28] P. 152.

so far that they do more harm than good are one form of miscarriage in this direction. The display of "uncalled-for ferocity," as Lindsay characterizes it, for the protection of young, is in point. Lindsay says: [29] "I have been assailed in spring by fresh- and sea-water birds on unwittingly nearing their nests or themselves—the supposed intruder or threatener of danger did not dream of the existence of a nest till his attention was called to it by the mistaken behaviour of the ruffled and angry mother, whose own best policy would obviously have been to have maintained a discreet silence in hiding her young."

I have had a similar experience with the ruffed grouse (*Bonasa umbellus*). While studying beaver work at Bald Mountain Pond on June 2, 1921, I was suddenly startled by a great puff and flutter and rustle coming from the hillside behind me. Looking in that direction I recognized a bird, probably a female, about thirty feet away, crouching close to the ground with wings partly spread and feathers much ruffled. I naturally stopped and faced the would-be terrible creature. She came on some distance, but before getting very near, assumed her normal attitude, sheered off somewhat, and ran on through the brush and rocks in the general direction I was traveling. There is hardly a doubt that she had either a nest or a brood of young near by. Except for all this fuss I should not have had the slightest notion that I was intruding upon the precincts of grouse of any kind. Her performance was the more stupid in that I was oblivious of grouse until she thrust herself upon my notice, and was going in the opposite direction from that whence she came. Had she kept still, in a very few moments I should have been beyond possible danger to either her or any of her family. This misfunctioning of the protective instinct of birds is common, however efficacious it may be generally.

The vast amount of fighting that goes on among birds in

[29] *Mind in the Lower Animals*, 1879, Vol. III, p. 204.

connection with reproduction often results in useless injury to both sexes. "The contentious pigeon," says Craig,[30] "as every fancier can testify, brings disaster not only to his neighbors but also to his own cherished home and family."

There is no question that the sex act proper at times runs wild among birds and results in deeds that from the human standpoint are horrible. An instance in point is that of several male mallard ducks taking turns at "treading" one and the same female until she was so exhausted that she could no longer hold her head above water and died of drowning.

AMONG MAMMALS

Passing now to injury to kind among mammals, we glance first at the hard treatment which the young frequently get at the hands of their parents. Cannibalism practiced by mammalian mothers and fathers upon their own offspring is familiar for many species. We may safely say, however, that no mammalian mother eats her own young habitually and under perfectly normal conditions. When the female domestic hog or cat or dog or rat or mouse or rabbit or guinea pig devours her little ones the assumption is commonly made that the act results from some unusual condition. Hunger rarely plays a part in the practice so far as domesticated animals are concerned, for it operates in the presence of abundant food. As to its occurrence among wild animals, we have not been able to find much information. When carnivorous species are sorely driven by hunger, they in all probability do eat their young and one another at times. It is well known that when impairment of strength, as by injury or disease, has befallen a wolf or wild dog, its companions are likely to devour it if short of food.

---

[30] "Why Do Animals Fight?" by Wallace Craig, *International Journ. of Ethics,* Vol. XXXI, April, 1921.

The tendency of mothers to eat their young because of some disturbance, as through confinement, needs further attention. "Any disturbance of whatever kind," writes Lindsay,[31] "of the female or her surroundings, while she is in the highly excitable, morbid condition that succeeds parturition for a time, may precipitate or produce destruction and cannibalism of the young." This author, an experienced medical man, calls attention repeatedly to the morbid appetites and impulses attending the puerperal state. The making stronger in a mother of the impulse to destroy her young than is her impulse to preserve them, by "any disturbance of whatever kind," involves the question of adequacy of adaptation. If a mother hog or rabbit eats her young when there is not the slightest need for doing it so far as food is concerned, but does it because of some not very fundamental change in her surroundings or in her physiological state, her adaptation is sorely defective as judged by the criterion of success in perpetuating her kind.

Another form of mammalian cannibalism is illustrated by a case reported by E. A. Goldman,[32] who was in charge of rodent control for the American Expeditionary Forces in France during the war. In a lecture before the Biological Society of Washington entitled "Rats in the War Zone," he stated that rats caught in traps were frequently eaten by their companions. This was not done from lack of other sources of food since a superabundance was always available from the supplies of the troops.

Akin to the injuries inflicted by members of mammalian species upon one another, already noticed, is the well known treatment dealt out to weak or injured members of a herd of cattle by the able members. "If an individual in a herd happens to be sick or wounded the others, instead of showing sympathy, attack it and either drive it away into solitude

[31] *Mind in the Lower Animals,* Vol. II, p. 63.
[32] Biological Survey, United States Department of Agriculture.

or gore it to death." [33] This sort of thing is characterized by Darwin as the blackest spot on the moral character of the animal world.

Robertson thinks the case ought to be considered "in the cold light of science" and without mixing "human sentiments with bovine codes of morals." Various authors have surmised that this practice may after all be an adaptation. If so, it would not belong to the category of activities which is occupying us. Since, however, individual animals obviously do suffer harm at the hands of their own kind as a result of this practice we must examine the case to ascertain whether the usefulness assumed is valid and is unattainable by any less injurious method.

This habit might be explained on the basis of its hypothetical usefulness in minimizing the danger to the herd of attacks from carnivorous beasts. The supposition is that a sick or wounded member of the herd would be more liable to attack by such enemies, and that such attack would in turn expose the well members. This is logically sound, but no specific facts in support of it have been presented so far as I know.

Another form of the hypothesis is that eliminating diseased members from the herd might lessen the danger of spreading the malady in the herd generally. This is also good logically. Whether it is supported by facts is, so far as I am aware, unknown. But if a member of a herd, stricken down by an injury, is set upon and gored by its companions, merely through the operation of an instinct that was once useful but has none of its usefulness now, the act by which the harm was done falls under the head of maladaptation. The persistence of activities as instincts, long after their original usefulness is ended, is a common form of imperfection in adaptation, and is specially needful of correction if the persisting activity results in useless injury and waste.

[33] *Wild Traits of Tame Animals,* by Louis Robertson, p. 157.

The activity among mammals which probably results in more far-reaching injury to kind than any other is the sexual activity. The "law of battle," as Charles Darwin and others have called the pugnacious operations of the males, seems to reach its culmination in this class. Almost everybody has seen more or less of it in some species, wild or tame. One would expect that an impulse so pervasive and intense as this is would run to excess and perversion and would often do harm in various ways. This expectation is realized. Undoubtedly much more fighting is done, and more injury is inflicted upon one another, by the males of many species than is necessary for the legitimate ends of offense and defense. In a vivid account of the fighting of wapiti or round-horned elk (*Cervus canadensis*) Theodore Roosevelt writes, "The only danger comes when the beaten party turns to flee. The victor pursues at full speed. Usually the beaten one gets off; but if by any accident he is caught where he cannot escape he is very apt to be gored in the flank and killed." [34]

Relative to the protection of mother and young by the father, in the case of the mule-deer (*Odocoileus hemionus*), Roosevelt says: "While the fawn is so young as to be wholly dependent upon the doe, the buck never comes near either. Moreover, during the period when the buck and the doe are together, the buck's attitude is merely that of a brutal, greedy, and selfish tyrant. He will unhesitatingly rob the doe of any choice bit of food, and although he will fight to keep her if another buck approaches, the moment that a dangerous foe appears his one thought is for his own preservation. He will not only desert the doe, but if he is an old and cunning buck, he will try his best to sacrifice her by diverting the attention of the pursuer to her and away from him." [35] Nor is the male wapiti any better, according to

---

[34] *The Deer Family*, by Theodore Roosevelt, T. S. Van Dyke, D. G. Elliot, and A. J. Stone, p. 142.

[35] *Ibid.*, p. 51.

Roosevelt. "The mother of this species will fight desperately for her calf, but the bull leaves his family to their fate the minute he thinks there is any real danger." [36]

The male of the most common American deer, the white-tailed, or Virginia deer (*Odocoileus virginianus*) is said by some writers to defend its doe and fawn at times. If this is true (some of the most competent naturalists do not confirm it) we should have to rate the species distinctly above the mule-deer and the wapiti. This would accord with the estimate placed upon the intelligence of the white-tail by several writers. There seems to be no trace of generosity in deer nature. At the fighting time if the "deer is the conqueror, he never ceases to batter, spear, and trample his victim as long as any sign of life remains." [37] The most experienced observers of this deer testify to its exceptional viciousness. By November, Seton says, the bucks are "blind and mad with desire, as well as ready and eager to fight any of their own or other kind that seems likely to hinder their search for a mate." [38] W. T. Hornaday [39] issues this practical warning: "The strength and fury of a buck of insignificant size are often beyond belief. The loving pet of May readily becomes the dangerous, fury-filled murderer of October. . . . Do not make a pet of any male member of the Deer family after it is two years old."

The Alaskan Fur-Seal (*Callorhinus alascanus*) presents another instance of the treatment which the females among mammals are subject to from the males. This seal is highly polygamous, the "bulls" while on the breeding-grounds each collecting around him and keeping near him a group of about three dozen cows, the groups being known as the harems. The male is much larger and stronger than the female, so

---

[36] *Op. cit.*, p. 142.
[37] Ernest Thompson Seton, *Life Histories of Northern Animals*, Vol. I. p. 197.
[38] P. 106.
[39] *American Natural History*, p. 121.

much so that he readily picks any rebellious or disobedient spouse up in his mouth and puts her where she belongs. Owing to the extensive monopolization of the cows by the bulls, many males in a rookery (the name given to the whole breeding colony) are always left out in the cold, so to speak. As a portion of these are full-grown and have the common sexual desire, they naturally strive to get a share of the females. This of course makes trouble. While the fighting is, according to Jordan's report, somewhat less extensive and destructive than has sometimes been reported, it is liable to have consequences particularly for the females that are significant from the standpoint of maladaptive actions. We read: "When an idle bull steals a cow, he is usually attacked by her master. Sometimes he drops the cow, which returns to the harem while the bulls settle the account. It sometimes happens, however, that the master or perhaps a third bull seizes the cow and she is pulled about until one or the other hold loosens. Doubtless a certain number of cows are literally torn to pieces in this way. One was seen on Kitori rookery to lie limp and insensible for five minutes after being thus treated. She afterward crawled away, evidently seriously hurt. That the number of cows killed by the bulls in their struggles or by the rough treatment of the harem masters is considerable is shown by the fact that no less than 42 dead cows were found in the one season of 1897 on Reef rookery, the majority of which were so torn and mangled as to point to the harsh treatment of the bulls as the probable cause." [40] Most of the steps in one murder of this sort were observed by the naturalists of the Jordan commission.

"Living cows, cut and slashed and torn, are everywhere visible," we are told. Apparently the ugly work is all done by the bulls. Nothing indicates that the cows "fight back"

[40] *The Fur Seals and the Fur-Seal Islands of the North Pacific Ocean*, by David Starr Jordan et al., Vol. I, p. 62.

with their masters, or fight one another. Credit is given the bulls for doing what they do accidentally rather than intentionally. The wounds inflicted upon one another by the seals seem to have little effect on the health and strength or even comfort of the animals, even though the lacerations are extensive.

Before leaving the subject of injury to kind during the breeding-time activities of male mammals notice should be taken of the periodicity of the activity in the larger species and of the profound mental as well as physical change which characterizes it. Hornaday's statement is illuminating for the deer family. "During the season immediately following the perfect development of the new antlers—say September, October, November—male Deer, Elk, Caribou, and Moose sometimes become as savage as whelp-robbed tigers. The neck swells far beyond its natural size, the eye-pits distend, and the buck goes stalking about with ears laid back and nostrils expanded, fairly spoiling for a fight. I have seen stags that were mild and gentle during nine months of the year suddenly transformed into murderous demons, ready and anxious to stab to death any unarmed man who ventured near." An overpowering desire for a particular gratification on the one hand, and on the other "fairly spoiling for a fight" with anything that might, even possibly, thwart that gratification, is the substance of what is here before us.

Our presentation has taken cognizance of only two mammalian groups in relation to the injuriousness of secondary sexual behavior, as the animal activities connected with but incidental to reproduction might be called. Something similar to what we see in deer and seals is found in every group of mammals. Especially would this be the case with all groups in which there is a sharp physical difference between the males and the females.

This section on injury to kind among mammals, resulting from activities which must be recognized as imperfectly adapted because of such injuries, will be concluded with the case of injury and death inflicted upon the young by their parents through what, from the human point of view, would be called heedlessness and stupidity. Any farmer who has raised hogs knows how liable young pigs of a litter are to be badly hurt, even crushed to death by their mother and other adults if several are shut up together. If a mother with a large family of very young pigs is confined in quarters that are somewhat close, either as to total space or as to eating and sleeping quarters, she is very apt to trample on or lie down on some of the youngsters. This is particularly so if she happens to get a bit excited. There is of course no intent or no purpose in such injuries. They happen wholly incidentally to certain normal activities which in themselves have no relation to the rearing of young.

No matter how extensive or heinous or revolting, as humanly viewed, the injury or destruction wrought, there are the barest traces of regret, sorrow, remorse or sympathy connected with the deeds. The indifference of other near-by frogs or ducks or deer or seals to such doings as we have mentioned is very striking. We are not raising the much discussed question of whether any animals below man possess the germs of moral consciousness. To insure ourselves against misunderstandings, we unhesitatingly express our belief that many mammals and birds do possess not merely the germ but considerable sprouts of such consciousness. But even in its very highest development it is still so very young and small and tender as to be scarcely recognizable in comparison with what it is in the highest human development.

CHAPTER 11

MALADAPTIVE ACTIVITY RESULTING IN SELF-INJURY

OF the four classes into which we have divided maladaptive activity among animals, this class is the most important. Since any individual's activities are performed by itself and by no other individual, they necessarily concern the individual itself more closely than any other individual. Innumerable acts of any individual may be entirely without significance for any other individual. Every single act in the life of an organism, no matter how trivial, whether of the organism as a whole or of any part of it, must have some significance for the organism itself, because it is part and parcel of the life itself. Every act in an organism's life has some significance for that life. If it is demonstrable that some portion of the acts of organisms make not for the preservation but for the injury or even destruction of the organisms performing the acts, this fact is of prime significance. That such injurious or destructive activities do occur among animals on an extensive scale, it is now our task to show.

This mass of raw data is especially abundant and varied; the material to be presented has been selected largely from that group of animal activities by which brute animals meet the changed conditions of life forced upon them by the coming of civilized man into their environments. A man is as definitely a factor in the environment of a mosquito as is a mosquito in the environment of a man. Civilized man, armed with window-screens, drainage systems and kerosene from the bowels of the earth, is an even more considerable factor than savage man.

The coming of man into the environment of a brute animal creates sharply changed conditions. Most changes in environment are slow. The span of human life is not long enough to trace any modification of the activities of the living things affected by them. Such sudden and far-reaching changes as the coming of man may precipitate, furnish the most searching of all tests under field conditions of psychobiological adaptability.

In very many cases, especially among the highest subhuman animals, the new conditions imposed upon the creatures by the presence of man and his works result in a competition between them and man for the necessities of life. This competition may become so keen that its outcome is life or death for one or the other of the contestants. Such a situation gives us opportunity to study the matching of human wits against brute wits, where one or both are subjected to the strongest possible spur to use all the wits of which they are possessed to the best possible advantage. For our more general purpose of comparing man's adaptive abilities with those of other living things, both as to common traits and those peculiar to him, these cases are of special value.

Finally, the material to be presented has been chosen with a view to making obvious the truth, not very clear to cursory observation, that animal activities are imperfectly adaptive when performed in response to nature untouched by man, in essentially similar manner and degree as when performed in response to changed environic conditions which manifestly result from the presence of man. These principles of maladaptive action are seen to be factors in animal evolution, regardless of whether man is or is not involved as one of the environmental factors.

AMONG INVERTEBRATES

Our marshalling of data will begin with a lowly creature, the common earthworm, and with an instance coming under my own observation. The case is one with which many people are more or less familiar. It is that of the slaughter of these animals which frequently occurs when they live where much-traveled human roads pass through their territory. During a rain the worms appear on the walks and roads and are trampled upon and killed in great numbers. The cement walk on a certain piece of New Jersey Avenue, City of Washington, is flanked on the inner side by a coping, also of cement, which rises above the walk from a few inches at one end to a few feet at the other. The area beyond the coping is filled to the top of the wall with earth of the sort these worms frequent. A slight crack, large enough for a worm to crawl through, intervenes where the sidewalk abuts against the coping. During several days of rain early in May, 1921, this sidewalk became strewn with angleworms in all stages of demolition, from small pieces of skin to flattened sections of bodies, on up to worms still having life enough in their mangled forms to enable them to move a little. Since the walk was laid off into squares of equal area, it was easy to estimate the number of worms which had died in this way on the one piece of sidewalk, the length of a double city block. On the series of 88 squares adjacent to the coping there was an average of about eight worm carcasses per square. This would give 704 for this series of squares. The second tier of squares had about half as many remains. On this basis these two tiers or rows of squares had 1056 dead worms. Beyond the second series of squares the number of corpses fell away sharply. A very conservative estimate of the number to be added from the rest of the broad walk would bring the total to 1100, representing the earthworm mortality on one short piece of sidewalk during one rain storm. What it would be in an entire city during an entire season, the reader may speculate for himself.

Another observation on this same piece of sidewalk deserves recording. Rain occurred again on the seventh to the ninth of May and again on the 11th. But this time not a single worm did I find on the walk. Had the slaughter accompanying the rain of a few days previous wiped out to such an extent the worm population of the earth next to the sidewalk that there were no worms left to come forth and die during the next rain? This seems hardly likely. Nevertheless the fact surely presents itself as a possible explanation of the absence of worms at the second rain; for the drain upon the population by the first slaughter was certainly considerable.

Whatever the cause that brought all these earthworms on to this piece of sidewalk, there to be trampled to death, the loss of life must be accounted so much needless destruction wrought upon the creatures by themselves. There is no evidence that anything in earthworm economy makes it necessary for them to crawl out when it rains upon hard surfaces where people walk. Some persons speak of these occurrences of worms on the surface during rains as due to their being washed out of the ground. This explanation is wholly out of the question for the case here cited, where the conditions of sidewalk, coping, level ground firmly turfed, made such a thing impossible. Darwin [1] believed that some of these striking appearances of worms upon the surface are due to sickness of the worms. The death of the sick worms is, he thought, "merely hastened by the ground being flooded." [2] Darwin gives little reason for his belief, and other observers have not, so far as I am aware, confirmed his view. [3]

[1] *The Formation of Vegetable Mould through the Action of Worms.*
[2] P. 14.
[3] See a considerable correspondence on this and related points of earthworm habit in *Nature,* Vol. CVII, 1921.

All who have given attention to worm mentality would now agree, I presume, that the reactions of the poor creatures which I have described were simple tropisms, and that their death was a mere incident to the activities. The rain-and-the-sidewalk presented the conditions for a particular set of responses of the "forced" type. Accordingly the movements were certain to occur regardless of what the results might be. This furnishes another illustration of the contention that the persistence of an ancient type of action, formerly useful, after that activity becomes useless or destructive, is exactly one of the chief things that makes activity imperfectly adapted.

Our treatment of self-inflicted harm among insects will be facilitated by recognizing three major forms of misdirected action, resulting from: (1) Failure to discriminate between objects or conditions that are the aim of the action, and others that resemble these more or less but cannot be substituted for them. Under this class are easily recognizable several sub-classes, dependent upon the different purposes served by the objects sought as food, means of conveyance and sex. (2) Failure to adjust after interruption of the stereotyped activities of the instinctive routine type mentioned on page 184. (3) Action in excess of what is essential to attain the ends sought. Several sub-classes arise here dependent upon the character of the end sought. Of these ends the most important are those connected with nourishment and propagation.

In the first class under the head of nourishment come such mistakes as that of butterflies attempting to feed on artificial flowers made to imitate real flowers of the kind the insects are accustomed to. This sort of thing is far from rare. A case was reported by E. E. Barnard [4] of an effort of a butterfly to feed on a peacock feather stuck in a man's hat. Blunders as gross as this are probably not very common

[4] "A Mistaken Butterfly," *Nature*, 1915, Vol. XCV, p. 174.

under natural conditions and do not lead to great injury. But identification failures of a more subtle kind become a serious matter in many cases. Such a case is that presented by a member of the blister beetle family (*Sitaris humeralis*). The quite remarkable career of this animal during its larval life was followed through by Fabre. The larval life of the beetle is dependent upon a solitary bee of the genus *Anthophora*, the bee's egg constituting the food of the larva during one of the larval stages of the beetle, and the bee's honey serving the purpose during another larval stage. The bee nests in the ground, the nest being constituted of several cells in each of which honey is stored and an egg is placed.

The kernel of this part of the story is that relating to the way the recently hatched larva of the beetle reaches the egg of the bee. "The eggs of the *Sitaris* are deposited in the earth in close proximity to the entrance to the bees' nests, about August. They are very numerous, a single female producing, it is believed, upwards of 2000 eggs. In about a month . . . they hatch; . . . the larvæ do not, however, move away, but, without taking food, hibernate in a heap, remaining in this state till the following April or May, when they become active. Although they are close to the abodes of the bees they do not enter them, but seek to attach themselves to any hairy object that may come near them, and thus a certain number of them get on to the bodies of the *Anthophora* and are carried to its nest. . . . They attach themselves with equal readiness to any other hairy insect, and it is probable that very large numbers perish in consequence of attaching themselves to the wrong insects." [5] One obviously large chance of getting on the wrong insect is the fact that the male instead of the female bees appear to be the ones commonly used as carrier by the larval beetles. This makes the larva's chance of success contingent

[5] Fabre, retold by David Sharp, "Insects," *The Cambridge Natural History*, Vol. VI, p. 273.

upon its passing later from the male to a female which has not yet deposited her eggs, for it seems necessary to conclude from Fabre's experiments that the larvæ reach the eggs by actually slipping from the body of the bee to the egg at the moment the egg is deposited. The reason why the larvæ first attach themselves to a male bee in the species studied by Fabre, is that the males hatch about a month earlier than the females. Since the youngsters are emerging from several months of hibernation when the bees begin to come out, the impulse to seize the first objects that give them a chance may be very strong.

This life career of *Sitaris* is manifestly adjusted for a great amount of waste by self-destruction, due to an instinctive activity which fails regularly in a large number of instances to accomplish its purpose. This failure may be traced to the existence within one complex of activities of certain acts which are wonderfully well-fitted to meet the needs of the species and certain others which are very illfitted to meet these needs. There are not many performances among animals below man known to us that look more like thoughtful planning and skillful executing than those of the passage of the *Sitaris* larva from the malé to the female bee and again from the body of the female to the egg.

But why is the male bee included in the plan at all? If the larvæ were not in so much of a hurry in the spring to attach themselves to something but waited until the female bees hatched, they might avoid entirely the large chance of failure involved in attaching to the male first and afterward transferring to the female. This attainment of the egg by the beetle larva through starting out on a male bee and then making a skillful transfer to a female that is going to lay the egg seems quite comparable to the attainment of his dinner by an aviator through starting out on one plane and skillfully transferring himself to another en route which should be carrying his meal. Such an aviation feat might be all right as a "stunt"; but to make the life not only of the aviator himself but of the whole race of aviators dependent on the performance would hardly be counted a wise general aviation policy.

Another example of self-produced mortality from lack of knowledge of the factors involved in the means of conveyance regularly used is furnished by the "ballooning" of spiders. The habit especially of the young of various families of climbing to some elevated place on quiet days, elevating the abdomen to a nearly perpendicular position, spinning out several threads to be carried up and off by air currents, and then letting themselves go when the pull is felt, is described in all general works on spiders. The breeze-borne aeronauts are known to be carried long distances in this way and the mode of travel is counted an efficient means of distribution for the animals. It at least appears to be an efficient means of preventing the crowded condition that would result if all the young were to remain at the old homestead. It seems inevitable that so random a kind of travel would be full of hazards. That it is so is proved by such observations as one recorded by Darwin.[6] On November 1, 1832, when the *Beagle* was sixty miles from land on the coast of Patagonia, "The weather had been fine and clear, and in the morning the air was full of patches of the flocculent web, as on an autumnal day in England. Vast numbers of small spiders, about one tenth of an inch in length, and of a dusky color, were attached to the webs. There must have been, I should suppose, some thousands on the ship. . . . The spiders were all of one species, but of both sexes, together with young ones."

As a "steady but light breeze" was blowing from the land, there could be no doubt where the spiders came from. But where were they going? Just with the wind. That seemingly is the whole answer so far as their active part in the

[6] *Journal of Researches*, by Charles Darwin, Appleton edition, p. 159.

performance is concerned. Possibly a few of the several thousands that happened to be caught by the *Beagle* may have survived the journey. But what about the thousands upon thousands that did not happen to be caught thus or by any other ship? "They put to sea and were never heard of again," would have to be the record of their kindred on shore if a record were kept by them. This is by no means an isolated case, as is indicated by Darwin in his comments on the one observed by him.

Nor is it among spiders alone that self-destruction occurs by being blown to sea. Many species of flying insects have been reported in large numbers at distances from land that make any chance of their being saved out of the question. The interesting problem of wingless insects and birds on islands is closely connected with this.

An example of self-injury through failure to readjust after interruption of activities of the instinctive routine type relates to one of the wolf spiders (Lycosidae) and is taken from Warburton.[7] The large species of southern Europe, the true tarantulas, live for years. Until the fall of the first year, the youngsters are wanderers over the earth. When fall comes and they have attained maturity they burrow into the ground and establish their permanent homes. "Curiously enough," Warburton writes, "if disturbed, they entirely decline to burrow unless it be the proper season for that operation, but remain inert and helpless on the surface till they die. If, however, a tunnel is provided for them, they enter it at once and adapt it to their needs."[8] The apparent explanation for the spider's behavior in "entirely declining to burrow unless it be the proper season for the operation," is that burrowing for the particular species is an activity which has a place in a whole series of activities; in that place it must come or not come at all. Burrowing, for

---

[7] *Spiders*, by Cecil Warburton.
[8] P. 72.

this spider, belongs to a routined set of activities, a set for which a route exists and has existed for countless generations of the animals.

Our presentation of self-injury among insects due to excessive activity will have to limit itself to one example of excess in pursuit of food, and to one example of excess in connection with mating. The domestic honey-bee will furnish the example of the first. The observations are reported by an English bee-keeper, Herbert Mace.[9] Bee-keeping being a business with Mr. Mace, he determined to get more information than the works on bee culture contain, about the conditions under which his colonies produced the most and the least honey. To this end he weighed each of two hives daily through a honey-producing season, selecting for the purpose one of his strongest and one of his weakest colonies. He then studied the weight records in connection with the weather records for the same period. "The average results when the wind was light or moderate in force were in both cases more than four times better than when the wind was blowing freshly."[10] This does not mean that the bees stayed at home on windy days. There is nothing in Mr. Mace's account that indicates that fewer workers leave the hive when the wind is blowing hard than when it is not. The chief cause of the difference in weight noted was the difference not in the number of bees leaving the hive, but in the number returning to it honey-laden. "High winds cause great loss among the colonies, and it would be advisable when such prevail to keep the bees confined in the hives, unless there are sources for honey-gathering in the immediate vicinity." Mace concludes that the stronger colonies suffer more than the weaker ones from this source of loss. The chief reason for this conclusion was the fact that the only

[9] "The Influence of Weather on Bees," *Nature*, March 21, 1912, Vol. LXXXIX, pp. 62-65.
[10] P. 64.

time when the weak colony showed better than the strong one as judged by the weighings was when the winds were high. The explanation of this, Mace thinks, is that the "strong stock, being able to send out a larger proportion of foragers, suffered proportionally heavier losses of bees."

Another interesting fact noted by Mace in regard to the meteorological influences upon bees is their sensitiveness to sunshine and shadow. When they are working in the open field on a bright sunny day, they "hurry home as soon as a cloud comes up. Sometimes, in the height of the honey flow, a cloud passing over the sun will bring them home at such a rate that on one or two occasions I have gone out, thinking they were swarming." Perhaps it is not justifiable to suppose serious injury results from such home-rushing. So far as it occurs as a response to passing clouds which bring neither rain nor much lowering of temperature, it must be done with considerable useless expenditure of energy, and wear and tear of wings.

This study of Mace's is impressive as revealing how little we know, compared with what we do not know, about the way animals below man, and especially those well endowed with locomotive and mental powers, solve their problems of existence in nature. Probably not one among the innumerable host of insect species has been studied more than the honey-bee, and certain aspects of its life as independent, isolate individuals are known in great detail. They have been studied vastly more as objects in themselves than they have been as objects in relation to all other natural objects upon which their existence is absolutely dependent. Extensive observational and experimental investigations have been made on what senses they possess and how these may and do operate under humanly imposed conditions. But when it comes to questions of how the bees use these senses and for countless ages have used them, in their efforts to live and flourish under conditions imposed by nature, a bee man

like Mr. Mace finds no answer to such practical matters, as
that of how effectively the bees are able to cope with the
difficulties and dangers from the vicissitudes of weather
which beset them in their food gathering. One of the things
of most importance to the bees themselves and to the bee
keeper, the experimentalist is likely to exclude from his
program. To get the information which specially interests
the experimenter it is necessary for him to guard against
some of the very conditions which would give information
specially important for the bee man and specially interesting
to the naturalist. A situation like this, which reveals the
meagerness of our knowledge of the working life of so
familiar a creature as the honey-bee, makes us feel the truth
of Forel's words: "Comparative Psychology is an as yet
almost unexplored territory and but little understood, for
want of approaching it by the best side, that is to say, by
carefully made observations." [11]

For our example of self-injury from excessive activity in
connection with mating, we go to the May-flies (Ephemer-
idæ). The facts are furnished by Vernon Kellogg. [12] They
pertain to an incident witnessed by Kellogg at Lucerne,
Switzerland, in August, 1897, and involved one of those
familiar gatherings of May-flies around electric and other
bright lights. For the benefit of those of my readers who
are not entomologists, a brief interpretation of this phenomenon may be useful. The only object of the May-flies'
few hours of adult life is reproduction, this being dependent
upon fertilization of the egg by mating of male and female
and the laying of the impregnated eggs in some body of
water. The act of mating is accomplished by the females
and males coming together in flight through their common
sensitiveness to light, both sexes being positively phototropic

[11] *The Senses of Insects*, Auguste Forel; Eng. trans. by MacLeod
Yearsley, p. 269.
[12] *American Insects*, p. 63; *Insect Stories*, pp. 191-210.

in a high degree during the first part of their adult life. The electric lights introduced into the May-fly environment by man being specially bright and specially localized, the creatures are irresistibly "drawn" to them. Since these lights are usually, as in the case of this Lucerne arc lamp described by Kellogg, over the land and not over the water, the tropism in the absence of any adequate inhibiting or guiding counterforce, proves fatal to the insects.

Beginning with a remark about his attention being called to a crowd of people around a brilliant arc light near the Schweizerhof Hotel, Kellogg goes on: "The light seemed to me curiously hazy, and even before I got near the crowd I had made a guess at what was going on. My guess that it was a May-fly dance of death was quite right. Perhaps it would be better to call it a 'dance of life,' for it really was a sort of a great wedding dance. But it was a dance of death, too, for the dancers were falling dead or dying out of the dizzying whirly circles by thousands. How many hundreds or thousands or millions of May-flies there were in the dense circling cloud about the light, I have no idea. But the air for twenty feet every way from the light was full of them, and the ground for a circle of thirty or forty feet underneath was not merely covered with the delicate dead creatures, but was covered for from one to two inches deep." [13]

The number of dead flies on the ground is the measure of useless destruction the creatures had brought upon themselves by this dance. The justification for calling the destruction useless is that by dying as they did the females were prevented from leaving any progeny. In other words, they were prevented from accomplishing the chief end toward which the whole dance business was directed. It was as though a pair of birds were to court so strenuously and work so hard at nest-building that they should kill them-

[13] P. 201.

selves before the eggs were laid. Another sentence of Kellogg's brings this fact out positively: "In the first place, after the dance of death, the few that don't die fly out over the lake or river or pond, and drop a lot of little eggs into it. Then they die happy—if May-flies can be happy. Mind you, I don't say they can. We are the only animals that we know can be happy. And we mostly aren't."

It was Kellogg's knowledge of the extremely stereotyped, mechanical character of the performance that enabled him to make the remarks quoted about happiness in May-flies and in men. Being both scientific and poetic, it was possible for him to say something wiser than either a scientist with no poetry in his soul or a poet with no science in his soul could say.

The remarkable scheme by which propagation is accomplished in the May-fly family involves remarkable modifications in structural and functional aspects of the life of the creatures. Consider what is implied by the very brief life of the adult, the winged stage of their existence. While some of the species are said to live several days, others live only a few hours. They emerge at sunset and their career is ended before the next morning. They never see full daylight. As light is a factor essential for the completion of the life-cycle, their sensitiveness to it, so much of it as occurs in their career of darkness, is excessive. This naturally implies an unusual development of eyes. Accordingly we find in the males of some of the species the most remarkable ocular equipment for perceiving light and objects in motion possessed by any animal whatever. Not only is each of the paired eyes highly compounded according to the regular insect scheme, but each of the pair is divided into two parts, one on top of a thick post and the other level with the surface of the head at the base of the post. There are in addition three smaller, simple eyes, called ocelli. Exactly how such eyes work, especially in seeing objects, nobody knows. That they play an important part in such intense responses to light as these animals show is a safe inference.

Reflecting again on the brevity of the winged period of May-fly life, we naturally infer that the nutrimental apparatus would either be adjusted for the taking of nutriment fast and furiously or it would be adjusted for taking no nutrition at all. As a matter of fact the latter alternative is the one realized. The mouth parts, highly elaborate in typical insects, are so changed retrogressively that scarcely a trace of such parts can be recognized. The intestinal tract, wholly unused and useless for its original function, has become transformed into a thin, distensible-walled sac inflatable with air, the inflation being accomplished by the muscular action of the body, and a set of valves so arranged that the air can enter the sac from the mouth, but cannot escape. The creature is converted into a sort of balloon fitted out with wings and a neuro-muscular system to guide its movements enough to bring the reproductive cells, male and female, which are likewise carried about by the balloon, into contact with each other. The reproductive apparatus is likewise greatly simplified as contrasted with its structure in insects generally.

In other words, the entire make-up of the adult May-fly consists of organ-systems coördinately modified in a wonderful way to correspond with the one function of this phase of its life. The "dance" is in reality a highly mechanical waggle of a body constructed as above described, in an unstable equilibrium, and having the end function indicated. That a mechanism of such inflexible type should miss its end in a large percentage of trials is certain on probability principles alone.

The enormous destruction we have been looking at resulted from an electric light, an entirely new and strange factor brought into May-fly existence. It might be said that such havoc as that wrought by it upon the insects can not be supposed to be of much significance for the evolution of this insect tribe. In reply to this I would say that ability to meet successfully new and advanced conditions is exactly the test of intelligent life; and that beyond question the propagative operation of May-flies misses its end to a considerable extent under natural conditions in much the same fashion as under the artificial conditions. Undoubtedly the destruction is rarely as great in the state of nature. And certainly, too, it succeeds far enough in nature to insure the perpetuity of the May-fly stock. But its success has been at enormous cost in individual adult lives. Indeed the cost may have been and may now be too great to be kept up, for the May-flies of the present geological era form an unimportant part of the insect tribe as compared with the number of their allies in the far distant past. Scudder, the eminent student of fossil insects, regards the May-fly tribe as the "lingering fragments of an expiring group." If this pronouncement of Scudder's is correct what causal explanation of the slow-impending doom of May-flies is closer at hand than that of the very maladjustment in activity here noticed? In all likelihood other causes have been involved, but the existence of other causes would not render the causal factor suggested above any less probable.

CHAPTER 12

SELF-INJURY (*con.*) : AMONG BIRDS

OUR further raw data as to self-injurious animal activity will be drawn from two vertebrate classes only, birds and mammals. The riches at our command are so great as to be quite embarrassing.

The behavior of wild yet semidomestic birds, as sparrows, linnets and swallows, which by chance fly into man-occupied buildings through open windows and doors has forced itself on the attention of many persons. Nobody who has seen one of these accidents can have failed to notice the "stupidity" with which the creatures miss the windows and doors opened by the human occupants of the temporary bird prison, as ways of escape for the prisoners. Their eyes appear to be useless so far as seeing the openings is concerned.

A common remark by those who would help the entrapped birds out of their trouble is that the "poor creatures are so frightened" as to be unable to take advantage of their chances for freedom. The eyesight of the birds is abundantly capable, so far as the mechanical structure of the optical apparatus is concerned, of seeing an open window. It is a question not of the competency of the eyes in themselves, but of how these are used. Without doubt, strangeness of the situation and fright contribute largely to the inability of the birds to make good use of their eyes. But another element is involved. The birds tend to stay in the upper parts of the room, going above the openings. The usual interpretation of this is as an effort on the bird's part to avoid being captured. In all probability this plays a part in the total activity of the unfortunates. But any one who has watched birds under these conditions knows that their tendency to keep in the upper part of the room is quite independent of any effort to capture them, or even of human activity of any kind. A much more potent factor is the fact that bird flight, especially as it starts from the resting state of the bird, is instinctively upward. For a bird to "take flight" means for it to move upward as well as merely off into the open air. This flight impulse is normally one of the strongest of all bird impulsions. Being further intensified by fear, this impulse becomes so much stronger than is the bird's ability to direct flight by sight, that the "senseless" dashings about take place. The birds may batter themselves to death by violent contact with solid objects of the room. Thus a type of action which in general is of the highest usefulness to birds may under special environic conditions, result not in the creature's good but in its harm, even in its destruction.

Another form of self-injurious activity resulting from defective employment of the sense of sight, is the fighting of a bird's own image reflected in the glass of windows, on the supposition that the image is another bird. This is a form of misdirected activity to which birds are quite liable. From the accounts I have come upon it seems that blackbirds are especially given to such performances. Moffatt [1] describes a case of this sort. Having been told that a blackbird was carrying on a contest with itself at a neighbor's house the author went to see it and "found that its action was exactly that which the cock birds adopt in fighting. In fact, it was obviously doing battle with its own reflection in the glass. For this purpose it repaired to the same window every morning during the whole of March and a greater part of April."

The almost universal tendency for such "blind" activity

[1] "The Spring Rivalry of Birds," *The Irish Naturalist*, 1903, Vol. XII, pp. 152-166.

to repeat itself almost exactly and well-nigh endlessly is illustrated by this instance. Moffat continues: "It never, so far as we could make out, noticed itself, or looked for itself in any other window—but used all its energies against this particular one." The following year the same bird returned and waged the same foolish feud in the same place and the same way. This year remarkably enough a cock chaffinch carried on a similar performance at another window of the same house. "So all through the spring of 1899 we had two daily battles going on. And in the third spring, 1900, it was exactly the same, the 'crazy Blackbird'—as he was called—fighting himself at one side of the house, and an equally infatuated chaffinch doing the same thing at the other."

In addition to other records of blackbirds waging such contests, robins, cardinals, and brown towhees have been observed to do essentially the same thing. While I know of no observations showing that anything quite comparable to this particular form of maladaptive action among birds occurs where man has not intruded any of his handiwork into their environment; and while proof seems wanting of serious injury to the birds, it appears to me likely that fuller knowledge of bird life in nature would produce positive evidence that similar things occur in nature and to the positive injury of the birds.

EXTINCTION OF SPECIES PROMOTED BY MALADAPTIVE ACTIVITY

Instances of birds becoming extinct "at the hand of man" are only too well known. A fact which has been largely neglected by writers is that *the birds themselves have contributed to their own destruction.*

We will first notice two cases in which the men responsible for the fatality to the birds belong to primitive races. Take the extinction, or near-extinction, of several species of

Hawaiian birds. Almost everybody knows something about the famous feather robes worn by the kings and warriors of the native Hawaiian people. So many and so elaborate were these garments that the drain on the birds which yielded the most highly prized feathers was very great. The birds were therefore protected by royal edict and by taboo. With the downfall of the monarchy and the dying out of the taboo the native hunters were left with a free hand to slaughter the beautiful birds. The O-O (*Moho nobilis*) was one of the species most sought, and the part it played in its own destruction is told by H. W. Henshaw.[2] "When feeding in the morning," Henshaw says, "and particularly when with the young, the calls of the O-O are almost incessant, and it is this loud and constantly repeated call-note which has led to the easy destruction of the species. The poor bird has yet to learn that its appreciation of the joyousness of existence and its love for its mate and young can be expressed only at the cost of its very life." [3]

Hawaiian natives, birds and men, furnish another and somewhat different illustration. The Hawaiian goose (*Bernicla sandvicensis*) which has undergone the remarkable change of habit of becoming entirely a land goose has at the same time adopted certain habits which make it an easy prey to the native hunters. It attaches itself so rigidly to certain localities for breeding-places that it returns to them year after year. This the hunters learn and take advantage of for making prey of the geese, old and young. The rigidity of habit is the more destructive to the birds in that when the young are being led around by the parents, neither old nor young being able to fly, the old because moulting and the young because not mature enough, the hunters are able to run the birds down and kill them with clubs and stones.

[2] *Birds of the Hawaiian Islands,* 1902.
[3] P. 72.

Certain species of small Australian Parrots (Lorikeets) have become nearly extinct, partly from exposing themselves to the depredations of hunters by habits some of which are very similar to those of the unfortunate species of Hawaiian song birds. The facts as here presented are taken from G. M. Mathews.[4] Concerning the Musk Lorikeet, Mathews quotes F. P. Godfrey of Victoria, as follows: "The birds quickly betray their nest by harsh screeching, and only have to be watched for a few minutes in order to detect the nest."

Of another species, the Purple-crowned Lorikeet, we have the following, quoted from E. B. Nicholls: "If you fire a gun or shout out loudly the whole flock dart toward the ground like a flash, and fly with amazing speed only a few feet above the grass. The aborigines, taking advantage of that peculiarity, used to build a sort of brush fence, white-washing it with the pipeclay mixture they used in their corroborees. When the birds passed overhead, the blacks raised a great clamor, and the panic-stricken parrots, dropping to earth, flew into the brush and were caught in hundreds."

The Musk Lorikeet furnishes another example of the fatality there is likely to be in this place-habit. After describing a snaring device used by the native hunters for capturing the birds, Mathews writes: "It seems strange that these birds, when once they alight on one of these poles, repeatedly come back until they are eventually entangled in one of the many horse-hair nooses with which the forked extremity of the snare pole is covered." At this point the author mentions a fact which is doubly significant for our general discussion. The hunters, he says, keep on catching the birds by this snare method, "even though they can get little or nothing for them." Man, though able to outwit the senselessly repetitious birds, is not yet able to correct his own senselessness in the same direction!

The excessive gregariousness of these parrots and their

[4] *Birds of Australia*, Vol. VI.

dullness of perception as to where danger lies have contributed to their undoing. "I have seen as many as fifty-six shot off one large tree," Mathews quotes G. A. Kearlland as saying, "without the rest of the flock taking alarm." Take the following concerning the Dowitcher (*Macrorhamphus griseus*), one of the shore birds likely to be regarded by hunters as a "kind of snipe." "This gregarious instinct combined with its gentleness, is a fatal trait, and enables gunners to slaughter them unmercifully and sometimes to exterminate every individual in a 'bunch.' "[5] Something similar to this, so far as gregariousness is concerned, could be said of at least a great majority of flocking birds which for any reason are hunted by man.

No more striking example of this could be cited than that of the passenger pigeon (*Ectopistes migratorius*). The story of this bird from the coming of white men to North America to the extinction of the species within the last few decades, is one of the most dramatic in bird life. The phase of it with which we are specially concerned is the way the habits of the birds contributed to their own destruction. In the first place the prodigious numbers of individuals in the heyday of the species must be clearly before our minds. On this as upon other points connected with the habits of this pigeon, the two famous American ornithologists of the early nineteenth century, J. J. Audubon and Alexander Wilson, are our main sources of information. What Audubon thought the largest flight of the wild pigeon he had ever seen occurred during the autumn of 1813 in the vicinity of Louisville, Kentucky. As he traveled one day from Hardensburgh on the Ohio river to Louisville, a distance of fifty-five miles, the pigeon myriads filled the air during the entire day, so that the "light of noonday was obscured as by an eclipse." For three days this kept up. The air during the time was filled with the odor of pigeons. An attempt to estimate the

[5] *Birds of North America*, by Robert Ridgway, Vol. I, p. 230.

number of birds in such a mass as this would seem useless. Both Audubon and Wilson did make such attempts on flocks that were somewhat more restricted. Thus Wilson estimated a flock which passed over him in the region of Frankfort, Kentucky, to be two hundred and forty miles long and at least a mile wide, and to contain over two billion two hundred million individuals. The testimony of many observers for many parts of the United States makes it impossible to regard these as fabulous stories. My own recollection of the spring visitations of the birds to Wisconsin during the sixties and seventies of the nineteenth century makes my mind easily receptive of the Audubon-Wilson statements.

What can we recognize in the career of this species that seems to have contributed most to its great numerical success? The bird was wonderfully fitted in structure and mode of life for utilizing the almost boundless materials on which it fed. That appears to tell the story. "Mast" (nuts of all sorts, but particularly of the beech and oak) seems to have been the great staple originally, though many kinds of berries and seeds were eagerly consumed. Nor was the vegetable world alone capable of ministering to their food requirements. Insects, especially grasshoppers and caterpillars, earthworms, snails, are said to have been extensively utilized at times. When agricultural grains were introduced into their ranges, these were pounced upon with great avidity. From this brief inventory of food sources, something of the extensiveness of the raw materials upon which the birds could draw will be readily understood by those acquainted with the vastness of the forests which originally overspread so much of North America east of the Rocky Mountains, and with the great areas covered with vegetation of less size than forest trees, but greatly prolific in seed production.

The food-seeking habits of the species were of exactly the

right kind for making the most of these bounties of nature.
The birds migrated northward and southward with the
change of season, going wherever food was abundant with
the greatest facility. A mile a minute was the rate of flight
attributed to them by Audubon and other observers.
Whether this figure is exact or not, certain it is that they
flew with astonishing speed and endurance. On this aspect
of their habits we read: "The Wild Pigeon appears to be
almost entirely influenced in its migrations by the abundance
of its food, except in those parts of the country in which it
had not been known to remain during the winter. Even
in these movements it is largely influenced by instinctive
considerations of food. Evidently the temperature has but
little to do with their migrations, as they not infrequently
move northward in large columns as early as the seventh of
March, with the thermometer twenty degrees below the
freezing-point.[6]

The vast quantities of food material available for the birds
and the facility with which they utilized it enabled them so
to adjust their breeding habits as to become enormously
prolific even though each pair normally produced but one
young at a sitting. The smallness of the brood was offset
by the fact that a pair produced several broods a year (one
every month, some authors say) as long as the food supply
was abundant. There is evidence that the birds were rather
long-lived and enjoyed a considerable period of fertility.
The mode of dealing with the nestlings increased the net
productiveness. The single young was subjected to a nutritional forcing that reduced the parental period of responsibility for its welfare to a minimum. Both mother and
father produced the well-known pigeon milk which, mixed
with the contents of their own crops, they fed the one nestling. This rich early diet followed by the mast with which

[6] Baird, Brewer and Ridgway, *A History of North American Birds,*
1874, Vol. III, p. 370.

the young is said to have been "stuffed" brought the bird to the squab stage in a condition that caused it to be spoken of as a mass of fat. It was then pushed out of the nest by the parents and for a few days while scarcely able to fly was an easy victim to hungry or greedy creatures (including man) which preyed upon the birds. The young are said to have been ready to begin reproducing at the age of six months.

This presents with extreme brevity our information on the question of how it came to pass that this species of pigeon flourished probably for thousands upon thousands of years in such almost incredible numbers.

Now something on the equally interesting question of how it came to pass that the species disappeared from the earth as in a single night, one may say without exaggeration, if the period of their going be compared with that of their entire existence. "The belief that the Passenger Pigeon was a bird of remarkable vitality, endurance, and powers of flight undoubtedly has a good foundation, but all these powers combined might prove useless against that dominating fear which compelled the bird to turn from the known dangers of civilization—the ax, the gun, and the forest fire, toward the inhospitable and semi-arctic regions of the north. We may hope that a remnant of the great hordes which once swept over our state still exists somewhere and may eventually restock our forests, but it must be confessed that this is far more a hope than an expectation, and with each succeeding year this hope grows fainter." [7] Today (July, 1926) there no longer remains a trace of such hope in the minds of most ornithologists.

A variety of explanations have been suggested to account for the phenomenon. None of them are weighty except that which recognizes the hand of the white man as the chief agent in the deadly work. Destruction of the forests and other sources of food and of the nesting and roosting places

[7] W. B. Barrows, *Michigan Bird Life*, p. 251.

contributed much to the end finally reached, but the enormous slaughter of the birds throughout their wide area was the greatest factor in their final annihilation. The story of this is as tragically impressive as anything of the kind that has ever had to be told. The accounts of how the pigeons were attacked in their roosting places at night by "guns, clubs, long poles, pots of sulphur, and various other engines of destruction," of how farmers for miles around drove their hogs to these places to fatten them on the carcasses which the people themselves could not use; and of how the great flocks were warred upon as pests because of their destructiveness to grain and other agricultural crops, are revelations of the destructiveness to which the species was subjected in the earlier periods. In the later period, after the netting and other specially effective methods of capture were fully developed and the fruits of the pigeon industry had found an almost unlimited market in the great cities, destructiveness reached its climax.

What, if anything, was there in the activities of the birds that contributed to their own undoing?

For one thing the prodigious numbers of individuals involved combined with certain aspects of their gregariousness greatly facilitated human depredations upon the birds. In addition to the great massing of individuals in the flights, there were two distinct forms of herding when the birds were not on the wing. One of these constituted the "roostings"; the other the "breedings." The former were the great assemblages for purposes other than reproduction; the other chiefly for reproduction.

At the roosting places the birds assembled only at night for the most part, the day being spent in excursions after food. Something of the character of these is portrayed by Audubon in his *Ornithological Biography*, the example being a roost which he saw on Green River, Kentucky. This was forty miles long and three miles wide. At evening the birds came to spend the night, settling on the trees in such great numbers that "Many trees two feet in diameter, I observed, were broken off at no great distance from the ground; and the branches of many of the largest and tallest had to give way, as if the forest had been swept by a tornado." As a result of this overcrowding and the activities of hunters and farmers, many of the birds were killed and injured. With the break of day the able-bodied birds were all off again for the feeding ground. The quantity of food consumed by such hordes of voracious creatures must have been enormous. Consideration of this aspect of the matter enables one to see why the birds were treated as pests. "They often descended upon all the fall-sown wheat and rye fields in such numbers that the farmers had to watch their fields or lose their crops." [8]

The havoc-production of the breeding assemblages was even greater than that of the roosts. One of the last of these, that in Emmet County, Michigan, in 1878, has been often described. This is said to have covered an area of from twenty-eight to forty miles long, and from three to ten miles wide. One hundred and ten nests are reported to have been counted in a single tree, and almost every tree had some nests. How the birds fared at the hands of pigeoners in this instance is indicated by the following: "For many weeks the railroad shipments averaged fifty barrels of dead birds per day, averaging for the season about 12,500 dead birds daily, or 1,500,000 for the summer. Of live birds there were shipped 1,116 crates, six dozen per crate, or 80,352 birds." Besides these railroad shipments great numbers were shipped by steamer from various ports. The squabs found an eager market; they were taken in vast numbers by shaking them, like fruit, from the smaller trees, and by cutting down the larger trees. Great numbers were taken, some

---

[8] E. H. Forbush, "Birds of North America," p. 46, *Nature Lovers' Library*, Vol. II.

for immediate consumption and some for preservation and storage as winter supplies by the residents of the surrounding country. Many of the live birds shipped to the cities were used in trap shooting: a form of sport that is highly significant from the standpoint of animal and human instinct.

The great ease with which the birds were taken was a very important factor in this wholesale slaughter. "A most remarkable attribute of the Pigeon was its disregard of the presence of human beings in its roosting and nesting places. Any one who entered quietly one of these spots when the birds were there would be surrounded by the unsuspicious creatures in a few minutes. The nests formerly were placed in trees of great height . . . but after the primeval forests were cut off the Pigeons nested sometimes in low trees. This contributed to their doom." [9]

This lack of caution combined with excessive gregariousness promoted the success of the netting method of capture which seems to have been the chief reliance of the market pigeoners. It is of record that by making "grain beds" and allowing the greedy birds to collect on these for feeding, as many as two hundred and fifty dozen were sometimes taken at a single haul of the net. Another effective kind of bait was salted mud. It having been discovered that the birds had a great liking for this, especially at the breeding time, extensive "mud beds" were made in the neighborhood of the breeding assemblages. Upon these the birds would gather in multitudes and so fall easy victims to the previously prepared nets. Still another device utilized by the hunters was the decoy or "stool pigeons." These were captive live birds blinded in some way, placed where they could be easily seen by the great migratory flocks, and made to flap their wings by manipulating a string attached to them. The "foolish" birds were drawn to their unfortunate fellow

[9] *Ibid.*, p. 45.

creatures, and so to their destruction, in great numbers. These habits of the birds unquestionably aided man in his terrible onslaughts upon them.

Under some circumstances, the birds' activities were highly self-destructive in the state of nature. Audubon refers to the considerable mortality which at times they brought upon themselves by overloading the trees on the roosting and breeding places. Another source of natural destruction was through drowning and unfavorable meteorological conditions. Forbush writes: "Undoubtedly thousands of Pigeons were destroyed occasionally, during their flights, by storms or fogs at sea or on the Great Lakes." He cites Schoolcraft as stating that in 1821 he saw on the shore of Lake Michigan great numbers of skeletons and half-consumed bodies of Pigeons which had been drowned in the lake while attempting to cross it. This early observer is quoted as saying the birds were often overtaken by tempests while crossing the lake and were "drowned in whole flocks."

Another way in which they fell victim to the storm king was by nesting too early in the spring. Thus Barrows relates that one of the last nestings in Michigan "was broken up by a heavy fall of snow after the nests had eggs. All the old birds left in a body and never came back." Such instances of the destruction of birds and other forms of animal life by occasional and unusual climatic changes (and they are known to be by no means infrequent) tend wholly to disprove any half-mysterious weather-forecasting power widely supposed to be possessed by animals, and to prove that they are peculiarly liable to fatal disaster from adverse weather because of a lack of good sense, as humanly viewed, relative to such conditions.

Although this review of the dramatic life and death of the passenger pigeon as an animal species is very brief, it is adequate to substantiate the charge that while upon civilized man rests primarily the responsibility for this zoölogical tragedy, the birds themselves must be recognized as having been closely accessory in this responsibility.

SELF-INJURY DUE TO DEFECTIVE FEAR

An important type of maladaptive activity among birds is that involving the impulse to run away from danger. The rôle of this impulse is of vital importance in nearly all birds and mammals. The maladaptiveness of the bird activity due to this impulse may be traced in certain cases to its under-functioning, and in others to overfunctioning.

One of the most striking instances of the complete absence or very poor development of this impulse known to me among birds is presented by the Franklin Grouse (*Canachites franklinii*) of Oregon, Washington, and British Colum-ɔia. So disregardful of danger, at least from human beings, is this bird that its common local name is "fool hen." "Though almost any of the grouse on occasion may be foolishly bold, none approaches the present species in fatuous absence of fear. Not infrequently one will espy the birds sitting composedly watching the observer from a distance of 10 or 20 feet. Snyder . . . says, 'One sat sedately on a limb while a revolver was emptied at her. The shots having missed, roots and stones were thrown, which she avoided by stiff bows or occasional steps.' It would often be easily possible apparently, to kill the bird with a stick. . . . Considering the foolish boldness, or lack of fear, of this species it is small wonder that it has suffered an alarming decrease practically throughout its range. . . . In 1920 practically everybody in the woods, sheepmen, hunters . . . were freely taking toll of the gentle birds, even though the State law prohibits their being shot at any season of the year." [38]

Seemingly every writer who has had opportunity to observe

[10] Kenneth Racey, *The Murrelet*, Bull. Pacific Northwest Bird and Mammal Club, Sept., 1921, Vol. II, p. 6.

this grouse has testimony of similar character to give. There is evidence that hunting dogs give the bird as little concern as do men. How it is that so fearless a species should have survived as long as it has in the struggle for existence is not clear. Red men surely inhabited its native country ages before white men came, and it would seem inevitable that these aboriginal hunters should have preyed upon it as well as do their white successors. How, furthermore, has it escaped the depredations of the coyotes, lynxes, martens, and other animals which are supposed to prey upon any birds which occupy the same territory with them, and which are certainly abundant in the Pacific Northwest? Probably fuller knowledge of the life habits of the species will furnish at least a partial answer to this question.

On the whole the evidence does not warrant the belief that lack of fear has contributed very largely to the destruction of birds. Such cases as those mentioned appear not to be common, at least among modern birds. There are instances in which birds have been nearly devoid of fear of man at their first meeting with him, but if the meeting has proved destructive, the species has soon become sufficiently wary.

We have next to notice fear that overfunctions, that is to say, fear that is so strong and violent as to make it a danger rather than a safeguard under some circumstances. Cases of bewilderment and paralysis from fear may be regarded as coming under this head. A naturalist-hunter relates that a dove just after having been shot at and missed by each of three hunters, "flew down the canyon and passed me at about forty yards' distance. I fired once and missed. Instead of flying on out of danger the dove flanked sharply and landed right in front of me and began to eat." [11] The sight, hearing, and past experiences of the dove (*Zenaidura*

[11] E. K. Lipking, "Is the Dove Bag Limit too Large?" *California Fish and Game,* January, 1922, Vol. VIII, p. 48.

macroura) are adequate to enable it to behave more pre-
servatively than this in such a situation. Its defect was
mental. Its landing close to one of its sources of deadly
peril, and especially its beginning to eat, indicate mental
confusion. It is very improbable that the eating was done
because the bird was really in need of food. The more
likely explanation of the act is that food material of some
sort happened to be present where the dove landed, and that
this as a stimulant to the naturally strong food-taking impulse, brought out the appropriate response, quite regardless
of the immediate food needs of the bird.

Another example of disaster-producing fear of a different
type is described as follows: "On the pampas the gauchos
frequently take the black-necked swan by frightening it.
When the birds are feeding or resting on the grass, two or
three men or boys on horseback go quietly to leeward of
the flock, and when opposite to it suddenly wheel and
charge it at full speed, uttering loud shouts, by which the
birds are thrown into such terror that they are incapable
of flying and are quickly dispatched." [12] In the same connection Hudson tells of frequently seeing the native boys
catch another bird, the Silver-bill (*Lichenops perspicillata*)
by hurling something at it and then rushing upon it, "when
it sits perfectly still, disabled by fear, and allows itself to be
taken."

In these cases it is man in his primitive state who fatally
outwits the birds. In any complete history of bird destruction by man, the part played by the hunter's taking advantage of the bewildering or paralyzing effect of fear upon the
bird would loom large.

[12] W. H. Hudson, *The Naturalist in La Plata*, p. 202.

CHAPTER 13

SELF-INJURY (*con.*) : AMONG MAMMALS

IN mammals we reach the zoölogical class to which the human animal belongs, in which our own basic instincts and activities find their most immediate forerunners. In man as in all the members of the class, the new-born young are nourished by a milk produced by the mother. For a considerable period before birth the young are borne within and nourished by the uterus of the mother. The sexual activities involved in propagation are fundamentally the same in all the class.

We will study self-injurious maladaptive actions in mammals under the following heads: sucking by the new-born young; food-getting by adults; avoidance of danger.

The sucking activity. This rests upon a reflex, called forth by the stimulus of contact with almost any object. Ancestral habit as a causal explanation of the phenomenon has been resorted to in connection with miscarriages of this as of so many other instinctive actions. This explanation tends to divert attention from the most significant part of the phenomenon, the injuriousness of it. It is well known that tufts of the mother's wool will bring out the sucking response in new-born lambs quite as readily as will the mother's nipple, and that the "foolish" little creatures will suck away on these so energetically and persistently that starvation might result did not the mother sheep or the shepherd intervene.

If the sucking mechanism and impulse of lambs is of such character that the act of sucking is apt to be so performed as to yield no milk to the lambs, the question which concerns us is how far this useless action may be carried. It may be carried to the extent of death by starvation of the creature. This inference rests on a large body of observation. As far down the mammalian scale as the marsupials, we know that the movement of the very immature young toward the teat is essentially tropistic, the direction being upward; and that this direction will be maintained even if it takes the creature *away from* instead of *toward* its source of food. Normally the direction of movement is against gravity, and brings the young to the teat only in case this happens to be in that direction, which it is ordinarily.

Going through the whole scale of mammalian life to man, we should find the human infant at birth only slightly better off, so far as the sucking instinct is concerned, than is the new-born marsupial. The finger or almost any other object brought into contact with the infant's lips will evoke the sucking reflex. If the object is one that can be taken into the mouth, and at all resembles the nipple, the sucking activity will occur and would go on to complete exhaustion were the infant wholly dependent upon its own resources and upon this one instinct.

Summarizing the results of his examination of the evidence on the general question of the nursing ability of infant mammals, C. Lloyd Morgan gives us the following: "In the absence of further evidence, we may perhaps accept the view that the young are drawn to the mother by the sense of warmth, and come in contact with the teats either as the result of random movements and vague attempts to suck something (other parts being often sucked as well as the teats), or in response to stimuli affecting the sense of smell or through some external guidance." [1]

Probably in no mammal whatever is the sucking activity sufficient of itself to insure the wholly unpracticed young from death by starvation. Given the new-born mammal en-

[1] *Habit and Instinct,* 1896, p. 116.

dowed with this food-securing ability and given a food
supply furnished by the mother such as that which actually
is furnished, it seems necessary to recognize that without the
interposition of a third agency of some sort every new-born
mammal would starve to death without ever tasting its
mother's milk. The sucking activity of the new-born mammal is an extremely capable and important element in meeting the nutritional necessities of the creature; but it is not
sufficient of itself to accomplish this, as it is incapable of
making sure of a source of nourishment. The infant mammal's ability to suck is abundantly adequate for its needs;
but its ability to get at the right object to suck is not
adequate.

Food-getting by adults. Every experienced raiser of any
of the domestic mammals has had many chances to observe
the occasional "senselessness" of these animals in relation
to their food. On small, well-regulated farms where the number of animals involved is not large, this is less likely to
show itself than on the great ranges where natural conditions are much more varied, where regulation by man is far
less complete, and where the number of animals involved is
much greater.

When "range" cattle have to be fed for a portion of the
year because of shortage of pasturage from drought or other
cause, it is important not to feed them long and constantly
on a single small area lest they become so attached to it
that when the range grass is again ready for them they will
not recognize the fact and turn to the pastures, but will
keep on hovering around the feed place even though nothing
is found there. Mr. W. C. Barnes, Chief of the Grazing
Division of the United States Forest Service, and Mr. J. E.
Nelson of the same division, both practical stockmen and
competent observers, confirm and extend such statements as
to the tendency of cattle, sheep, and horses to return to the
places where they have been fed, watered, or salted, so per-

sistently after there is no longer anything to be got from so doing, that serious harm may result to them therefrom. Mr. Barnes says that cattle will continue to visit their accustomed water hole after it is completely dry, until they die of thirst, even though there may be other holes near by which contain water, but which the animals have not been in the habit of visiting. Such a thing as going definitely in search of a new supply of water or food when the old supply is gone appears to be beyond the mental capacity of any of the domestic mammals. Such an effort for finding food is very different from a general wandering about under the stress of thirst or hunger.

Nor is danger of death from thirst or starvation the only one to which these animals may subject themselves by their tendency to repeat the same acts. Mr. Barnes once helped the same cow out of the mud three times, where she had mired down while after water. Despite this experience, into the same mudhole she went again, this time to her death before anybody could help extricate her. All this while water could have been safely reached not far away. When their accustomed water ponds are covered with a thin film of ice, cattle will suffer from thirst although water could be readily secured by breaking the ice. Horses will paw and break the ice under such conditions, Mr. Barnes says; and cattle will follow the horses if they have a chance, to take advantage of what their more resourceful neighbors have done.

So far as this particular matter is concerned horses would seem to be possessed of considerable "sense." However, when they are brought to the test in other ways, they do not make so good a showing. Mr. Nelson tells of an experience of his own in which he had great difficulty in getting a horse to put down its head to drink from a pond because it had been long accustomed to drinking from a bucket held up to its head. I have known of the actual death from thirst of a horse from failure to make this same adjustment in its mode of taking water.

On the question of how far this sort of thing is applicable to mammals in the state of nature there does not seem to be much direct information. However, there is little or nothing to justify the supposition that wild brutes have more ability for adjusting themselves to new situations than have their domesticated relatives. Ability to meet new conditions is the crucial thing. A search of writings on the habits of the larger wild mammals, giving special attention to the question of how these habits have operated in the face of the great changes wrought upon the environments of the animals by the coming of man, particularly of civilized man, indicates extremely little of such ability. We read: "Of the larger wild game about the Painted Woods (North Dakota) and vicinity, after the buffalo and bear, the elk were the next to disappear, which owing to a kind of domestication or attachment to the points where they were born and raised, they usually remained in the one neighborhood until exterminated by the great influx of hunters that came in with or followed the building of the Northern Pacific railroad." [2]

Of like import is the testimony of Mr. Barnes and of the members of the U. S. Biological Survey, Doctors E. W. Nelson, T. S. Palmer, and others, who have had much to do with the elk herds of the West, particularly with the government-protected herd of the Yellowstone National Park and Jackson's Hole. The narrow restriction of the elk "runs," and the rigidity with which the animals cling to these greatly increased the difficulty of preserving the remnants of the great herds that existed in these regions before the white settlers and hunters came. The elk show little ability for hunting out new grazing grounds under the stress of immediate need. What is here said of the elk would be more or less true of many species of the large herbivores

[2] J. H. Taylor, *Beavers and Their Ways*, p. 135.

which have suffered extinction in several parts of the world at the on-coming of civilized man.

This statement must not be understood to imply that such animals have no adaptability whatever relative to changing conditions in their food supply and other life necessities. Extensions and changes of habitat are definitely known for some species. Dr. Nelson tells us: "During recent years, the moose has been extending its range in various parts of northern Canada, having even descended to the delta of the Mackenzie River." The evidence for this presented by Nelson seems conclusive.[3] Undoubtedly many other instances of this sort might be cited, but this one will suffice to illustrate the point that while the large gregarious herbivores have considerable facility for meeting changes in their food and other life necessities, this appears to be general rather than specific. No one would doubt that the moose's extension of habitat as indicated might be, in fact probably would be, advantageous to the species. But that it was deliberately done to meet some particular requirement or emergency no one well acquainted with the ways of animals would be likely to contend. A herd of elk who have become hungry from shortage of forage at a particular spot, in moving away would likely be guided by some condition of momentary betterment, quite regardless of whether the direction was right or wrong for permanent betterment. To choose to endure still greater deprivation of food for today in order to cross a barren ridge to reach a valley on the other side where much better grazing would probably be found, would be quite beyond the mental capacity of any elk or other mammalian species below man.

Another form of animal improvidence which brings special disaster upon the creatures themselves when they become competitors of civilized man, is illustrated by stock-killing

[3] *The Big Game of Alaska,* by E. W. Nelson, Bull. of the American Game Association, April, 1921.

dogs and wolves. The waste touches the welfare of man as well as that of the improvident animals, to such an extent as to cause him to wage war of self-defense upon the marauders. This is especially evident in the case of sheep-killing dogs. Those who know most of this matter insist that the only real safety against these dogs is in the prompt killing of them. This fate is pronounced upon the dogs as the result of actions which are "senseless" so far as meeting any real food need of the dogs, such need being otherwise provided for. With the wolves the case is different, their food supply being derived more or less from their killings of stock animals. Nevertheless, the wantonness and wastefulness of their depredations often impel the stockmen and hunters to redoubled efforts against the offenders.

Much the same reasoning holds for such cases as that of the wasteful Adirondack beavers.[4] The destruction of timber by flooding is injurious to man as well as to the beavers. Man, unlike the beaver, has wit enough to see this. And in addition he sees how to remedy the evil, by destroying some of the beavers in order to protect them and himself against their wholesale destructiveness. This beaver case illustrates a very widely operative principle in man's relation with many animals. His preservation of them ("conservation" is the current word) largely for his own benefit, consists in part in destroying *some* of them in order to prevent them from inflicting injury upon *all* of themselves, such injury resulting from their lack of wit in using their food and other natural resources, and from their great and imperfectly regulated capacity for propagation.

Another aspect of food habit among mammals which may subject them to danger is the tendency for the food-taking impulse to be so dominant under some conditions as to inhibit the sense of outside danger. Describing some of the habits of the short-tailed shrew of Ontario, a recent

4 See pp. 157-158.

author says, speaking of the greed of the animals: "Their particular delight was to get into the frying-pan and feed on the cold fat which it contained. So engrossed did they become in their gormandizing on this fat that they paid no heed to my presence and several times I took up the pan and walked about with it while they were thus engaged." [5]

The perils of the feeding time, to which so many animals are subject on account of watchful enemies, are largely provided against by the keenness of sense with which many mammals are equipped. Their mental alertness while eating, and the prevalence among them of such devices as lookout individuals for the feeding groups in the case of gregarious herbivores, are familiar and conclusive proof that adaptiveness with reference to danger of this kind has reached a high development among them. When this adaptiveness comes to involve the adjustment among instincts which are rather sharply antagonistic to one another, as in the case noticed, its defectiveness comes to view. Most of the imperfectly adapted activities we have been looking at, involve antagonisms among instincts of one kind or another. In the relation between the sexes in mammals this fact becomes even more plainly evident.

UNDER-ACTIVITY IN THE PRESENCE OF DANGER

Among mammals activities arising from the impulse to escape from death or injury threatened by some external agent present an important type of maladaptation. The failure in adaptiveness in these activities can be traced to the two sources of underdevelopment of the sense of danger, or insufficiency of fear, and of overdevelopment of this sense, or excess of fear.

[5] "Notes on the Habits of *Blarina brevicauda* in Ontario," by A. Brooker Klugh, *Journ. of Mammalogy*, Feb., 1921, Vol. II, p. 35.

Instances of underdevelopment of the danger sense in the relation of wild animals with men are so plentiful that it is hard to select the few to which space can be given. Perhaps no case of animal destruction could be mentioned that would appeal more strongly to American readers than that of the great bison (*Bison bison* Linn.) which originally inhabited the whole territory of the United States between the Alleghany and Rocky Mountains, and much of Canada. This species exists no longer as a wild animal except in one small herd in the Yellowstone National Park where it has the benefit of rigid government protection. So far as its own self-preservative ability is concerned the Buffalo would surely have gone the way of the Dodo and the Passenger Pigeon before now. Its existence in small numbers today is wholly dependent upon the fact that man has seen fit to stay his own hand before his work of destruction was quite complete.

The belief seems to be widely held that for this great zoölogical tragedy the ruthlessness and greed of man are solely responsible. That upon the animal itself rests any of the responsibility appears to occur to very few persons. Yet Dr. Hornaday, one of the most earnest, active and efficient of those who have espoused the cause of the buffalo, does recognize such responsibility. This zoölogist enumerates five causes that have operated in bringing about the virtual extermination of the buffalo as a wild species. Of these, four are in man himself, but the remaining one is "the phenomenal stupidity of the animals themselves, and their indifference to man." [6]

"Still-hunting" is generally recognized as one of the most disastrous of all the methods of buffalo slaughter. The still-hunt was based on the fact that if the hunter could manage to hide himself completely from sight and smell of

---

[6] *The Extermination of the American Bison*, etc., by William T. Hornaday, 1887, p. 465.

the animals, he could shoot them down one after another without their recognizing danger in the fact that their companions were dropping dead all about them.

In the following paragraph Hornaday gives particulars of this mode of killing: "Having secured a position within from 100 to 250 yards of his game, . . . the hunter secures a comfortable rest for his huge rifle, all the time keeping his own person thoroughly hidden from view, estimates the distance, carefully adjusts his sights, and begins business. If the herd is moving, the animal in the lead is the first one shot. . . . If the herd is at rest, the oldest cow is always supposed to be the leader, and she is the one to kill first. The noise startles the buffaloes, they stare at the little cloud of white smoke and feel inclined to run, but seeing their leader hesitate they wait for her. She, when struck, gives a violent start forward, but soon stops, and the blood begins to run from her nostrils in two bright crimson streams. In a couple of minutes her body sways unsteadily, she staggers, tries hard to keep her feet, but soon gives a lurch sidewise and falls. Some of the other members of the herd come around her and stare and sniff in wide-eyed wonder, and one of the more wary starts to lead the herd away. But before she takes half a dozen steps 'bang!' goes the hidden rifle again, and her leadership is ended forever. Her fall only increases the bewilderment of the survivors over a proceeding which to them is strange and unaccountable, because the danger is not visible. They cluster around the fallen ones, sniff at the warm blood, bawl aloud in wonderment, and do everything but run away." [7]

Concerning the effectiveness of this method, Hornaday says: "The highest number Mr. McNancy ever knew of being killed in one stand was ninety-one head, but Colonel Dodge once counted one hundred and twelve carcasses of buffalo inside of a semicircle of 200 yards radius, all of

[7] P. 469.

which were killed by one man from the same spot, and in less than three-quarters of an hour." This description seems to justify Hornaday when he says: "The buffalo owes his extermination very largely to his own unparalleled stupidity; for nothing else could by any possibility have enabled the still-hunters to accomplish what they did in such an incredibly short time. . . . A single still-hunter, with a long range breech-loader, who knew how to make a 'sneak' and get 'a stand on a bunch,' often succeeded in killing from one to three thousand in one season by his own unaided efforts. Capt. Jack Bridges, of Kansas, who was one of the first to begin the final slaughter of the southern herd, killed by contract, one thousand one hundred and forty-two buffaloes in six weeks." [8]

Without stopping to analyze the mental processes of animals thus permitting their lives to be snuffed out, this much seems obvious: Failure to recognize danger from the several sensory impressions received, sight of the smoke, direction of the sound of the shot, and the behavior of the wounded companions, must be interpreted as indicative of a very low order of intelligence and a very poorly developed sense of fear. The whole story of how stupid fearlessness of these animals contributes to their destruction could hardly be told without telling the whole story of the destruction itself. Another aspect of it is found in the evidence of great destruction coming upon the animals from the same defects, wholly independently of man's depredations. Fearlessness owing to lack of sense wrought great havoc upon the herds in several ways but particularly from their sinking inextricably into quicksand or other soft earth, and from drowning through venturing upon ice not strong enough to hold them.

As an illustration of the first mentioned we take the following: "In this manner, in the summer of 1867, over two

[8] *Ibid.*, p. 465.

thousand buffaloes, out of a herd of about four thousand, lost their lives in the quicksands of the Platte river, near Plum Creek, while attempting to cross." [9] And to the same effect this from the Journal of John McDonnell: "Observing a good many carcasses of Buffalo in the river and along the banks, I was taken up the whole day in counting them, and to my surprise, found I had numbered when we put up at night 7360 drowned and mired along the river and in it." [10] In the same volume we find the following concerning the icy road to buffalo destruction: "Treacherous ice on the rivers took greater toll of Buffalo life than any other natural enemy of the animal. Under date of May 2, 1807, Alexander Henry records: 'The number of Buffalo lying along the beach and on the banks passes all imagination. They form one continuous line and emit a horrible stench. I am informed that every spring it is about the same.' " [11]

It would probably be wrong to suppose that all destruction in these ways was attributable to stupid fearlessness; or rather to suppose that all such destruction might have been avoided had the creatures been more liberally endowed with intelligence and a sense of danger. Even the wisest, most cautious of men may be caught at times by death-dealing instrumentalities such as those here mentioned, but there can be no question that the buffalo lack of "sense," especially sense of danger in many situations, contributed enormously to its death rate. This appears to have been particularly so when the herding and migratory instincts were in full swing. Seton, speaking particularly of the destructiveness due to ice too weak to bear up the load which the great herds often put upon it, writes: "All winter the buffalo herds of the colder range were accustomed fearlessly to cross and recross the ice-bound rivers. Springtime comes

[9] Hornaday, *The Extermination of the American Bison*, p. 420.
[10] "Mammals of North America," in *Nature Lovers' Library*, Vol. IV, p. 43.
[11] P. 43.

with the impulse to wander farther north; the herds are more compacted now; they slowly travel on their route; river after river is crossed at first. But a change sets in; the ice grows rotten; to all appearances it is the same, but it will no longer bear the widely extended herd; the van goes crushing through to death, and thousands more are pushed in by the oncoming herd behind." [12]

On a later page this author touches the subject of the powerful and blind on-pushing of the migratory instinct. "Cold weather and more snow may follow, but the impulse to travel possesses them now. Once it is given command, it changes not in force or direction till the remembered pastures are reached. Rivers may cross their path. These, if frozen, are unnoticed; if open, they are swum; if covered with rotten ice, the ice is broken eventually by the weight of the herd, and many are drowned, but the rest swim through and continue their march." [13]

Perhaps even so scant a review as this of the causes which brought to an end the natural life of this mighty species, is sufficient to convince the reader of the justice of Hornaday's including among these causes "the phenomenal stupidity of the animals themselves, and their indifference to man."

The migratory or travel instinct may go to remarkable extremes in mammals. A case in point is the often-cited one of the occasional mass movements of the Scandinavian Lemming (*Lemmus lemmus*). The typical habitat of this rodent is the high tablelands of the Scandinavian peninsula where it occurs in great abundance. At irregular intervals, once in from five to twenty years, it increases enormously in numbers and, descending to the lower country, overruns even the cultivated lands. The hordes "steadily and slowly advance, always in the same direction and regardless of all

[12] *Life-Histories of Northern Animals*, 1909, Vol. I, p. 271.
[13] P. 274.

obstacles, swimming streams and even lakes of several miles in breadth, and committing considerable devastation on their line of march." In turn "they are pursued and harassed by crowds of beasts and birds of prey, as bears, wolves, foxes, dogs, wild cats, stoats, weasels, eagles, hawks and owls, and never spared by man." The onward march may continue two or three years, till those which survive the depredations of enemies reach the seacoast. But even this does not stop them, for into the water they plunge and swim straight off from shore as far as their strength will carry them. "Those that finally perish in the sea, committing what appears to be a voluntary suicide, are only acting under the same blind impulse which has led them to cross shallower pieces of water with safety." [14] It is said that none of the migrants ever return to the original home.

A much-quoted causal explanation of this remarkable performance is that the westward drive of the animals is inherited from ancestors which used to migrate to the west when, in geological times, the European continent extended much farther to the west and north than it does today. The species seems to have inhabited the British Islands in Pleistocene times. If the creatures have been going through such self-destroying experiences as this every twenty years or oftener since the Pleistocene age and have learned nothing therefrom, the fact is certainly disparaging evidence as to their grade of mental development.

An example of a type of dangerous fearlessness dependent, not upon mental dullness, but upon alert curiosity is furnished by the American or pronghorn antelope (*Antilocapra americana*). Observers of this animal in its wild state refer to its curiosity and the fatal costliness of this to the animals themselves. The combination of this attribute with the keenness of sight and fleetness of foot of the creatures is widely commented on. One of the early records to this

[14] W. H. Flower and R. Lydekker, *Encyclopædia Britannica*.

effect occurs in the *Journal* of the Lewis and Clarke Expedition. In the entry of April 29, 1804, we read concerning the antelope: "These fleet and quicksighted animals are generally the victims of their curiosity. When they first see the hunter, they run with great velocity; if he lies down on the ground and lifts up his arm, his hat, or his foot, they return with a light trot to look at the object, and sometimes go and return two or three times, until they approach within reach of the rifle. So, too, they sometimes leave their flock to go and look at the wolves, which crouch down, and, if the antelope is frightened at first, repeat the same maneuver, and sometimes relieve each other, till they decoy it from the party, when they seize it. But generally the wolves take them as they are crossing the rivers; for, although swift of foot, they are not good swimmers."

Many observers of more recent times give evidence to the peculiar mentality of these animals as to their sense of danger. "It is a queer animal," says Roosevelt, "with its keen senses, but with streaks of utter folly in its character. Time and again I have known bands to rush right by me, when I happened to surprise them feeding near timber or hills, and got between them and the open plains. The animals could have escaped without the least difficulty if they had been willing to go into the broken country, or through even a few rods of trees and brush and yet they preferred to rush madly by me at close range, in order to get out to their favorite haunts." [15]

It seems to be generally agreed that these "streaks of utter folly" in the character of these animals have contributed not a little to the near-extermination which has befallen the species.[16] Nor do such streaks appear to be

---

[15] *The Deer Family*, p. 105.
[16] Several good observers of recent times are certain that not only the pronghorn but also the buffalo and several species of big game animals whose complete extinction seems avertible only by man's effectively pitting his own left hand of preservation against his right

limited to this single American representative of the Antelope family. Observations could be cited tending to show that some at least of the species of African and Asiatic antelopes, which are quite different from the American species suffer from similar maladaptations. When the curiosity of the animals takes the form of gazing at its object, it may exhibit distinct resemblances to hypnosis in humans. Thus narrating how a solitary buck once stood gazing at him till he came well within 100 yards of it, Nelson writes: "It actually closed its eyes and appeared to be dozing, as its head nodded slightly up and down, apparently in complete indifference." [17]

Another form which the fearlessly curious activity of this animal takes is especially well illustrated by Nelson in the same article. This consists in its racing for a considerable distance parallel with, and not far from, its potential enemy. We read: "When traveling on horseback and happening upon antelope in such places the writer often amused himself by spurring his horse to a gallop and continuing his course in a direction which would take him by and away from the animal. . . . This procedure almost invariably brought the expected response, and the animals began racing him until they had gained a slight leadership, when they would dash by in front across the road or trail."

Another example of dangerous fearlessness in a mammalian species is selected because of the absence in crucial circumstances of instinctive fear and of the seeming independence of this absence. By independent absence of fear, I mean the complete absence of fear, in contrast to seeming absence, where fear is present but overcome by some stronger

---

hand of destruction, have gained wisdom, as we may call it, from the deadly follies of their progenitors. It is said that today successful hunting of the few individuals that remain is a very different matter from what it was in the early period when the numbers were almost limitless. Both the evidence for this and the significance of it, if it is really true, will have to be considered later.

[17] E. W. Nelson, *Status of the Pronghorned Antelope, 1922-1924,* U. S. Dept. of Agriculture Bull. No. 1546, Aug., 1925, p. 6.

and partially antagonistic instinct. The case in mind is furnished by the Elephant Seal (*Mirounga angustirostris*). This giant seal was formerly very abundant on the west coast of North America from central California to near the southern extremity of Lower California. It is a valuable oil-producing animal and has been so persistently and ruthlessly hunted that it is now reduced to a small herd which has its headquarters on Guadalupe Island off the coast of Lower California. The evidence of independent absence of fear in these animals comes from the observations of a party of naturalists who visited Guadalupe Island in July, 1921. A herd of more than two hundred was found hauled out on one of the beaches. It was composed almost entirely of full-grown males. This shows that the creatures were not under the domination of either the mating or the parental instincts. Since they were all resting more or less quietly on a barren beach, the nutrimental set of instincts was not in evidence. Nothing was seen by the party either at this point or elsewhere of the great majority of the females or any of the young of the year that must be supposed to be constituents of this herd.

The party's approach to the closely crowded herd was from the sea in a boat. As the main purpose of the visit was to study the animals and get pictures of them, the approach was made unobtrusively, but there was no attempt at concealment. Photographs were taken of them from as many points of view and degrees of nearness as was desired without in the least disturbing them. The men went among the creatures without let or hindrance, slapping them, putting their feet on them, and even, in one case, sitting down on one. This last seems to have been carrying the familiarity a little too far, for the individual sat upon vigorously and menacingly protested. Nor was the herd much perturbed by the shooting, killing, and skinning of two of their members, this having been done to secure museum specimens.

The experience here narrated with this remnant of the elephant seals is confirmed by other visitors to their island home. It is agreed that the life customs of the animals dependent upon their bodily structure and ways of behaving are such as to make their complete extermination at the hands of men easy and certain unless man interposes against himself and stays his own exterminative propensities.[18]

We are obliged to conclude that the nearly complete extinction which has befallen the once widespread, abundant, and valuable species of elephant seals, is due in no small degree to the stupidity of the creatures themselves. The attribution to them of self-preservative foresight enough to make them post sentinels around the sleeping herds [19] must rest on defective observation or interpretation or both. No one else who has observed the animals has reported anything of the sort so far as I can discover.

[18] Is it really true that the animals do nothing toward their own preservation? Have the disastrous experiences they have undergone in their contact with man for three quarters of a century taught them nothing whatever as to how they can thwart this deadly enemy? There is some evidence that the case is not quite so discreditable to their mentality.

It was mentioned in the above narrative that the party had no difficulty in approaching the herd from the sea by boat. A careful observer told me that on several visits to the Guadalupe herd, he had noticed that whereas the animals were almost entirely heedless of men if approached from any direction on land, they exhibit considerable shyness when approached from the water in boats. This he assumes is due to the fact that the usual way of attack upon them by hunters is from this direction and by this means. The same observation and interpretation are expressed by H. N. Moseley concerning the "Sea-elephants" of Kerguelen Land. This author tells us (*Notes by a Naturalist on the "Challenger,"* p. 201) that he went close to a large male and excited him with the hope of seeing him do something with his peculiar proboscis, but that his efforts had had no effect in making the beast "move from his ground or frightening him at all." When, however, the ship's cutter containing several men came toward the beach, the "Elephants became immediately alarmed as if accustomed only to expect danger from boat parties."

[19] See Anson's *Voyage Around the World in 1740,* etc.

OVERACTIVITY IN THE PRESENCE OF DANGER

Manifestation of fear so excessive as to interfere with activities necessary to escape from danger is familiar to all in cases of *panic*. These same elephant seals, whose fears were so slow-stirring, when once aroused suffer equally from the destructive effect of their panic.

This story is told in Captain C. M. Scammon's account of the mode of capturing the animals in the palmy days of the oil industry of which they were the basis, on the coast of the Californias. He writes: [20] "The sailors get between the herd and the water; then, raising all possible noise by shouting, and at the same time flourishing clubs, guns, and lances, the party advance slowly toward the rookery, when the animals will retreat, appearing in a state of great alarm. Occasionally an overgrown male will give battle, or attempt to escape; but a musket-ball through the brain dispatches it; or some one checks its progress by thrusting a lance into the roof of the mouth, which causes it to settle on its haunches, when two men with heavy oaken clubs give the creature repeated blows about the head, until it is stunned or killed. After securing those that are disposed to resistance, the party rush on the main body. The onslaught creates such a panic among these peculiar creatures, that, losing all control of their actions, they climb, roll, and tumble over each other, when prevented from farther retreat by the projecting cliffs." On one occasion when sixty-five seals were taken several of the dead bodies showed no signs of having been clubbed, lanced, or otherwise mutilated. The assumption was that these had been "smothered by numbers of their kind heaped upon them." This is panic pure and simple.

[20] *The Marine Mammals of the North-Western Coast of North America*, p. 118, 1874.

The story recalls the behavior of a terror-stricken human crowd; for example in connection with theater fires. Such panics, whether among seals, buffaloes, men or any other creatures, are incontestable proof of a rather high degree of mentality. Sea anemones and starfishes are never panic stricken in the face of danger. What part "pure" instinct and what part "pure" reason takes in the panics of different species is an extremely interesting and complex problem, but one not to be dealt with here.

Striking examples of the deadly possibilities there are in panic from fear are abundantly supplied by the horse. "A horse will dash himself to death getting out of the way of a swaying shadow or whirling leaf." [21] G. J. Romanes says: "I think I am right in saying that the horse is the only animal which, under the influence of fear, loses the possession of every other sense in one mad and mastering desire to run. . . . The wholly demented animal may run headlong and at terrific speed against a stone wall." [22] Everybody who has had large acquaintance with these animals can recall instances enough in which he has seen this defect of character more or less distinctly manifested. Indelibly stamped upon my own mind are my experiences as a farmer lad with a mare which it fell to my lot to handle almost daily for many years. Her excessive fright at anything and everything unusual made getting on with her trying indeed. This animal would go into spasms of fear at the sight and sound of a railroad train running through the fields many rods from the road on which she was, while her harness mate would scarcely look toward it or prick up ears at its noise.

Panic-stricken horses may also meet their doom through their tendency to return to their places in a burning barn after they have been led away by human rescuers. An

[21] *Wild Beasts,* by J. H. Porter, p. 17.
[22] *Animal Intelligence,* p. 323.

instance of this kind occurred a few years ago in my neighborhood; I am reasonably certain as to the essential correctness of the report, especially as to one horse in particular.
This individual was a high-bred and valuable saddle horse
of whom the owner and the keeper were very fond. Special
effort was consequently made to rescue her. She had been
kept untied in a box stall. The rescuers succeeded in running her out before the fire reached her part of the barn.
But they were unable to prevent her from returning and
she was burned to death in her accustomed place.[28] Romanes' belief that the horse is the only animal in which desire to run results from its losing "possession of every other
sense" under the influence of fear, may be right, though
this is questionable. It is certain that there are animals
not a few in which fear and its allied emotions may upset
their mental equilibrium quite as disastrously, though in
other ways. Almost complete paralysis at the critical moment may be quite as seriously maladaptive as the horse's
blind running away. The horse itself furnishes a striking
example of how, under some circumstances, fear may have
the opposite effect from inducing flight. Inability to make
any effective movements at all sometimes results. Thus
Angelo Mosso tells us [24] that at the sight of a tiger a horse
may tremble to such an extent as to be no longer able to

---

[28] The unquestioned bewilderment or panic-producing influence of
fire on horses raises the interesting question as to how far this same
influence may have been operative with the ancestors of the modern
horse, and also with other animals than the horse. We have convincing
evidence that prairie fires destroyed great numbers of the American
buffalo. There is no evidence that panic and confusion of mind on
the part of the animals played a part in this destruction, neither is there
evidence that the buffalo showed any special wit for escaping from the
great fires that occasionally swept over the western plains. From the
knowledge we have of their mentality we should seriously doubt their
having any ability in this direction. From what we know about the
effects of intense fright in many animals, it seems probable that the
deadly havoc known to have been wrought upon various forest-dwelling
animals by forest fires has been partly due to the panic or other forms
of mental confusion produced in them.

[24] *Fear.*

run. The rabbit is another animal in which this sort of
thing is known to occur. Thus we read: [25] "The terrifying
effect of a stoat on a rabbit is perfectly extraordinary and
unaccountable. I have picked up hunted rabbits so petrified by fear that they have made no attempt to get away."
Lindsay [26] says: "But on the other hand fear, alarm,
terror, horror, in their major degrees at least, frequently
paralyze all power of self-protective action, creating a dangerous immobility of body, with an accompanying fixity of
stare. This condition is often described as a kind of *fascination* of which the main features are the powerlessness of
mind and body, with the gaze helplessly fixed on some
dreaded object—generally some powerful enemy, such as a
serpent. The spell-bound animal is otherwise said to 'lose
its head' or 'wits' in some serious, sudden, unexpected emergency in which presence of mind and readiness of action are
all-important. To terror in the victim is due the power of
the rattlesnake to 'charm' the said victim, to hold it as if
spell-bound, fixed in its position and gaze, insusceptible of
flight or motion. . . . Such is the dread of armed men, or
even of man's firearms, in certain baboons, that the mere
sight of a gun, or of the act of aiming one—though the
weapon be unloaded—begets sometimes paralysis of thought
and action with its consequences."

The reference to the power of the rattlesnake to "charm"
its victims may be looked upon by some critical readers as
weakening this whole idea of mental upset in animals by
fear, since at least one good authority on reptiles brushes
aside as pure myth the reputation which snakes have in this
way. Undoubtedly much that is fictitious and highly fanciful has gathered around this subject. Nevertheless that
many animals are subject to some kind of almost complete,

[25] "The Stoat," by Frances Pitt, *The National Review,* Vol. LXXV,
1920, p. 263.
[26] *Mind in the Lower Animals,* Vol. II, p. 235.

though temporary, overthrow of their ordinary mental processes under the fear of enemies, especially serpents, seems beyond question.

An illuminating general treatment of the snake's power in this way is given by W. H. Hudson in "The Serpent's Tongue." [27] Hudson maintains that whatever be the power of the serpent to "fascinate its prey" (the term *fascinate* he retains out of deference to custom, but he does not like it), its tongue is one element, though only one, in that power. He introduces his argument with the well-known fact that a frog will be thrown into a helplessly paroxysmal state by the approach to it of anything, even a stick, if the movements are "snake-like." Something of this is known by experience to every schoolboy who has had the joy of teasing either frogs or toads.

It is less easy to observe such defective self-control in birds and mammals than in frogs and toads. With reference to this Hudson writes: "We are now in possession of a very large number of well-authenticated cases of undoubted fascination in which the victims are seen to act in a variety of ways, but all alike exhibit very keen distress. The animal that falls under the spell appears to be conscious of his loss of power, as in the case of the frog pursued by the ring-snake. He is thrown into violent convulsions, or trembles, or screams, or struggles to escape, and sometimes rushes in terror away only to return again, perhaps in the end to jump into the serpent's jaws." [28]

These few examples of the mind-dethroning power which fear may exert upon animals constitute the merest glance at a vast and important subject which is now in a fair way to receive the attention from physiologists and psychologists which it deserves.

[27] *The Book of a Naturalist*, p. 134.
[28] P. 149.

DUE TO RAGE

The "senselessness" of activities inspired by excessive rage is even more familiar than the menace of panic. It is interesting that colloquially we use the same word "mad" for the human being who is insane and for the one who is overwrought with anger. Whatever we may think about the successful adaptiveness of human actions inspired by anger, there can be no doubt that among animals such actions can be highly destructive of the welfare of the enraged individual himself. Only one illustration will be given.

The instance concerns the California Elk (*Cervus nannodes*) and is reported by C. Hart Merriam.[29] An effort was made several years ago to remove a herd of wild elk from one locality to another. The reason for this effort lay in the fact that, owing to protection from hunters, the elk had so increased in numbers as to become more destructive to crops than the ranch owners chiefly affected were willing to stand for. The plan was to transfer them to a particular place in the Sequoia National Park, where they would be under government protection, but could find no farm crops to ravage.

The story is a thrilling one, but only a small portion of it is relevant to the present discussion. That portion concerns the performances of a large bull which was captured, tied, placed in a corral with a few of his companions, from whence he was forced into a heavily crated flat car, transported by railroad to the station nearest the Park (35 miles away), and thence taken to the destination in a heavy wagon drawn by a six-mule team. As to fear, Merriam says: "From first to last he had shown no fear and had fought every living

[29] "A California Elk Drive," *The Scientific Monthly*, 1921, Vol. XIII, pp. 465-475.

thing within his reach." It would be necessary to go back to the beginning of the efforts made by the vaqueros to "round up" the animals while they were yet free in the open, in order to prove the absence of fear, and this Merriam's reference does not do. "When in the corral, no sooner were the ropes cut than the bull charged with such earnestness—in spite of the fact that he was unable to stand still on his feet—that the men were obliged to escape over the fence with the utmost promptness." [30] The creature's inability to "stand still on his feet" was due to the hard treatment he had received while being brought "hog-tied" to the corral. Special notice should be taken of the "charging" despite the animal's weakened condition.

In illustration of the statement that the bull "fought every living thing within his reach," the author says: "Discovering the spike-horn bull, whose fetters had been loosed simultaneously with his own, leaning against the corral fence near by, he instantly lowered his head and charged, driving his strongly curved brow-tines into the side of the younger animal, which soon began to bleed at the mouth and the nose, and later died." [31] This incident belongs by right, it will be noticed, to the class of maladaptive actions designated as "injury to kind."

Now for the way it fared with the creature himself from his own activities. "While in transit he had fought and butted and kicked until he had splintered several of the side boards of the car. A half barrel of water that had been put into the car stood in the doorway. By means of a pole it was upset and pushed to one side. No sooner had this been done than the elk, seeing it in a new position, charged and dealt it a resounding blow that sent it rolling over the floor. This evidently pleased him, for arching his neck and leaping

[30] P. 468.
[31] *Ibid.*

forward he struck it again and again, making a great noise, and following it around the car, butting it furiously as if it were the cause of all his trouble." [32] At another juncture he became specially enraged, "butting furiously in one spot until the boards began to give way." Finally, having been so closely confined in the crate that he could not butt, he began to kick, first with one foot and then with the other. "The force and rapidity of the blows were astonishing; it seemed incredible that his strength could hold out." This was kept up almost incessantly for the entire way and so effectively that it was found necessary to stop several times on the wagon part of the journey and repair the damage the bull was doing to his prison bars. The place in the park where the animals were to be released was finally reached, only the old bull and one calf having survived the ordeal to this point. By this time the old fellow had finished his fight: finished it because he had finished himself. The hind wheels of the wagon were sunken into the earth so as to bring the floor of the crate down to the level of the ground, the crate was opened and the old bull, now utterly subdued, was given his freedom once more. "With his head bent to one side and back curved, with one ear up and the other down, and with a dejected helpless expression on his face, he hobbled wearily away, barely able to step without falling. Slowly he made his way to the river, waded in, drank, crossed to the far side, staggered laboriously up the low bank, and lay down. The next day he was found in the same spot—dead."

The sequel of the story is quickly told. Profiting by this first experience at attempting to move the elk, those having the matter in charge soon found a somewhat different method of capturing and transporting them so that later a goodly herd was established in their new home, where they them-

[32] P. 473.

selves are safer from harm than in the old home, and are unable to harm anybody else. Had that bull elk possessed sufficient control over his own emotions to prevent him from killing himself to no purpose he might have been one of the fortunate colonizers in the new and better country of which his kindred soon became the possessors.

CHAPTER 14

MALADAPTIVE ACTIVITY IN MONKEYS AND APES

THE whole monkey tribe are so much more like men in all structural attributes than are any other animals that the question of how far they are manlike in their mental lives is always recognized as one of peculiar interest.

How far does the round of activities of an individual monkey or great ape during its whole lifetime run parallel with that of a human being? That the life activities of individual monkeys or apes in their natural surroundings can ever be studied as fully as the life activities of individual humans already have been studied, is probably beyond the range of possibility. The habitats and modes of life of nearly all the primates, especially of the great apes, place special obstacles in the way of such studies. Opportunities of study on the activities of these creatures are at present restricted almost entirely to individuals held captive. There is unavoidable and incalculable difference between the best man-made surroundings of captive animals and the natural surroundings of them. Try to imagine what scientific knowledge of the mental life of man would be had it been built up exclusively on studies of individuals, mostly adults, and with little reference to sex, held in close confinement and carefully observed only in connection with set experiments! All the historic background, paleontological and archæological, and most of the comparative background, would be excluded from such studies. The radical shift of viewpoint now taking place in this matter has given us broadened and liberalized studies on anthropoids which have greatly increased our knowledge of their mentality. These studies, though necessarily restricted to captive animals, give them the largest possible measure of chance to act in their own way, these activities being watched continuously and with the greatest possible care, and interfered with for experimental control only with a view to getting information about the activities beyond that which the mere watching is able to elicit.

EXTENT OF ACTIVITY RESULTING IN EXCESSIVENESS: IN FOOD-TAKING

Despite the dearth of knowledge of the life activities of monkeys and apes in nature and of the necessary defectiveness of knowledge gained from the study of captives, we have unmistakable evidence concerning some of the characteristics of their activities. One of these characteristics is the generally active life they lead, the activity implicating especially the arms, hands, and fingers. Any reader who has access to a zoölogical park may test the truth of this statement for himself. Let him visit in turn one animal house after another with the question in mind, "In which are there the most things going on?" After testing the matter repeatedly and for different hours of the day he will hardly be in doubt as to what answer must be forthcoming. The bird house and the monkey house are preëminently the ones in which activity is greatest both as to quantity and variety. Great in quantity and variety as are the activities in the bird house and significant as these are from the general zoölogical standpoint, they are obviously out of line with human activities.

Comparing what goes on in the monkey house with what happens in any of the places in which terrestrial mammals are confined, two contrasts are striking: The greater total amount of activity, individual for individual, in the monkey cages as contrasted with that in the cages of any other mammals; and the greater variety of activities, especially those involving arms and hands, in monkeydom. Any one who has had opportunity to observe members of the monkey tribe has noticed the busy fingers presented by the creatures. The amount of poking and pulling at wisps of straw, or fur, tails and legs of companions; of picking up and eyeing or smelling or biting sticks, straws or other small objects from floor or shelf or food receptacle; and of fingering irregularities on surfaces of cage sides, is remarkable when viewed in comparison with what can be seen among animals of any other group. How far are these activities subject to the defects as well as to the merits which we have seen among animals generally? That the tendency to excessiveness of action is manifest in many kinds of monkeys and apes there appears no room for doubt. A little experimental observation of my own on a half-grown female mandrill in the zoölogical park at Cincinnati is illustrative of one phase of excessive activity. The rule against promiscuous feeding of the animals by visitors not being here enforced, by mid-afternoon on days when visitors were numerous the monkeys would be so "fed up" on peanuts and other things that their need for food would be wholly gone, and their desire for it and tendency to respond positively toward it almost gone. When a peanut was offered to the individual in question she would slowly and as it seemed absent-mindedly reach through the bars for it, take it in her hand and put it into her mouth, crack it and perhaps eat a portion of the meat, casting aside the rest, or perhaps not eat any of it. Such was her procedure when no resistance whatever was put in the way of her taking the nut offered to her. But when I held the nut where she could not quite reach it or so tightly that considerable effort on her part was necessary to get it away from me, the whole proceeding took on quite a different character. Anger was manifest in all her mien and effort, eyes flashing, teeth showing, and all arm and body movements greatly quickened and intensified. The most significant thing done under the altered state was to the nut, once it was secured. With steel-trap-like speed it was carried to the mouth, with equal force and speed smashed to bits by a single snap of the jaws and teeth, and the whole mass of fragments, meat and shell commingled, thrown away with a speed and force in keeping with all the rest of the performance. Not the slightest move to eat the nut was made in any of the many instances in which I balked her taking it.

Two points here illustrate the principle of excessive activity. First there was the obvious fact of going through the whole food-taking operation when there was no need or real desire for food, just because there was food in sight and in reach. The other point was the apparent necessity for the performance to run its course once it was started. This was especially conspicuous when the action-cycle was done in anger from the creature's being somewhat thwarted in the initial stage of the cycle. Clearly the wrath was excited by my interfering with the monkey's getting the nut into her hand. Why then should not the performance have stopped with the accomplishment of that? The nut grasped by the hand must be carried to the mouth and put into it, the mouth must be opened and closed upon the nut for smashing it, and the rubbish must be spat out, because it had to be got rid of in some other way than that for which nut-cracking was originally and legitimately performed. Here was a series of acts unmistakably performed originally and basically in behalf of the creature's food necessities, but in a particular situation gone through repeatedly not only without answering in the least to the original purpose, but being actually contrary to that purpose. Instances like this furnish conclusive evidence against the generalization reached by some psychologists that the food-taking response occurs only when the stimulus thereto is accompanied by hunger.

I had no chance to test monkeys of other species in this collection to determine how interference with taking proffered nuts would affect them. However, so extensively were visitors amusing themselves by offering nuts to sated monkeys that there was ample opportunity to observe individuals of several other species going languidly through the operation of reaching for nuts, taking them, and then making little or no use of them.

IN MATERNAL SOLICITUDE

One other illustration of excessiveness of activity in the monkey tribe is in connection with the mother's solicitude for and care of her young. The particular phase of this to be noticed is what mothers may do with the corpses of their dead babies. The most fully described instance known to us is furnished by Yerkes.[1]

In this case the bereaved mother, a Rhesus monkey, clung to the remains of her child for five weeks, at the end of which time all that was left of the thing was a small mass of skin with the hair still on, the whole having no resemblance whatever to the original. The pertinacity and frame of mind of the mother during the period were shown by the fact that she carried the grewsome object with her most of the time and never went far from it or relinquished her watch over it when she laid it down. So vehement was her protection of it that "it was utterly impossible to take it from her except by force." Evidence is now available indicating that this sort of thing is rather general in the monkey-ape tribe. Several similar instances have occurred among the monkeys of the National Zoölogical Park at Washington, the Javan macaques, which breed readily in captivity, being specially mentioned in this connection. The

[1] "Maternal Instinct in a Monkey," by R. M. Yerkes, *Journal of Animal Behavior,* 1915, Vol. V, p. 403.

case of a female chimpanzee which gave birth to an infant that died in a few days [2] shows something of the same kind at this level of the primate scale.

MISDIRECTION OF ACTIVITIES RESULTING IN SELF-INJURY

Are monkey activities liable to go in the wrong direction as well as *too far* in the right direction, after the fashion we have seen the activities of other animal groups doing? Less evidence is available in this than in the other case. The most striking example we have come upon is the persistence of Köhler's chimpanzees in eating their own excrement. The author relates [3] that his vigilance against this habit, even his sharply administered punishment for it, was hardly successful in breaking it up. It may be that the idea of activity "going in the wrong direction" is too simple a statement for such a performance as this. Quite conceivably elements in the food and feeding or in the strange surrounding objects incidental to captivity play a part. But even so, that an activity (that of food-taking) essential to life is here persistently performed in a way not contributory to the original purpose of it, is certain. The ability of even the highest apes to discriminate between objects that are good for them and those that are useless or harmful is not high. Several other illustrations are given by Köhler for chimpanzees, only one more of which will be mentioned. Köhler found that his animals seemed to be quite as much afraid of roughly made images of different kinds of animals as of the animals themselves. "On one occasion, in the morning, I placed one of the stuffed donkeys in the ape's stockade and laid the banana bunch under him.—The apes crept together into a corner and only occasionally did one of

---

[2] "Notes on the Birth of a Chimpanzee," by W. Reid Blair, *Bull. of Zoölogical Society of London*, September, 1920, Vol. XXIII, p. 105.
[3] *The Mentality of Apes*, p. 309.

them venture a terrified glance at the dreadful being." [4]   In this particular matter it would seem, as Köhler points out, that chimpanzees are not much if at all superior mentally to dogs, horses, or various other brute creatures.

A. R. Wallace [5] gives two significant instances of mis-directed activity.   One of these is the behavior of the little ape toward a false mother which he made for the creature out of a bearskin.   That the infant went through the regular performances of snuggling up, nosing around for a nipple, and filling its mouth with hair and wool as an incidence to the sucking response are what would be expected on the basis of what is well known about infant mammals gener-ally, human infants not excepted.   Apparently the creature was ready to repeat the blunder as many times as it had a chance; for, says Wallace, after trying several times to give his charge satisfaction by this substitute for a mother, he had to give up the plan to save the infant from choking itself to death with wool.   How much farther would a young orang go than would a young human in this particular wrong course of action?   How much better would the human do both as to benefiting by experience and as to gaining ability with age so to benefit?

The other case given by Wallace in connection with the same specimen concerns the animal's liability to go wrong from not distinguishing parts of its own body from foreign bodies.   "It would hang for some time by two hands only," we are told, "and then suddenly leaving go with one would cross it to the opposite shoulder to catch hold of its own hair, and thinking no doubt that that would support it much better than the stick, would leave hold with the other hand and come tumbling down on the floor."   A performance like this, involving the problem of an animal's getting objective

----

[4] P. 334.
[5] "Some Account of an Infant Orang-Utan," *Annals and Magazine of Natural History*, 1856, Vol. XVII, p. 386.

knowledge of its own body, suggests that the striking way various monkeys will grasp and other wise manipulate their own body members, notably their feet, with their hands, is contributory to gaining such knowledge.

As a last example of monkey mistakes, a simple but ludicrous one recently noticed by myself in the zoölogical park at Washington may be mentioned. Following a sharp rain which left puddles of water in the out-of-door cage of a group of Bengal macaques, a female entertained herself for some time by sitting beside one of them, stroking the water with her hand quickly enough to make bubbles on the surface, then trying to pick the bubbles up in her hand and examine them; they had burst before she could get her hand into the range of her eyes. I could see no indication that she was surprised at her failure or that she really learned anything about the nature of bubbles by what she had done. My impression was that if she happened to start to amuse herself in this way again, her curiosity about bubbles would be as devoid of results for her knowledge of them the second time as it was the first time.

MISDIRECTION OF ACTIVITIES RESULTING IN INJURY TO KIND

Köhler's investigations on chimpanzees furnish the most important testimony, the most striking instance falling under the head of injury to kind. The case concerns the violent treatment accorded a small, weak, innocent individual of the species by other stronger, more robust members. The story is a special version of the old one, familiar from its exemplification among human as well as brute animals, of wholly unwarrantable fear of strangers. It concerns the addition to the group of a new member in the person of a "poor, weak creature, who at no time showed the slightest wish for a fight," and who exhibited nothing whatever to arouse the anger of the others "except that she was a stranger." The unsavory tale is best told in the investigator's own language: "She at once aroused the greatest interest on the part of the older animals, who tried their best with sticks and stalks put through the bars to indicate at least a not too friendly connexion with her. . . . When the newcomer, after some weeks, was allowed into the larger animals' ground in the presence of the older animals, they stood for a second in stony silence. But hardly had they followed her few uncertain steps with staring eyes, when Rana, a foolish but otherwise harmless animal, uttered a cry of indignant fury, which was at once taken up by all the others in frenzied excitement. The next moment the newcomer had disappeared under a raging crowd of assailants who dug their teeth into her skin and who were only kept off by our most determined interference while we remained. Even after several days the eldest and most dangerous of the creatures tried over and over again to steal up to the stranger while we were present, and ill-treated her cruelly when we did not notice in time." [6]

The similarity of a performance like this to what takes place among many animals and even among humans, especially of low culture, can hardly fail to strike one. Köhler has given considerable attention to the question of how apes are likely to fare at the hands of their own kind. He points out that so closely and constantly are the activities and attitudes of chimpanzees dependent on the relations of the individuals with one another that "it is hardly an exaggeration to say that a chimpanzee kept in solitude is not a real chimpanzee at all." "That certain special characteristic qualities of this species of animal," we are told, "only appear when they are in a group," is simply because the behavior of his comrades constitutes for each separate animal the incentive which will bring about a variety of behavior, and observation of many peculiarities of the chimpanzee

[6] *The Mentality of Apes*, pp. 300-301.

will only be clearly intelligible when the behavior and counter-behavior of the individuals and the group are considered as a whole. In this, the part played by one animal may have definite significance for the observer, which it would not have if a human being were the partner. But, apart from this, the group connection of chimpanzees is a very real force, of sometimes astonishing degree.[7]

What does this group-forming tendency mean for the welfare of the individuals? Does it mean that the individuals are greatly concerned for one another's good? Because the members of a group are profoundly influenced by one another, does this imply a high regard for one another? Köhler's studies point to the conclusion that a high degree of group-forming influence among animals is not incompatible with a high degree of egoism and a low degree of altruism. For chimpanzees at least, it is first and foremost a question of *actual sensory presence*. The familiar adage, "Out of sight out of mind," applies with tragic (as humane humans would say) literalness among these creatures. "Unquestionably, their interest today in some fruit which they saw buried yesterday is greater than that taken in one member of the group who was there yesterday and who today does not come out of his room any more."[8] Köhler tells us: "More than once I established that the temporary (or permanent) disappearance of a sick (or dying) animal has little effect on the rest, so long as he is taken out of sight and does not show his distress in loud groans of pain, as chimpanzees so rarely do. This corresponds to the lack of concern of the group in the healthy ape that is segregated, as long as he does not whine too miserably; and if a sick animal dies in its own room, it is no use expecting any sign of sadness or of missing him, as there is no direct incitement to

[7] P. 293.
[8] P. 295.

mourning or excitement, and every animal in the group at the moment feels the group around him."

In appraising the results of the activities of individual chimpanzees in relation to the welfare of other chimpanzees, we have seen how unjustifiably individuals may suffer at the hands of other individuals, and how indifferent individuals may be to the welfare of others. We have also seen a measure of group-forming tendencies among individuals which in general would be supposed to have large possibilities of mutual advantage. Is there evidence of such advantage? Köhler shows that individuals having ample food which they like will definitely share it with other individuals which have no food and beg for some. He shows also that well and strong individuals will definitely assist ailing and weak ones. All this is contingent on the immediate presence of helper and helped.

Although the evidence thus presented of "injury to kind" as a maladaptive activity among anthropoids is admittedly very limited in quantity, its character is such that we seem justified in presuming further information will prove consequences of this nature to be nearly, though not altogether, as characteristic of these as of other higher mammalian species. Knowledge of the gorilla concerning this matter is awaited with special interest, for there are signs in what we already know of this species that the conclusion just stated may have to be modified.

SELF-INJURY FROM NORMAL TYPES OF ACTION

The question of whether monkeys and apes are liable to self-injury from their own normal types of action may next receive attention. In discussing the intense stimulatory effect on individual chimpanzees of one another's sensible presence Köhler writes: "Bigger animals, who do not show signs of actual fear, cry and scream and rage against the walls of their stockade, and, if they see anything like a way back, they will risk their very lives to get back to the group." [9] This refers to the experimental isolation of an individual from the group for the purpose of testing its efforts to reëstablish connection with its comrades, the isolated animal being in plain sight of the others. Unfortunately the author does not tell us very definitely about the risks the animals would take in such situations, this apparently not having been a phase of the phenomenon that interested him much. He mentions that an isolated animal will refuse food altogether for a while at the beginning of the isolation, so preoccupied is it with its desire and efforts to regain its lost associations. Information is very desirable as to just how far under such conditions interference with the nutritional activities would go and with what consequences.

The main source of risk to which Köhler seems to refer is the emotional and activational violence incited by isolation from companions, or by the dissatisfaction due to the stimulus of the visible but untouchable presence of companions. It is a question whether the incitements due to isolation may be injurious to the incited individuals themselves. Köhler speaks repeatedly of glottal cramps and spasms in his animals resulting from emotional excitement though we are not informed as to exactly how this may affect the creature's physical welfare. Might an animal choke to death in this way?

Something of the astonishingly violent performances chimpanzees may go through at times are referred to by various writers and may be observed by any frequenter of primate collections which contain one or more of these animals. One I saw by a huge male having a large cage all to himself in the zoölogical park at Sydney, Australia, made a great impression on my mind. It seemed to me there was

[9] P. 293.

plenty of chance for such a performance to have harmful consequences not only to any thing or any body who might be in the creature's immediate vicinity, but even to itself.

Köhler has considerable to say about the "spells of 'pure excitement' " apparently rather characteristic of this species, without being very explicit as to the effects on the excited individuals themselves. In one passage we read: "The Chimpanzee's register of emotional expression is so much greater than that of average human beings, because his whole body is agitated and not merely his facial muscles. He jumps up and down both in joyful anticipation and in impatient annoyance and anger; and in extreme despair— which develops under very slight provocation—flings himself on his back and rolls wildly to and fro." [10] Again, "They sometimes tear along (as if possessed) by the walls of their sleeping-dens, and kick them till the excitement subsides." [11] Whether these "explosive" performances are connected with sexual impulses or are of some other source Köhler is uncertain, though he favors a different explanation, for some of them at least. But he frankly admits them to be very much of a psychological puzzle.

We have here seen obvious possibilities of self-injurious activity. We should like more knowledge about the animals' risking their lives in their own performances. We would be glad to know what might happen to individuals from failure to take food, from throwing themselves to the ground, from kicking the walls of the dens, during easily induced "tantrums," "fits," and the like, whether of joy, fear or rage.

[10] P. 318.   [11] P. 326.

CHAPTER 15

MALADAPTIVE ACTIVITY AMONG LOW-CULTURED HUMAN BEINGS

RARELY have I told people of the futility or worse of what I have found ants, woodpeckers, beavers, and other animals doing, without getting the reply: "Why, human beings do just that way!" The reply is made as a justification of the creatures, on the ground that their doings are inevitable and irremediable if thus manlike, since human misdoings of this general kind are but part and parcel of man's fate, and so have to be made the best of, even though they are often useless or foolish and not infrequently lead to disaster. The reply gives me the impression that the persons making it get considerable half-conscious satisfaction from what seems to them evidence that the fatefulness of human folly is sharable with animal life generally. My stock rejoinder is substantially the following: "I am well aware that men act in much the same way. But exactly what most distinguishes human animals from even the best-favored brute animals is the ability men have, if they will only use it, to avoid acting in this way."

The internal evidence of the whole animal world is unmistakably to the effect that the gradation there presented from minute, simple, and almost infinitely numerous creatures, up to large and complex creatures sharply limited in numbers, is a manifestation of nature's way of enabling living beings to act ever more effectively for their own welfare. Acting more effectively to this end consists largely in avoiding wrong tendencies of exactly the kind we have been examining in this section on maladaptation. We need now to examine human activities to see how much truth there is in the statement that "people act just that way."

Perhaps the most convenient basis for such an examination is the two main ways we have seen animal activities to be maladaptive, namely through excessiveness and through misdirection. The nutritional needs and activities of humans will first receive attention.

The saying is well known that the lives of savages are either "a feast or a famine"; along with this goes another that most savages "live from hand to mouth." These sayings are likely to be understood to refer more to the environmental conditions under which savages live than to activities of the people themselves. As a matter of fact it is usually more a question of what people do to and with their surroundings than what those surroundings are. The environment of the people now living in Winnebago County, Wisconsin, is the same as that of the Winnebago Indians who lived there in pre-Columbian times, except for what the white people themselves have done to make it different. If the original Winnebagos lived more "from hand to mouth" or more on the basis of "a feast or a famine" than do the present-day pale-face Winnebagoites, the sole difference is in the different activities of the two groups and kinds of people concerned.

FOOD-TAKING AMONG SAVAGES

Evidence on this point is furnished by the way savages conduct themselves with reference to their food-taking, using food in the broadest sense. Evidence of this sort is available from many peoples. As one example take the Fijians. The islands are prolific in many kinds of raw food materials, and the people know "just where to go for what they need. There is little time or labor wasted in the search for food." [1] What prevents Fijian well-being from reaching its acme so far as sustentation is concerned? Feasting, this writer says,

[1] W. Deane, *Fijian Society*, p. 207.

is "inextricably interwoven with his [the Fijian] etiquette and social organization." Numerous inevitable occurrences of the community, births, marriages, deaths, are taken as opportunities for feasts. "Unfortunately, at times, the preparation for them becomes a burden on the people, especially when the spirit of emulation enters into them. During such a season of rejoicing, lasting only a week, hundreds of pounds have been wasted in riotous living, leaving the clansmen a load of debt which takes months to remove. The local Chinese storekeeper, who has an eye to business always, has often, to my knowledge, established a lien on the following year's crop, by advancing provisions to the enthusiastic customers who crowd his small shop." [2]

One of the wasteful practices connected with the feasts is in the etiquette of giving to fêted visitors. Deane says: "On my first visit to a certain town in Kandávu, I was presented with twenty-two fowls for my Sunday dinner. Those I could not eat, my boys carried away. . . . The visitor is often thus considerably hampered, and good food has not seldom been thrown away when the outskirts of the settlement have been reached." [3]

Nor can the question of the effect of the gorging on the health and general character of the gorgers themselves be ignored. Were it possible to apply the rigorous methods of scientific dietetics to answering the question it seems probable that bad nutritional customs would be found to be potent causes of the cultural backwardness of savages. The customs of savages in this and other matters are not so-and-so because the people are savages, but the people are savages because their customs are so-and-so.

Consider a performance like the following occurring among a group of Shoshone Indians and reported in the journal of the Lewis and Clark expedition. The Indians came upon one of the hunters of the expedition just as he had killed and

[2] P. 208.   [3] P. 210.

dressed a deer. "They dismounted in confusion and ran tumbling over each other like famished dogs. Each tore away whatever part he could, and, in short, no part on which we are accustomed to look with disgust escaped them. One of them who had seized about nine feet of the entrails, was chewing at one end, while with his hand he was . . . discharging the contents at the other." The narrator philosophizes: "It was, indeed, impossible to see these wretches ravenously feeding on the filth of the animals, and the blood streaming from their mouths, without deploring how nearly the condition of savages approaches that of the brute creation." Performances more or less like this seem to be rather characteristic of savages under the stress of hunger; numerous queries arise concerning them. Is the feeling of disgust with which we are accustomed to regard certain parts of a dead animal and to which the writer refers, really a mark of superiority of civilized as compared with primitive peoples or the reverse? Does our fastidiousness as to what parts of a carcass are and what are not edible rest on anything else than a sentiment that counts for nothing when our food necessities come down to a physiological basis pure and simple? This question is particularly pertinent now that we have scientific grounds for believing that some civilized peoples have gone too far in excluding the viscera and blood of animals from their meat diets.[4] But aside from the nicer questions of nutrition thus raised, it is fair to ask whether, if these savages were able to escape death or serious exhaustion by eating such food as came in their way, it would not be to the advantage of cultivated people to retain at least the ability to be equally unsqueamish in case of food crises, for crises are sure to occur now and then among the civilized as well as among the uncivilized?

Beyond a doubt civilized men taken as a class far excel

[4] E. V. McCollum, *The Newer Knowledge of Nutrition*, p. 393 especially.

their savage kindred taken as a class, in ability to forestall situations in which they must eat whatever comes in their way or suffer the consequences. When a single instance like this is viewed as one element in the general conduct of the people concerned, there can be no doubt that maladaptive activity is involved. The trouble is partly covered by the charge that savages are given to living "from hand to mouth."

Then there was in this instance the "confusion and tumbling over one another," by the Indians, "like famished dogs." According to the ordinary standards of conduct among civilized people, such behavior would be unseemly. On its face it has the marks of both excessiveness and ill-direction of action. Whether it would come under the head of maladaptiveness in the strict sense in which we are using the term would require closer examination to decide than we are at present ready to make.

SAVAGE FESTIVALS

The most immediately and obviously self-injurious practices of savages occur when eating and drinking are combined with festival performances involving sexual and religious activities. It is this sort of combination that makes conduct orgiastic in the strictest and fullest sense. A great majority of all people, no matter what their cultural level, manage to provide themselves with something liquid or solid to "get drunk on." This exceedingly wide appetite for intoxicants, with the endless forms of expression in word and phrase and song connected with it, is only one manifestation of the tendency of all animal activity to excessiveness. Substances having intoxicating effects have played such an outstanding rôle in human life that the terms "stimulus" and "stimulant" often have no other meaning than this, even though all organic activity whatever is dependent on stimulus in one way or another and on stimulants of one kind or another. In a strict psychobiological sense the smell of savory, wholesome food is just as truly a stimulant to a hungry boy or girl as a drink of whisky is to a red Indian or a white American. Drunkenness from strong coffee, alcohol, morphine, or any other intoxicant is only one expression of the general tendency to excess in seeking stimulation.

The records of primitive people afford numberless examples, concerning eating, drinking, dancing, religious rites of some sort, and sexual indulgence. The Guiana Indians furnish examples of this sort.[5] Eating appears to play a relatively minor part in the festivals of these people, but the minor rôle of eating is amply offset by the major rôle of drinking. "Every Indian party, from a private 'social' to a public ceremonial, is practically a drinking bout, interspersed with more or less music, and its necessary corollary, a dance." One of the favored beverages is "black drink" made from the cassava by a fermentation process. An Indian "is never satisfied," Roth writes, with drinking this stuff. He quotes another observer: "I saw men emptying at one draught calabashes that certainly contained two or three quarts, hurry off to a tree where they will squeeze in their stomachs so as to vomit their contents, and directly afterwards accept from the hand of the woman waiting for them the newly filled calabash, the contents of which they will again guzzle at one pull."[6]

Roth's general account of a "festival" is brief and pointed. "In general terms . . . without drink there is never any dancing, which will continue so long as the former lasts, and thus a dance may often continue a couple of nights, including the intervening day. The entertainment . . . generally

[5] W. E. Roth, *An Introductory Study of the Arts, Crafts, and Customs of the Guiana Indians*, Thirty-Eighth Annual Report of the American Bureau of Ethnology, 1916-1917, Government Printing Office, 1924, pp. 27-745.
[6] P. 470.

begins and ends with a deafening yell; in the former case
it may be done to exorcise the evil spirit and so prevent him
spoiling the merrymaking." From this account this yell
seems to be the only touch of the religious factor, the people
apparently being much more taken up with other elements.
The story continues: "The whole affair, furthermore, usually
ends up with a sexual orgy, or, as Barrère naïvely puts it,
'to wind up, they all intermix.' Sad to relate, however, this
intermixing really occurred, as it still does, throughout the
whole performance, so soon as the effects of the liquor are
felt."

The only other example of the fully rounded type of orgy
to which we will give space is from New Guinea. The ceremony described was connected with the presentation of
skulls to the visitor. "Though our hosts began the party in
our honor, now all are joining in for the sheer pleasure it
gives them, with no thought of us. . . . As the excitement
heightens the affair becomes a wild orgy in which all par-
ticipate. . . . Long into the night the mad festival continues
until one by one the participants drop out from utter exhaustion. . . . Unaccustomed to violent exercise such as
that of the night before, some of them wearily drag themselves to the shade of the groves with the air of persons trying to show signs of animation merely to save their friends
the trouble of a funeral. The women seem to be utterly
fagged out, and their feet drag as they prepare food for
the men." [7]

The drink called wady used by these people is made from
cocoanut, certain roots and leaves, mixed with saliva and
sugar enough to make it ferment. To its efficacy the author
testifies as follows: "After a wady party of this kind the
men do not fully recover for days, for the stuff is almost
paralyzing in its effect." [8]

[7] W. F. Alder, *The Isle of Vanishing Men*, p. 140 et seq.
[8] P. 147.

It would be quite unfair to give the impression that all primitive peoples are orgiastic to the extent that these two groups are. With some peoples, many of the tribes of North American Indians for example, one of the chief orgiastic elements, the sexual, does not appear in some of the most important performances. The significance of this may be that the possibilities of harm from this source are recognized and guarded against by the people themselves. Just how far the rigid exclusion of women from many of the ceremonies of North American Indians and of savages of other parts of the world is on account of this would be an interesting thing to know. Drunkenness is not universal in the festivities and ceremonies of savages. There appears not to have been much of this originally among the North American aboriginals. Their bad reputation in this regard does not come from practices in their original state but from their slight ability to withstand the white man's influence as a guzzler himself and a trafficker in grog. Nor is there lacking evidence of moderation in drink among primitive peoples of other parts of the world, as for instance, with some of the Dyacks of Borneo, according to Lumholtz.

It must be recognized that while a given group of people may exercise a large measure of control over some of their activities their excesses in other activities may be great. As experienced and friendly a student of Indians as Moorehead can say that although he has seen thirty or forty Indian dances, he has "never seen a really immoral dance." [9] But at the same time, the author gives the following concerning the Ghost Dance by Sioux on Pine Ridge, South Dakota: "During the height of excitement, those worshipers most deeply affected cut small particles of flesh from their arms, and thrust these, also, between the rushes of the holy tree. Henry Hunter (the Weasel 'Itonkasan') informed me that after the dance had been running some days, the rushes

[9] W. K. Moorehead, *The North American Indian*, p. 223.

covering the base of the tree were literally besmeared with human blood." [10]

Moorehead continues: "One by one the dancers fall out of the ranks. Some staggering like drunken men, others wildly rushing here and there almost bereft of reason. Many fall upon the earth to writhe about as if possessed of demons, while blinded women throw their clothes over their heads and run through brush or against trees." This sort of thing may not be properly called immoral. It may properly be labeled fanatical or epileptiform, or with some other supposedly explanatory adjective. All this does not alter the fact that it is a form of human activity, and that judged by any criterion that can reasonably be applied it is largely excessive, useless, and injurious. In short, it is maladaptive.

Much of what peoples of low culture do in the use of their food and other external necessities of life and of their own bodies is excessive and improvident. What a well-known anthropologist has said of a group of Indian tribes on whose ways of life he made extensive studies would be applicable equally well to all primitive people (to say nothing about many people not generally supposed to be primitive). We read: "The most striking and far-reaching characteristic of all the Indians visited, even from the medical standpoint, is their improvidence and seemingly a decided inability to take advantage of some of the lessons of experience. This keeps them disarmed against all accidents and diseases." [11] The author says that abundant harvests are pretty sure to be accompanied by frequent feasts in which much of the food supply is consumed. As a consequence before the next harvest comes, suffering from shortage of food or from the use of poor food is often severe.

[10] P. 112.
[11] Ales Hrdlicka, *Physiological and Medical Observations among the Indians of Southwestern United States and Northern Mexico*, Bull. 8, Bureau of American Ethnology, 1907, p. 31.

Such instances of improvidence should be regarded in the light of what we learned about the intense preoccupation of Köhler's chimpanzees, and also of other creatures, not so much with their eating (though this may be great) as with the presence of bodies useful for food and for other purposes. The conclusion seems unescapable from such facts as we have presented under various heads, that the activities of animals toward external bodies are by no means limited to the utilization of the bodies in satisfying necessities, but are largely determined by the sensory presence of the bodies. Beavers do not limit their tree-felling operations strictly to their food and other needs, but extend them to many other things as dead trees, fence posts or railroad ties, quite useless to the creatures, doing this because gnawable bodies are near by. Monkeys do not reach for peanuts when they are hungry merely but because nuts are extended toward them. Chimpanzees are greatly influenced by their companions not so much by their affection for and real need of one another, as by the mere sensory presence of one another. On the same principle people make feasts at which they are wont to eat and drink more than they need, and frequently to destroy or otherwise dispose of valuable food substances largely because such bodies are within sense-experienceable distance. People who act thus on a large scale and habitually are characterized, in the language of advanced industrial and social life, as improvident, and are familiarly known as backward or primitive, or savage, or barbarous peoples. That much of what is comprehended under these common terms falls within the scope of maladaptive activities of the variety we have called excessive, we may assume to have been established by the foregoing presentation.

MISDIRECTED ACTIVITIES

Misdirected activities, the other form of maladaptive activities recognized by us, play a specially large part in the lives of savages.

By misdirected activities are meant chiefly those which in their original form may have been thoroughly contributory to welfare, but as now practiced are not thus contributory, if indeed they are not the very opposite. The activities under this head are not necessarily wholly distinct from those under the head of excessiveness previously discussed. When food-storing animals like ants, wasps, woodpeckers, wood-rats, gather and stow away objects they cannot possibly use as food or for any other purpose, the uselessness of the performance may be partly attributable to the tendency to over-activity and partly to the wrong direction of the activity.

Some of the most striking examples of misdirected activi-ties among savages are connected with the food problem. In this case the maladaptiveness is involved in food-getting more than in food-using. A few minutes' reflection on the difficulties which have to be overcome in fishing and hunt-ing, in searching for wild plants suitable for food or other human needs, in searching for water under conditions of scarcity, and in bringing to maturity agricultural crops, makes patent the chances of doing the wrong things.

The passage quoted from Hrdlicka relative to the improvidence of Indians speaks of their "seemingly decided inability to take advantage of some of the lessons of experience." While there can be no doubt of limited ability in this regard of Indians and of other primitive people as compared with cultivated people, neither can there be any doubt of their great ability as compared with the most advanced brute animals. Even the most primitive peoples have a very considerable number of discoveries and inventions to their credit. We have but to contrast the stick-splicing and using performance of chimpanzees for getting food (probably the climax of invention among brute animals) with the innumerable implements and devices for the same purpose found among savages, to be reminded of the immense advantage even the lowest savages have over the highest brutes in this matter. Beyond question a great majority of the inventions made by savages represent benefiting by experience sometime by somebody. Undoubtedly chance and accident played considerable parts in some of them. But were these the main factors there would seem to be no reason why the higher anthropoids should not do about as well as the lowest men. The many weapons, tools, utensils, fabrics, dwellings, processes, produced by primitive people the world over are the results of efforts to find better, more effective ways of doing things, better ways of living. They are expressions of improved goals reached by improved activities.

MALADAPTIVE ACTIVITIES DIRECTED TOWARD SECURING FOOD

Though savages have won great advantages for themselves over their brute ancestors, so enormous and subtle are the difficulties in the way of securing creature necessities and comforts that the problem is only approximately solved. This is true even for peoples the most advanced in culture. We should be prepared to find our low-cultured kindred carrying on some of their most seriously misdirected activities, and making some of their worst mistakes, in their efforts to get possession of the indispensable sustentatives of life. We will look first at some of the absurd practices (as present-day knowledge enables us to see them) of savages, designed to make their hunting and other necessity-securing activities more successful.

"With the object of winning success in the chase, the hunter will submit to various purposely inflicted inconveniences and sufferings (i.e., he voluntarily undergoes certain ordeals)." [12] Several of these are described by the author. One is the use of the "nose-string." This, briefly stated, consists of a string passed through the nostril into the back of the mouth via the posterior nares and pulled forward until this end projects from the mouth, the other end still projecting from the nose. In order to make this performance more efficacious the string (called "bina" by the people) is treated in various ways. One of these we will learn from Roth's own words. "Robert, at the Makusi village of Maripai, uses a certain bright green arboreal frog, known as kopé, for a bina. When fresh, he rubs the slimy material from off the animal's back onto his chest, which he has especially incised for the purpose. When smoke-dried, he soaks it in water contained in a little gourbi (calabash cup), and after moistening the bina string with the same water, pulls it through his nose." [13]

Performances quite as little relevant as this for securing food or other necessities, for protection against disease and the violent forces of earth and atmosphere and for assuring success in childbirth, are so common among savages that it is hardly possible to read a chapter on the customs of any group of them without coming upon some such instances. For example, during pregnancy of a Kasungan wife (of Borneo), both she and her husband must desist from splitting firewood in order to protect the anticipated child from being harelipped or double-thumbed.

The most astonishing and, as judged by civilized standards, the most reprehensible of savage activities for bringing good luck is head-hunting, widely practiced among peoples of the Pacific Islands. Probably this custom is not regarded as a good-luck bringer for getting food and other physical necessaries among all the peoples who practice it, for it seems to be considered useful in a great variety of ways.

[12] Roth, *An Introductory Study of the Arts, Crafts, and Customs of the Guiana Indians*, p. 178.
[13] P. 114.

But that it is supposed to help in this way among some people appears certain. Thus from Lumholtz we have concerning the Penihings of Borneo: "If no heads are brought in there will be much illness, poor harvest, little fruit, fish will not come up the river as far as our Kampong, and the dogs will not care to pursue pigs." [14] Similar conduct, whether occurring among savages or among their superiors, has been much discussed under such labels as fetishism, animism, superstition and magic.

Foolish, ineffectual, and often harmful as this class of maladaptive activities is its ability to work positive injury is small as compared with that of activities aimed at getting possession of things needed or desired which are already possessed or claimed by other people. Since the food and other necessities of one person or group of persons are basically the same as those of another person or group, if one of these is already in rightful possession of the wherewithal to meet these necessities while the other is not, for the second to take the articles from the first to the latter's injury is clearly not contributory to the equal welfare of both parties, and hence is maladaptive in the strict sense in which we use the term. So here we are in the presence of the great problem of rightful possession, which includes the endlessly discussed question of property rights. Thieving, robbing, marauding and wars of conquest are the outstanding forms of maladaptive possession among savages and half-civilized peoples. So well do we know the general meaning of these terms that specific instances can give place to certain elements in the activities which will help to an understanding of the point of view of savages relative to this matter.

The most fundamental element is the absolute necessity of all human beings, like all other living beings, for food. We shall later have much to say under the captions life-or-

[14] *Through Central Borneo,* Vol. II, p. 258.

death needs, life-or-death utilities, and life-or-death activities. Since these categories are universal for the living world they are not less real, ever-present, and potent with the most primitive of primitive men than with the most culturally advanced men. There is probably no better starting-point for gaining the deepest possible insight into the nature of human conduct than is afforded by the difference between the attitude of brute and human creatures toward objects of life-or-death utility. This difference lies in the entirely unmindful, unhesitating, way any brute creature whatever (so far as we yet know) will take and consume whatever it needs wherever it finds it, regardless of the welfare of any other creature. Probably no brute animal ever hesitated a moment to eat food that might be before it if it felt the least impulse to do so, though the doing it would be a fatal deprivation of companions, even mates and offsprings. This is not to say that brute animals never share with others food which they themselves might eat to their advantage. That parent birds will hunt food and feed it to their young so assiduously as to reduce their own bodies almost to the condition of skin and bones is too familiar a fact to leave room for any such idea as that individual animals never share food with other individuals. The crux of the matter is the question of one's sharing food with another when that one has the chance, the impulse, and the ability to eat it himself. Almost certainly the feeding activities of parent birds and of some carnivorous mammals are as purely a physiological adaptation as is the mammary glandular mode of nourishing the young. The vigorous defensive actions shown by a dog or cat at the least sign of being interfered with while eating are an index to the part theft and robbery (as viewed from the human standpoint) have played in the brute part of the animal world. The tendency among humans to take what they need or want wherever they find it, regardless of any injury to others that may result from doing so; and the counter tendency to protect and defend possessions, is almost as manifest among low-cultured peoples as among brute animals. The chief difference is in the greater resourcefulness shown by humans in both the aggressive and the protective devices and operations. An especially important aspect of the matter is the methods of protecting possessions devised by various peoples. Robbery was taken for granted to such an extent among some of the Maoris that in case a community's agricultural efforts resulted in a good crop, the fact was concealed as carefully as possible from neighboring communities to safeguard the garnered stores from attack and plunder. The harvesting was done at night, as quickly as possible, and the food stored in inconspicuous places. Furthermore, producers might try to deceive their neighbors as to the extent of their possessions by misleading statements.[15]

All this clearly implies a measure of foresight as to life-or-death necessities; of knowledge as to ways-and-means of providing these; and of the character of neighbors, entirely without counterpart among brute animals. But perhaps the most significant way of protecting possessions among savages from the thieving and other appropriating tendencies of neighbors is the placing of prohibitory commands or declarations upon the articles which the would-be appropriators do not dare to trespass upon. This sort of thing, now known as taboo in the language which civilized people use for describing the customs of other people regarded by them as uncivilized, appears to be in principle a universal means employed by human beings for controlling the actions of other human beings. We shall give this matter more attention in a companion volume, in which many subjects merely touched on in this volume will be treated more fully and critically.

[15] *Old New Zealand*, by a Pakea Maori.

As to humans of this cultural grade at least, the remark "men act as animals do," obviously contains very much truth. In every one of the life-or-death activities; in securing and using food; in reproducing kind; in escaping death or serious injury from disease and the violent forces of inanimate nature; and in guarding against would-be human despoilers, all men are on common ground with all animals. For uncultured men, at least, all are on common ground with animals in the tendency to excessiveness of action and in the likelihood of misdirectedness of action. The whole difference, great as it is, between the activities of men of low culture and of animals seems to resolve itself into the greater skill with which men work toward their welfare; the greater ability of men in restraining themselves from going too far in the right direction; and their greater ability to go in the right direction; or, what is nearly the same thing, their greater ability to avoid going in the wrong direction.

While primitive people undoubtedly "act as animals do" even to all the forms of maladaptive activity, they have gone far ahead of the very foremost of their brute kindred in correcting this maladaptiveness. The facts which constitute the most convincing evidence of the superiority of the conduct of human animals as compared with that of brute animals are those which show that many primitive peoples are in some measure aware of the deleteriousness of their tendency to excessiveness in activities, and of the likelihood of their doing the wrong things, this awareness being accompanied by corrective measures in both directions. An illustration of measures to guard against excessiveness of action is furnished by the Fijians, as given by Thomas Williams.[16]

"Few things go more against a native's nature than to be

16 *Fiji and the Fijians*, Vol. I, p. 122.

betrayed into a manifestation of anger. On this restraint and concealment of passion he greatly prides himself, and forms his judgment of strangers by their self-control in this particular. When the hidden flame bursts forth, the transition is sudden from mirth to demon-like anger. Sometimes they are surprised into wrath, or vexed beyond endurance; when they throw off all restraint and give themselves up to passion. The rage of a civilized man, in comparison with what then follows, is like the tossings of a restless babe. A savage fully developed—physically and morally—is exhibited. The forehead is suddenly filled with wrinkles; the large nostrils distend and smoke; the staring eyeballs grow red, and gleam with terrible flashings; the mouth is stretched into a murderous and disdainful grin; the whole body quivers with excitement; every muscle is strained, and the clenched fist seems eager to bathe itself in the blood of him who has roused this demon of fury. When anger is kept continually under curb, it frequently results in sullenness. Pride and anger combined often lead to self-destruction."

Additional evidence of the store placed by savages on self-control is the belief held by some good observers that at least a portion of the self-imposed torture which occurs widely among primitive peoples is to the end of proving their ability to endure pain without performing the bodily acts characteristically connected with it. Not all such torture is for this purpose. Some of it has a self-purifying motive; and this suggests at once a sense of sin, of wrong, as by a "penitent" or one who sorrows for bad deeds he has committed. In some cases, self-torture is without doubt propitiatory, that is, it aims to gain the favor and help, or escape the vengeance of the gods. This clearly involves a consciousness of needs and also of difficulties and dangers in the way of getting them. If anything at all of this kind occurs among even the highest brute animals it is only in the merest traces.

CHAPTER 16

MALADAPTIVE ACTIVITY AMONG HIGH-CULTURED HUMAN BEINGS

OUR VERDICT ON OUR OWN ACTIVITIES; COMMON KNOWLEDGE OF MALADAPTATION

THE remark, "human beings do just that way," made in response to my stories about the maladaptive performances of animals, always has reference to humans like our very selves, not to savages. Another familiar expression is that so-and-so is given to "running a good thing into the ground." Defectiveness of character is so clearly implied here that the statement is not likely to be so worded as to implicate the speaker himself, as do the "human beings" or "men" of the other phrase. For some purposes and as to certain activities all high-cultured people see the necessity for self-restraint at least as clearly and prize it at least as highly as the native Fijians, regardless of what theoretical views they may hold concerning the good there may be in "self-expression" and the bad that may result from "repression."

A more personal form of the idea of running a good thing into the ground is seen in the statement that so-and-so "never knows when to stop." This form of the expression shows that the more personal the recognition of the tendency to excessiveness becomes, the greater the inclination to attribute it to some other person than one's self. One rarely admits that he himself "never knows when to stop." Thus it is indirectly recognized that there is virtue in "knowing when to stop."

How much truth is there in these folk expressions implying popular recognition of maladaptive activity? Is common knowledge confirmed and extended by scientific knowledge in this as in so many other cases? Our quest will be for evidences of excessiveness or the reverse, and misdirectedness of action under these four heads: Lost motion and waste of energy and time; waste of useful material; injury to kind; self-injury.

One of the commonest of human "frailties" is undue haste, especially in situations that are a bit out of the ordinary. "Don't be in a hurry; take your time," is a familiar admonition of the street-car conductor, gatekeeper, or other person whose function it is to control crowds of people passing through narrow or otherwise difficult places. The panics of audiences in burning buildings or other imminent dangers resolve to a large extent into action by those individuals involved who are too hurried and precipitate. Speeding is the particular bane of automobile driving. Eating too fast as well as too much is undoubtedly a prolific contributor to indigestion. That children and young persons are given to playing too much and too hard is now recognized as one of the very real and very difficult problems with which training of the young must cope.

To no small extent skill in doing anything consists in doing it just fast enough but not too fast. Who that has ever watched a game of base-ball by the most expert of players has not found himself on nettles at the seeming slowness with which a fielder throws to a baseman to head off a runner? Most hand-fumbling turns out to be more acts than are necessary to accomplish the ends sought. A certain amount of unavailing action may be a useful preparatory step for the real act; this is a very different thing from unmitigated fumbling. The good base-ball pitcher or golf player goes through his getting-ready movements quite as deliberately as he performs the culminating act. On the contrary, many of the preliminary hand-and-arm motions of the half-skilled automobile driver or typist are entirely useless. Any one who will watch his own movements for a single day of his ordinary life will hardly fail to catch himself fumbling once at least. All this and much more of similar import in our everyday speech and action is expressive of our verdict upon ourselves as resembling the rest of animal creation in the matter of maladaptivity of our actions.

Waste of useful materials. Is there real similarity between "waste" in the rather technical sense in which we are using it, and "waste" as economists and industrialists use it? The similarities between some of the work of beavers and some of the work of men is widely known. But always, so far as I have noticed, the similarities recognized relate to constructive activities of the two kinds of organisms. Are there similarities between their destructive activities? Since both are builders and hence users of raw materials, they must both be destroyers to some extent. When a tree is cut down by a man's ax or a beaver's chisel-teeth, that tree is destroyed. As a tree it no longer exists; and whether it is built into a beaver's hut, into a man's palace, or rots where it fell, makes not the slightest difference so far as its treehood is concerned. If both beaver and man perform their acts of destruction to the end of promoting their own well-being, and if they actually make the trees contribute to that end, in neither case is the destroyed tree wasted. If either beaver or man fails to make the destroyed tree contribute to beaver or human well-being, the tree is wasted.

I do not believe any one who has had opportunity to study on the ground the operations of a live lumber camp, and also opportunity to study on the ground the operations of a live beaver colony, can have failed to recognize resemblance between the destructive work in the two cases no less striking than that of the constructive work: tell-tale stumps, more or less fresh, all about; prostrate trees here and there pointing in various directions, and in various stages of being worked up; litter of chips and other fragments of wood in abundance; roadways worn on the ground here and there where the workers have traveled and hauled their loads. The differences between the two cases is more quantitative than anything else. The results at the human camp are usually on a much larger scale than are those at the beaver colony; and the skill and effectiveness of the activities, both destructive and constructive, are much greater in the former than in the latter.

As to usefulness and wastefulness of the operations in the two cases; that a large measure of useful results are attained in both is beyond question. These useful results are accompanied by a large measure of wasteful results so far as beavers are concerned. How about waste in the case of human lumbering? Not merely the destructiveness but the wasteful destructiveness of the lumbering activities are now recognized to be enormous, "appalling" in the view of some of the students of the subject, when the well-being of the country, in the present and for the future, are taken into the reckoning. The conclusion to which we seem driven by comparing beaver activities and human activities in the one industry of lumbering, is that both groups of operations, as actually carried on contain certain elements of disastrous wastefulness for the organisms themselves when their well-being is considered relative to all the members of the organic groups involved, existing at the present time and to exist in the future.

Judging from statements made by competent students, much the same wastefulness is going on in oil and other industries engaged in the utilization of mineral resources; in the use of agricultural soils; in the use of food resources, and in various other domains. The pronouncement of one recent writer [1] may be overdone. We read: "Half and more of the yearly output of natural resources heedlessly scattered and destroyed . . . a billion slaves of energy turning useless

[1] Stuart Chase, *The Tragedy of Waste.*

wheels, dragging unneeded loads. Motion, speed, momentum unbounded—to an end never clearly defined, to a goal unknown and unseen." Even if this is no more than half true, taking it with much evidence to the same general effect we seem justified in concluding that waste among high-cultured humans is an almost tragic reality and that it is essentially the same psychobiologically as waste in the animal world generally.

Injury to kind. No one would contend that human culture has ever reached a level at which those who are considered as living at that level never injure any other in any way. May the various forms of injury which high-cultured humans receive at one another's hands and the ways these come about be described and interpreted as we have the activities of the brute animal world and the low-cultured part of the human world? Most of the injuries to life and limb which cultured peoples suffer in travel, in industrial employment, in homicide, in personal fights, and in war, are the results of human activities. A man who is knocked down by a fist blow from a fellow man or the kick of a mule is hurt by the activity of an organic being just as truly in the one case as in the other. There seems no room for questioning the legitimacy of bringing injury-dealing human conduct into the same class with injury-dealing brute animal conduct, regarding both as maladaptation and resolvable into excessiveness or misdirectedness of action.

Murder is the climax of destructive injury inflicted by civilized man on his fellow man: if a person kills another by deliberate intention, he achieves the end he sought, his act appears to be a success, and hence should pass as adaptive rather than maladaptive. How is it, then, that such an act is held everywhere among high-cultured peoples as a major crime? We have here a more sharply defined conflict between welfare of the individual (as he supposes) and welfare of kind, of community, than we have found else-

where. What is a crime but an act the consequences of
which, however much the one performing it may consider it
to have contributed to his personal good, are considered by
the community at large contrary to its good? The evidence
of extremely slight consciousness of such opposition among
brute animals and scant perception of it among low-cultured
peoples is one of the striking results of our comparative
study of injury to kind. Recall the utter indifference of
some animals toward their disabled companions, and the
actual hostility toward such in other instances. The vigorous defense of the very young by the mothers among birds
and mammals generally, and the apparent dawn of real
fellow-feeling among chimpanzees, mark the extent of this
recognition of welfare of kind in the brute creation. But
the readiness with which mothers become cannibalistic to
their own young even among high-grade mammals; and the
out-of-sight-out-of-mind sort of regard of chimpanzees for
one another, indicate how weak and fitful is the perception
of community well-being as contrasted with that of individual
well-being among any of the brutes. As to primitive mankind, the low value placed on human life, shown by the
commonness of such practices as head-hunting among some
tribes, of murder, and of human sacrifice among many
others of relatively advanced culture, should impress us with
the slow and faltering way this latent attribute of living
nature has come to actuality.

The history of criminal law might well be taken as a
marker of the cultural advance of mankind from its lowest
to its highest level. Such law seems to show that human
individuals recognize the lives of other individuals as having
worth and right in and for themselves, just as their own
have. The history of law against theft and other violations
of property rights and against all other ways in which the
acts of individuals injure other individuals reveals upon
analysis conformity to the principles of maladaptive activity

recognized in our studies. He who takes what, according to generally accepted rules, belongs to another, performs an act which from his own point of view contributes to his welfare. Yet by his disregard of the welfare of the one from whom he stole, he aligns against him, so far as this act is concerned, the community at large on the ground that any other member of it may suffer like injury from the same source. While from the thief's own standpoint his act is successful, is adaptive, from the broader standpoint it is not successful, since it not only loses the advantage temporarily gained, but lands the actor in prison. Being both a failure as to the actor himself, and an injury to another person, it answers fully to our criterion of maladaptivity, falling under the head of misdirected activity.

Self-injury. As under "injury to kind" homicide stood out sharply as the climax of harm one person can do to another, so in this discussion of injury to self suicide holds first place. The statements by suicides explaining that their acts were done because the actors were "tired of life" make it necessary to recognize these as successful acts so far as the immediate purpose was concerned. The terms "success" and "failure" are often used with just these applications in cases of attempted suicide. The suicidal act may result in death outright, in which case it is a complete success; or it may accomplish only a serious injury from which the would-be self-destroyer finally recovers. In this case the act was only partially successful. Finally, the act may produce only the slightest injury or none at all; in which case the act was a total failure. All this reasoning carries on its face ample evidence of the pitiful inadequacy of such meanings of success and failure when it comes to high-level human affairs.

The suicide's announcement of weariness of life as the motive of his act says that his life is not, so far as he himself is concerned, worth carrying through to its natural end.

It is a failure. The successful act of self-destruction is, as a matter of fact, the culmination of a series of life activities which in the judgment of the destroyer himself contain more of failure than success. Suicide may be looked upon as a self-acknowledgment of self-maladaptation.[2]

Dueling. Dueling is a form of human activity which is designedly injury-inflicting and is peculiar to high-cultured peoples. It might seem that treatment of this topic would fall more properly under the head of injury to kind. If two men fight a duel and one kills the other, the dead man has received a fatal injury at the hands of a fellow man, and that, it might seem, is all there is to it. Apparently such is the legal view sometimes taken of the matter, for we learn that in England as the law has looked upon the killing of man in a duel, the deed "differs nothing from ordinary murder."

This is a very inadequate view. Essential to the technical idea of a duel is a definite agreement of the antagonists not only to fight each other, but as to place where, time when, kind of weapons, and mode of procedure. It is a well-thought-out plan by which each agrees to try to injure the other even to the death. Each agrees to take the chance of being himself the victim, with considerable chance that neither will be seriously hurt, or that both will be. Dueling is a form of human activity which in its results is something of a combination of murder and suicide. There is present in it an important element that is not present in either of the other forms of activity, the element of regulation by collective agreement. In neither murder nor suicide are there fixed "rules of the game." Dueling proper is always conducted in accordance with definite and elaborate rules and in the presence of other persons whose function it is

[2] This analysis of suicidal conduct has reference to normal-minded persons only. Maniacal self-destruction involves factors not involved in such cases as those here contemplated.

to see that the rules are lived up to. Dueling may perhaps better be compared to a combination of capital punishment with such self-destruction as that practiced by the Japanese under the name *hari-kiri*.

If one is himself killed while deliberately taking his chance of killing another, his act is surely a failure. His primary goal was not the injury of his antagonist but the attainment of something (his "honor" or some object, perhaps a woman) supposedly attainable only by this means. Since he attained neither his primary nor his secondary goal but suffered grievously himself, his failure was double. The maladaptivity of his performance is increased as compared with self-injury-producing activities among brute animals. Brutes probably never deliberately expose themselves to self-destruction.

What we have learned about the tendency to excessiveness in the instinctive and emotional forms of activity prepares us to learn without surprise what the history of dueling actually shows as to the extremes to which the custom has sometimes gone. Thus a French writer is cited as authority for the statement that during the eight years, 1601 to 1609, two thousand men of noble birth fell in duels in France. The duelists, we are told, "fought by night and day, by moonlight and torchlight, in the public streets and squares. A hasty word, a misconceived gesture . . . such were the commonest pretexts for a duel. . . . Often, like gladiators or prize-fighters, they fought for the pure love of fighting.[3] The victor in an English duel during the reign of Queen Anne is quoted: "I come to relate my sorrow, a sorrow too great for human life to support. Know that this morning I have killed in a duel the man whom of all men living I love best."

Though dueling exhibits maladaptation which is in a sense greater than any shown by brutes or low-

[3] Francis Storr, *Encyclopædia Britannica*.

cultured humans, when regarded from the standpoint of community welfare it is seen to contain elements of better adaptation. As pointed out long ago by Francis Bacon, it is a "sort of wild justice." It is a check on the impulse felt by one person to inflict injury or death on another in retaliation for real or imagined injury. Such an impulse is quite customary among children and low-cultured adults. The young Fijian killed by his father-in-law for the affront of having accidentally broken off a cooked lizard's tail which he was serving as the older man's meal would at least have had a chance of a fair fight for his life under a dueling system. The elaborate systems of etiquette and other forms of regulation of social, political, and industrial intercourse among the members of a community that have grown up at almost all cultural levels, observance of which must be secured at whatever cost of fine or bodily punishment, is a sufficient reminder of the stake which the community at large has in regulating, if not wholly preventing, the slaughter of its members on purely personal grounds. Assuming that George Canning and Lord Castlereagh, Alexander Hamilton and Aaron Burr, really were valuable men to their respective countries, it would surely be wise public policy to try to prevent them from killing each other in personal quarrel. Assuming that the two thousand French noblemen duelists killed in eight years really were noble (on the whole a community appraisal), it is natural and reasonable that the community should take measures to prevent such destruction. Governments and enlightened social conscience have made strenuous efforts to suppress dueling despite the modicum of justification and usefulness it undoubtedly has. Regarding human conduct as presenting different degrees of effectiveness in the effort to attain welfare, the prevention of dueling could be accomplished only by recognizing both its advantages and disadvantages. It would have to be retained until a less injurious and more effective way could be found of accomplishing the desirable ends aimed at by the custom.

War. Certain resemblances between dueling and war as conceived by civilized nations are obvious. In both there is the setting up and striving after a goal which neither of the parties is willing to grant the other; in both this encounter is conducted professedly and in some measure according to certain rules previously agreed on by the larger community; and in both there is the avowed effort of each side to injure the other side at the same time that each takes the chance of injury to itself.

The chief difference between the two is that, whereas the injury to the community caused by dueling is in the destruction of human lives alone, in war the injury is from the destruction of objects and materials of many kinds essential to the general welfare. The magnitude and complexity of the operations in such a war as that which civilized mankind has lately passed through tend to obscure the basic principles of human conduct involved.

If doubt be expressed as to the justification of considering war as "self-injury" we think the doubt is fully met by referring to the considerations in favor of ranging dueling under this head; by calling attention to the fact that the subject could not have been adequately treated under the previous head of "injury to kind"; and to the overwhelming evidence furnished by the history of all wars that victors as well as vanquished are sufferers, frequently to such an extent that there is doubt as to which suffered most.

Fighting is a type of animal activity in which the emotional phase of psychic life gains undisputed ascendancy over the rational phase. It matters not whether the particular performance is a cock-fight, a dog-fight, a clench-and-bite encounter between two men, a formal, well-seconded duel, or a military battle on land or sea. The ear-marks of the type, tendency to excessiveness and to misdirectedness, with the resulting waste and destruction, are everywhere unmistakable. So recent are our experiences of the World War that no one can have forgotten that the most distinctive characteristic of "war psychology" was the extreme sensitiveness of almost everybody in almost every relation whether for good or bad, and the exaggerated way in which almost everything, public or private, good or bad, was done and overdone.

As for misdirected action, the liability to mistakes stands out boldly and tragically in the history of wars. Think, for instance, of Napoleon's Russian campaign; of the British Gallipoli débâcle; of the German U-boat effort in the late war.

The devastated areas of the main European battle fronts, the western and eastern, supposedly the climax of wastage of the war, the reader may have had no opportunity to observe. Even so, impressive object lessons as to the waste of useful material may have been received elsewhere. Perhaps he has sailed down the James River of Virginia and seen the five hundred ships built and owned by the United States Government rotting and rusting there without ever having been used to transport a pound of cargo or a single passenger. Any one who has seen such unused products of human activity as these ships and such unused products of animal activity as the trees felled by beavers [4] can hardly avoid saying, "Yes, men act just that way."

The similarity of war to dueling extends to the problem of ridding the world as far as may be of this form of internecine conflict. We found on analysis of the effort against dueling that the community at large made the effort to secure its own good by finding a less destructive way of attaining the worthy ends at which the custom aimed. It was an effort to make a form of human conduct that was highly maladaptive into a form that is highly adaptive.

[4] Described on p. 153 et seq.

Modern war is the climax of maladaptive human conduct. The proposals for an international court and the "outlawing of war" resemble closely the efforts to suppress, to outlaw, dueling. The effort to do away with war merely because many of its consequences are terrible will probably never succeed. It does not accord with the basic principles of psychobiological activity. Brave and rational men do not give up long-established ways of seeking their ends primarily because these ways may bring immediate injury and pain and suffering upon them, but because they discover less destructive, more effective ways of attaining the ends than those originally used. Only by the most searching study of the way human welfare is involved in the causes of war and also the most searching study of peaceful means by which such welfare may be attained will high-cultured mankind succeed in freeing itself from war.

MALADAPTIVE ACTIVITY AS CORRECTED BY SCIENCE

Our discussion of maladaptive activity among high-cultured peoples has taken no account of the fact that whereas human conduct among such peoples is always assumed to be consciously aimed at the attainment of welfare, in the majority of instances there is uncertainty both as to what welfare is and to what course of action will attain it.

Cultured man has, by the very fact of being cultured, many more things to do than his brute or even savage human ancestors have, and this gives him just so many more ways for overdoing, and so many more chances of doing the wrong things. For the nutritional group of activities, one of the marks of high culture is increased dependence of the individuals on knowledge, common and technical, to protect them from increased danger due to increased complexity of food materials and general nutritional conditions, such knowledge being made essential by the absence of improvement in the inherent defectiveness of the instinctive basis of the nutritional activity.

Proof of the untrustworthiness of appetite, taste, "instinct," comes from the scientific study of nutrition. Depending on taste alone, anybody is liable to eat foods which, though ample as to quantity, are so deficient in some ingredients essential to complete nutrition that illness and death may result. Beri-beri, a disease common among those Orientals a large element of whose diet is rice, is a case in point. Polishing the rice to suit the taste of consumers deprives it of essential nutrient constituents. Something comparable to this occurs among all sorts of peoples. The robbing of wheat flour of some of its most important food elements by milling is a notable instance of the same sort of thing. The "new knowledge of nutrition" consists largely in discovering how far we civilized people are led by our tastes and appetites, worked upon by custom and advertising, into eating foods seriously deficient or positively injurious as to certain of their elements.

The human, like any other mammalian infant, would starve to death sucking a nipple that would not yield a drop of milk or anything else, so far as the sucking response itself is concerned. There is now abundant evidence that bottle-fed babies are liable to serious malnutrition, even to starvation, from lack of some essential ingredient of the food given. Every element of the nutritional activity, taking the nipple, sucking, swallowing, goes on quite normally. A sufficient quantity of what seems to be the proper food is taken. Yet the performance fails partly or wholly. Much more is involved in this maladaptive activity than would be involved in the case in which the child suffers from sucking a nipple that would yield nothing. In the defective food case there would be implicated not only the infant's defectiveness in taking defective food, but the parents or nurse's or doctor's or manufacturer's or somebody else's defectiveness in preparing or administering the food. So far as the food-taking instinct itself is concerned, the individual parent, nurse, or doctor (whoever is responsible for the defective feeding) is no better off than the infant; the only effective way of forestalling failure is through experience accumulated by each individual during his own life and by that of the lives of many other individuals.

As an instance of the general liability to misdirection of activity among civilized people, let the reader reflect on his ability to find his way in a complicated locality that is entirely new to him. To be rather exasperatingly concrete, let him examine himself as to his ability to go into the New York subway at Times Square for the first time, and catch the right train to take him to the Brooklyn Polytechnic Institute. If he has an hereditary tendency, an original endowment toward the Brooklyn goal, he need not, of course, be troubled by the maze of lettered signs; green or red lines painted on the walls to be followed for reaching particular trains for particular places; big black arrows everywhere, but each pointing the way to some special place; and so on. In fact it will be best for him to just shut his eyes and follow his inner leadings, so confusing, so bewildering are all these aids to the unfortunate travelers who have to depend (or suppose they have to) on what they and others have learned from experience of some sort.

The safety devices and measures connected with railroad trains, steamships, and automobiles; with hotels, school buildings, theaters and dwellings; with water works, electric systems, factories, are so many efforts to forestall liabilities to injury which civilized man has brought upon himself by the very activities which make him civilized, by making physical improvements and thereby multiplying dangers to be guarded against. The most highly cultured adult person among the most high-cultured people is not a whit better off so far as concerns the ability of his instinctive activities to reach the goals requisite to his welfare, than is any savage or new-born child. Such activities are always liable to go wrong and result in injury. Safety and effectiveness of action at all levels of human culture are dependent almost entirely on knowledge, to which objective experience by somebody, somewhere, at some time, is essential.

Many natural phenomena are altogether too subtle, too obscure, for ordinary experience to recognize, either as to their natures or as to their possibilities for human good. Bacteria are too minute in size, too elusive and pervasive in their modes of life, for common knowledge to encompass as to their beneficent or malevolent rôles in human life. The innate curiosity and love of truths concerning nature which so sharply differentiate the human from all other organic species contribute enormously to the guidance of human actions toward the attainment of the fullest measure of welfare. Research, preëminently in science, is the culmination of all forms of activity directed to the securing of new knowledge and making it available for human welfare, in fields where sources of positive good and of danger are obscure.

Human society in all grades and patterns is a necessary counterpart of human individuals. Whatever is done in such a group in terms of government, education, art, science, and religion, has as motive the guidance of the activities of individuals in the interest of welfare more effectively than the impulses to act would themselves guide it. Whatever else high human culture may be, it must contain high ability and high practice in individual self-guidance and social guidance of the instinctive and emotional types of action for the purpose of individual and collective well-being.

MALADAPTIVE REPRODUCTIVE AND SEXUAL ACTIVITY IN THE
HUMAN SPECIES

Were any one compelled to express an opinion as to which of all the sectors of human conduct get the largest number of persons into serious trouble he would be pretty sure to give the palm to the sector of reproduction and sex. There is a peculiar irony in the fact that while all organic beings bring trouble upon themselves by these activities, man appears to suffer more from this source than does any other kind of organism.

For one thing the "geometrical ratio of increase," especially dwelt upon by Darwin, presents excessive reproductive activity as a form of maladaptive activity resulting in injury both to self and to kind. That this interpretation of the phenomenon is justified has the confirmation of Darwin's own statement. "Every being," we read, "which during its natural lifetime produces several eggs or seeds, must suffer destruction during some period of life, and during some season or occasional year; otherwise, on the principle of geometrical increase, its numbers would quickly become so inordinately great that no country could support the product." [5] An activity wholly indispensable to the welfare of the species, yet ever tending to bring destruction upon the reproducing organisms, is the paradoxical situation here before us. The general facts are so familiar that surely they do not need to be further illustrated, to serve as a basis for our examination of human maladaptivity in this realm.

While the principle of geometrical ratio of increase as stated by Darwin has reference to organisms which reproduce sexually, as a matter of fact it is in reproduction without sex that the principle reaches its extreme exemplification. No plant crowds itself to degradation or death by seed-and-pollen reproduction with such rapidity and certainty as does

[5] *The Origin of Species,* Chap. III.

almost any plant which propagates by shoots or buds or runners or any of the numerous forms of asexual reproduction. Biological research having not only confirmed common knowledge in recognizing that reproduction is not dependent on sex, but having made it highly probable that the sexual mode of reproduction was grafted onto the sexless as a sort of afterthought, much theorizing has been resorted to in the effort to explain how and particularly why such a complication of the business should have been resorted to at all. If a single orange tree can (with a little help by man) give rise to millions of perfectly good trees, as was the case with a navel orange tree of Southern California; and if a single insect like an aphid can multiply a thousandfold in a summer; if such things can be done quite independently of any sexual intervention, why should not the propagative business of the whole living world have been arranged for without complicating it in such a way as the sexual relation does complicate it?   It is obvious that sexual reproduction operates as one means of curtailing the effects of reproductive activity.   Reflect on what would happen were all the germ cells, male and female alike, produced by every individual of every sexually propagating species, plant and animal, capable of developing into an adult by itself alone; that is, without having to fuse with some other individual.   What if every pollen grain of an oak or pine, which are hardly less in number than the grains of dust picked up from a dry road on a windy day, were capable of becoming, all by itself, a full-fledged tree!   Nor would the imagined possibilities in these species be much greater than for the male sex elements in almost all other species, plant and animal alike.

If in order to relieve our imaginations from such crushing reproductive possibilities as these, we limit ourselves to the possibilities that would be presented by female germ cells capable of development without fertilization, the relief is great, though the load to be carried is staggering. Few indeed are either the plant or animal species in which even the female germinal elements of each individual do not rise into the thousands. Terrible as are the implications of the "geometrical ratio of increase," even when the mode of reproduction is sexual, incomparably more terrible would that ratio be were each and every germinal element able to go on by itself and become an adult.

The two-individual mode of reproduction, the sexual mode, is in its very nature a check on the extent of reproduction. Glancing over living nature as a whole, we see several ways in which this checking comes about. For one thing the way the germ cells, both male and female, are thrown away by many organisms leaves so much to chance as to whether individual elements of the two sorts shall meet and fuse, that great numbers fail to make connections and so perish without issue. Many kinds of aquatic animals and plants dispose of their germinal elements in this manner; and since water currents are peculiarly indifferent as to what they do to objects which happen to be subjected to them, the losses here must be very great. Any one who has watched the stream of sex products being ejected into the surrounding water by a starfish or mollusc or worm cannot avoid being impressed by the phenomenon if he is biologically thoughtful. As far as the creature itself is concerned, the performance appears to be merely a getting rid of something no longer useful, for which it has no room in its body. Its sex products seem to be to it much what its excrementitious products are. In the one case as in the other, the organism appears to be relieving itself of an incumbrance, and to be wholly unconcerned as to what becomes of the cast-off materials.

As to what proportion of all the sex cells that mature and are cast away in the indiscriminate fashion above referred to fail to find mates, I do not know that biologists have ever tried to estimate. That the proportion must be very great appears certain.

Then there are the mediating schemes, almost numberless in kind throughout the whole sexually propagating world, through which the male and female elements have to pass in order to get together. All these involve much chance of failure. Reflect on the chances there must be in all cases among flowering plants where the only way the male elements have of reaching the female elements is by being carried from one flower, or even one plant, to another by some insect. Such passivity and dependence for reaching a goal involving the very continuance of existence is impressive, viewed from our human standards of effectiveness. The wastage is appalling. However, this very wastage, so far as the sex elements themselves are concerned, is a great means of rescue from the potential disaster there is in the geometrical ratio of increase.

Another check on reproductivity through schemes by which alone sex elements can get together is that of the periodicity of the sex instinct in many species of animals. The most familar and striking illustrations are afforded by the common birds and mammals, where it is largely a seasonal affair. A little reflection enables us to see that there must be something more to the phenomenon than season in the sense of temperature and other wholly external conditions. Since the body temperature of birds, and especially of the higher mammals, is influenced hardly at all by surrounding temperatures, there seems to be little or no reason from this direction why sex elements should not be produced and discharged at one season as well as at any other season. Nor do we know any other wholly external factor that should render the production of sex elements dormant for much of the year. So far as the male and female sex cells themselves are concerned, those of cattle and horses, let us say, would almost certainly be as competent to mature and fuse together in mid-winter or at any other season as in the spring. They have no chance to mature and mate at any other time than the rutting period of the organisms which produce them.[6]

Nobody questions that the dormancy of the sexual impulse during much of the year in many animals is a great check on the rate of reproduction of those animals, other things being equal. The rather rare cases among mammals where there is little or nothing of a seasonal curtailment of the sexual activity, the female's willingness to mate being limited only by her condition due to her last pregnancy, and the male's eagerness being limited by nothing except the limited capacity of the activity itself, are just the species in which the "geometrical ratio of increase" brings disaster to great numbers of the species most certainly and promptly. The self-devastation from overpopulation which some species of rodents, as certain rats and rabbits, may bring upon themselves is well known, these species being also well known to be but slightly restricted in their sexual activities.

In man we have a species which though a relatively slow reproducer and though possessed of remarkable abilities to provide itself with the essentials of existence, is yet so continuously and insistently active sexually that the problem of overpopulation always has stared the species in the face and seemingly always will. It will, unless man finds some way of adjusting the relation between his sexual responses and his reproductive activities as yet hardly intimated by the recognizable facts of the problem. The extent to which all

---

[6] There is a mode of interpreting the facts here referred to that is just end-for-end to that given. The reproductive elements themselves, the sex cells, and especially the sex internal secretions, according to this theory, explain the phenomena of rut and all else that the sexually mature males and females exhibit. Although this theory enjoys wide currency at present, it is almost certainly wrong, its error being involved in an inadequate metaphysics of the relations between bodies and the elements composing them. But the theoretical difficulty thus encountered need not trouble us at all so far as concerns the point here being made.

people, no matter what their mental endowment or cultural grade, have wrestled with this problem, both theoretically and practically, must be taken as proof of its great difficulty and so of the unlikelihood that its solution may be reached, even approximately, by any short cut, or stated in any compact, trim formula. It is, however, justifiable to presume, on the strength of scientific aim and method generally, that the more fully and clearly the problem can be stated the greater the chance of success in dealing with it practically.

The problem takes its place as a form of maladaptive activity due to excessiveness of action resulting in injury to the acting organisms. This statement furnishes a better formulation than any we have previously utilized for analyzing the situation, recognizing more clearly than ever before the sharp distinction nature herself presents between reproduction and sex. All biological research in this general field has undoubtedly led toward such recognition, and from the psychobiological standpoint the distinction is even more fundamental than morphological or physiological biology is in position to see.

Reproductive activities and sexual activities represent two forms of response dependent on two forms of stimuli which have no recognizably necessary connection with each other, and hence would seem to have acquired such connection secondarily in the course of evolution. No biologist would think of attributing the division of any cell to exactly the same causes that bring about conjugation of two protozoan cells or two metazoan sex cells. If a stimulus is a necessary factor in each case the presumption is strong that this factor is different in the two cases. When the phenomena are described in detail, down to the activities of the chromosomes in division (reproduction), on the one hand, and fusion (sexual union) on the other, the conclusion seems unescapable that the effective stimuli in the two cases are diametrically opposed to each other. The fusing bodies are so nearly alike, and their observable activities are such as to justify the supposition that the chief stimulus for each comes from the other. We must suppose that the set of causes, including the stimuli, which bring the elements together (basic sexuality) are essentially the opposite of those which make them separate (basic reproduction).

This is the way the matter looks when the "ultimate" elements alone are considered. The case is much more comprehensible when we consider the reproductive elements as minute parts of larger, more complicated and more active individual organisms. These elements come from individual organisms which are radically different in certain structural respects which have to do with the coming together and fusion of elements preparatory to the division of elements. The two sexes are individual organisms structurally so differentiated that while they continue their individual existence and give rise to reproductive elements they bring about, or greatly facilitate bringing about, the meeting and fusion of these elements.

The activities by the organisms involved in this operation of producing elements and bringing them together are what we know as sexual activities. These activities have their source in stimuli assumed to be essential to them but quite independent of the sex elements themselves. The stimuli belong to the large category of physical contact stimuli resulting in positive response. There is not the slightest ground for supposing that any of the touch stimulations which play so great a part in sexual activities are utterly different from touch stimuli which play important parts in many other activities, as for instance that of food-getting. The intimate rôle of facial and especially of lip contacts in both nutritional and sexual activities seems conclusive evidence of the basic identity of stimulus and response in these two activities. The biological evidence, especially from the side of comparative zoölogy, is overwhelming that positive responses to physically tactual stimuli are far older and more general than is anything connected with sex. The probable meaning of the special quality imparted to the tactile sensation and response to give the sex instinct, and of the overwhelmingly dominant place acquired by it in the total life of the organisms, does not fall within the scope of this presentation to examine.

There seems no escape from the conclusion that the sexual mode of reproduction as we find it in the higher animals, especially in man, has called to its help this ancient and apparently universal form of the stimulus-response duality, and has developed it to such a dominant place in the general scheme of stimulation and response as to mislead even highly trained students of human conduct as to the basic nature of sexual activity in human conduct. Freud and his followers, so far as they still cling to the idea that sex is the ultimate reality of human action, are conspicuous victims of this fallacious interpretation.

The two forms of stimulation and response here recognized belong to two widely different categories of activity already referred to as life-or-death responses and life-fulfilling responses. Life-or-death responses and activities are those concerned primarily with the mere continued existence of individual and species. The reproductive activity in the strict sense of the present discussion belongs clearly to this category, while the sexual activity belongs to the second category, that of life-fulfilling responses and activities. These are concerned primarily with all that makes human life valuable, worth while, as common expression has it. Notably sexual response and activity, esthetic instinct and impulses, and the religious and scientific modes of response and activity, all belong in this category of life-fulfilling responses.

Having been witnesses on a grand scale of the liability of

all activity to maladaptation, thereby exposing the actors to various dangers, and having noted the character and fruitage of the reproductive activity in its connection with the sexual activity, we should expect that the dangers to which organisms would be exposed in this realm would be proportional to the strength of the impulsions to respond to the stimuli definitive of the realm. In other words, we should expect that maladaptive reproductive and sexual activities stand very near the top of, if indeed they do not actually lead, the list of mankind's troublemakers. Experience here is so ample and intimate that illustrations, on which we have greatly relied in the previous discussions, may be dispensed with. A résumé of the main forms of maladaptivity will fall under the two heads of reproductive activity and sexual activity.

REPRODUCTIVE MALADAPTIVE ACTIVITY: OVERPOPULATION

It can hardly be doubted that from the standpoint of the species, the community, the nation, this is the most important category for man. Reminder of the great attention this subject has received by thoughtful students of human life, particularly since Malthus' time, will suffice for the needs of this discussion as evidence of the reality of this form of maladaptivity. "Injury to kind" is outstanding here; but it is also a case of *self-injury*, the welfare of the acting individuals themselves being closely involved.

DANGERS TO THE MOTHER IN CHILD-BEARING

In addition to overpopulation, there are a whole series of injurious consequences that may attend the reproductive activity. Natural dangers to the mother in pregnancy and childbirth may be due to physical defects which though not sufficient to prevent conception may seriously impair competency for normal pregnancy and parturition, one or both. The great efforts of scientific medicine to improve obstetrical care and to find safe and effective means of preventing conception are well known. Another category of dangers to the mother is dependent not on any natural physical defects of hers, but on efforts to prevent the natural results of conception through purposely induced abortion, with its train of probable consequences.

DANGERS ARISING FROM RELATION OF OFFSPRING TO PARENTS

Finally there is a large category of injurious reproduction that is dependent on the character of the offspring in relation to the parents, including the production of unmistakably inferior progeny, racially speaking (the "cacogenic" progeny of eugenics); and irresponsible parenthood. In view of the well-nigh utter helplessness of the just-born human infant, whenever one comes into the world through the mutual action of two adults, either one or both of whom fails to be responsible for their helpless product, an abnormal thing is done and one which is more or less harmful to somebody, usually to several persons. Illegitimacy comes under this head but does not coincide fully with irresponsibility. Offspring may be entirely legitimate so far as formal law or custom are concerned; yet parental responsibility may be defective or wholly lacking. Legal and social criteria of legitimate parenthood are very different from the criteria of physical and spiritual ability and willingness of parents to care for their offspring during the period of its inability for self-maintenance.

MALADAPTIVE SEXUAL ACTIVITY

Several categories are quite as obvious and familiar here as under reproductive activity. These fall into a group in which the activities involve two persons, and a group in which only one person is directly involved. The outstanding form under the first group in most civilized communities is prostitution; surely the merest allusion to this sufficiently establishes its place in our conception of maladaptive sexual activity. That every special act which would have to be listed under sexual prostitution is injurious perhaps could not be successfully contended; nor need it be to maintain our point. Nobody doubts that on the whole prostitution is and always has been a scourge upon mankind in a variety of ways. For one thing the woman who makes a single one of her functions, namely her sexual, the basis of her life career and thereby cuts herself away from participating, through her other functions and abilities, in the broader life of the community, injures by just so much both her personal life and the community life to which she should normally contribute. The physically impaired and shortened and the spiritually impoverished life of the female prostitute is sufficient evidence of the maladaptivity of this phase of sexual activity. Further evidence to the same effect that might be adduced from males who are the chief patrons of such females, we may justifiably neglect so far as the present inquiry is concerned.

The only other form of maladaptive activity under the first group that need be noticed is sodomy. A few writers have undertaken a measure of defense of this form of sexual gratification. It is hardly possible that anybody would seriously contend that so gross a perversion of an activity is not fraught with dire possibilities of physical and moral injury to both participants in the action. Probably the obviousness of these possibilities is exactly what makes the mere thought of them so repellent to us. Only the stringent demands of scientific description make it tolerable even to mention mankind's ability thus to pervert its own most vital processes.

The other group of maladaptive sexual activities which implicate only one person has its main exemplification in masturbation. It is not necessary for the purposes of this discussion to contend that every act of this sort is injurious. It is sufficient to recognize that a variety of bad consequences may and unquestionably do result from it. There seems to be a great dearth of accurate knowledge in this as in many other aspects of maladaptive sexual practices. Any consideration of sexual maladaptivity confined to the individual itself ought not to neglect entirely reference to the subject as it concerns the pre-adolescent life of the individual. It seems probable that closer researches in this field, from the standpoint of stimulus-response as we are conceiving it, will discover that wholesome sex life during and following adolescence is more dependent on how the individual gets acquainted with himself sexually than has been appreciated.

Meager as has been our examination of high-cultured man's liability to act maladaptively in his reproductive and sexual affairs, it has been enough to convince us that in its application to these affairs the saying that "human beings act just that way" is rather specially true. Thought-compelling as was our recognition of man's greater liability and his greater ability than the sub-human animals have, to act maladaptively in various sectors of his life, notably in industry and in war, even more thought-compelling is our recognition now of his still greater ability and liability to outdo the animals in bringing failure and pain and sorrow upon himself in this sector of his life.

Were it not that the same elements in man's adaptive ability by which he has gained his supremacy over the rest of the animal world make it possible for him to gain supremacy over his own tendencies to act maladaptively in all sectors of his life, reproductive and sexual included, we should have to conclude that, much of somberness as there has been in man's past career upon the earth, still more somber would be his outlook for the future. Human salvation depends on our race's ability to avail itself more and more of its already long-possessed and much-used adaptive capacity.

CHAPTER 17

THE ELEMENTS OF MAN'S PHYSICAL STRUCTURE WHICH ENABLE HIM TO BE THE MOST ACTIVELY ADAPTIVE OF ALL LIVING BEINGS

It would be obvious folly to affirm that in all his bodily structure and functions man is superior to all other animals. The ostrich is much fleeter of foot than is man. The elephant is many times stronger. The seal can outswim him with the greatest ease. When wholly unarmed his hunting ability is greatly inferior to that of the tiger or wolf. The dog excels him in sense of smell. Only when his physical nature is viewed in relation with his spiritual nature does his advantage over all other creatures come into clear light. Early in our discussion we noted the great rôle discovery and invention have played in bringing man to where he now is, as contrasted with the place still occupied by any of the other creatures with which he has had to contend. Attention was called to the part his brain and his hands have taken in these matters. We must now consider this subject more fully.

STRUCTURAL AND FUNCTIONAL ASPECT

The working together of head and hand in all the operations by which man has won his place in the world is apparent to everybody. The anatomist and the neurologist are impressed with the nice complexity of the structures by which head and hands are connected. The physiologist concentrates upon the special activities of muscles, nerves and blood vessels involved in this connection. The embryologist watches with never-ceasing wonder the structures gradually come into being properly ordered for making the completed organism. To comprehend the unitary whole seems to be a task reserved for the psychobiologist.

What would be the result were either head or hands, like those of man, to be combined in any other way than just as they are combined? What could result from combining a head like that of a man, with hands (fore limbs) like those of a lion? a horse? a walrus? an eagle? What could result from combining hands like those of man with a head like that of an elephant? a bear? an ostrich? an alligator? This query runs in the channel that pure fancy has followed throughout man's career as a rational being. The fact that such combinations have been made long and often as fanciful things to excite mirth or derision implies universal recognition that human hands and human heads belong inseparably together. They are inseparable both as to their present activities and as to their genesis. Had we not human heads we should not have human hands; and, per contra, had we not human hands we should not have human heads.

The terms head and hands as here used are highly figurative as well as very general. One's "head" is his best wit and wisdom. It is also his sense organs situated in that part of his body, and his brain, particularly his cerebral cortex. "Hands" symbolize his best manual skill, at the same time denoting the anatomical structures with their skin sensitiveness, and muscular suppleness and strength.

Certain well-known instances of animal achievement raise the question of whether we are really justified in speaking of man's great superiority over the animals concerned.

Such an accomplishment as the nest-building of orioles could hardly be duplicated by human handiwork. There happens to be before me as I work a nest of the Bullock Oriole which illustrates what these birds can do. This nest was built in a eucalyptus tree, from several slender pendant twigs of which it was suspended. Its framework is of threads taken from leaves of pampas grass, bunches of which were near at hand. These threads are interwoven with the twigs and leaves in such a way as to give both proper form and security of attachment to the nest. But the most surprising thing about this piece of construction is that in one place several of the threads are put through a hole in a leaf, the hole having almost certainly been made by the bird's beak, and securely inserted at both ends into the fabric of the nest, thus making the threads contribute definitely to holding the nest in place. In addition to the hole just mentioned, which is well toward the tip of the pendant leaf, near the base of the same leaf is another hole, undoubtedly made by the bird. Through the hole nearest the nest, a thread is passed, one end of which is attached to the nest, the free end being carried up and passed through the other hole in the opposite direction to its course through the first hole. The long free end is left dangling in the air, so contributes nothing to the support of the nest, its passage through the holes being very loose. Thus we have in this leaf a sewing stitch, crude to be sure, but nevertheless a typical stitch made by a bird. The nest construction here displayed could hardly be duplicated by human handiwork.

In view of such instances of animal achievement are we justified in speaking of man's great superiority over the animals concerned? Is it not permissible to hold that animals thus capable ought to be compared with very primitive rather than with civilized man, and then to assume that in time these dawn capabilities might become much what we see in modern man? But consider the anatomical conditions under which this piece of oriole work was done. Not hands, remember, but feet and mouth are the body members alone available for bird work. The "hands" (the whole fore limbs) are so completely given over in birds to locomotion that such uses of them as man makes of his hands are entirely excluded. If we inquire whether a bird capable as is the oriole, might conceivably grow in power and skill until finally its achievements might be comparable with those of civilized man, the question of physical means at the bird's command appears quite as important as that of mental means. By no possibility could an oriole's feet and beak be trained to produce, either directly or through bird-made tools and machines, thread and needles in any wise equal in quality to those produced by man. It is not conceivable that these members could be trained to do as good a job of sewing as a seamstress does no matter how good a brain might be possessed by the bird.

Similar considerations apply to any four-limbed animal below the primates. Think of the utter uselessness of the arms and hands of the horse and ox and all other hoofed creatures for any of the chief services to which the human arms and hands are put. Nor is there a single carnivore that is much better off so far as this is concerned. Even in animals of the squirrel kind in which the hands are better fitted for handling objects than in any other animals below the primates, the shortness and comparative inflexibility of the fore limbs and the structure of the hands, particularly of the fingers, limit their manipulative power very narrowly.

Many persons, including Francis Galton, have commented on the intellectual comradeship between man and his dog. Galton writes: "The animal which above all others is a companion to man is the dog, and we observe how readily their proceedings are intelligible to each other. Every whine or bark of the dog, each of his fawning, savage, or timorous movements, is an exact counterpart of what would have been the man's behavior, had he felt similar emotions. As the man understands the thoughts of the dog, so the dog understands the thoughts of the man, by attending to his natural voice, his countenance, and his actions. A man irritates a dog by an ordinary laugh, he frightens him by an angry look, or he calms him by a kindly bearing." [1] One

[1] *Enquiries into Human Faculty*, Everyman's Library, p. 187.

who actually experiences with his own favorite dog companion such dog qualities as these can hardly avoid questioning something in this wise: Well, Shep, bless your soul, so alike are you and I even to some of the finest of our qualities, what stops us from being equally alike in all our qualities? What is it that stands between us as to many other qualities? Since you can be so fond of me and will overcome so many difficulties to be with me, just as I am fond of you and will go to much trouble to be with you, how is it that you are not fond, as I am, of reading and writing books?

Without harrowing our minds for an ultimate answer to such questioning, this much is obvious enough: Were dogs to be fond of reading books, the only books they could have to read would be man's books; for man is the only creature in all the world capable of making writing tools and then holding them for the act of writing. Notice your dog's paws and you find yourself forced to the conclusion that no matter how much he might desire to write books, and even try to do so, he is forever debarred from doing so by the fact that he has no bodily means for doing it. This defectiveness in dog construction really affects the character of dog life much more extensively than merely in debarring him from becoming a writer and reader of books. It affects the most basic of all his activities, that of getting and using food. When you feed your dog what does he do? What can he do? Can he sit down or even stand up on his hind feet, take his meal in his hands, piece at a time, and put it in his mouth? Not at all. Straight at it he goes, and must, with his mouth. If his useless (for this purpose) paws can be made to help him at all, it is merely by way of stepping on and holding down some piece of food the better to be able to tear it into manageable mouthfuls or by way of poking some fragment into a more favorable position for getting at it with the mouth.

All this, however, is mere inconvenience for the dog as contrasted with the way man can manage his meal. The really vital thing comes in connection with the problem of getting food at all, the problem of capturing prey. All of the dog-kind, like all of the man-kind, are by nature hunters of animals to a greater or less extent. With man as with dog, modes of hunting the larger, more active, more wily species of animals which inhabit the same parts of the earth with themselves, constitute the major problem and some of the most vital activities of the species.

The most searching studies into the life-methods of primitive man are at one on the great rôle which hunting (including fishing) played with him. While all students of man's dawn life recognize this more or less, a few have specially emphasized it. One of these is Carveth Read.[2] We read: "The differences between Man and his nearest relatives are innumerable; but taking the chief of them, and assuming that the minor details are correlated with these, it is the hypothesis of this essay that they may all be traced to the influence of one variation operating amongst the original anthropoid conditions. That variation was the adoption of a flesh diet and the habits of a hunter in order to obtain it. . . . The adoption of the hunting-life, therefore, is the essential variation upon which everything else depends."[3] Whatever the truth may be as to how man originated, certain it is that hunting has played an enormous part with him and is almost a major impulsion with him still, even though living under conditions in which the original need for it does not exist. Similarly is it with the dog and his kind, wolves, foxes and so on. Hunters they all are in the strictest sense.

It is interesting to note the extent to which mankind and

[2] *The Origin of Man and of His Superstitions*, 1920.
[3] P. I.

dogkind have preyed upon the same animal kinds; especially on the deer and rabbit families, many mammals, and the gallinaceous and duck families among birds. Reflect on what the course of things is, and in all likelihood for numberless centuries has been, in the hunting business, with these two groups of hunters. As far back into the past as we can possibly see, dogkind has had to depend on almost exactly the same agencies and methods. Acuteness of sense in smelling, in hearing, in seeing, physical strength and endurance for the chase, sharp teeth and strong jaws, these alone have been the reliances. The chief reason for this has been that the unfortunate creatures have lacked any physical equipment by which the work could be done in any way greatly different. Given dog nature constituted as we actually see it, with body, limbs and head as they are, what possible methods can you imagine for capturing prey greatly different from those actually employed? Senses can be imagined keener than they are. Jaws might be stronger and be set with teeth sharper, more effective and more durable. There might be greater fleetness of foot and more endurance. But with limbs and feet fashioned as they are, by no possibility could they be used very differently from the way they are used.

With mankind the case is quite otherwise. Compare deer hunting by American sportsmen today in the Rocky Mountain wilds with deer hunting by the gray wolf in the same region. The American aboriginal hunting the same game in the same region a thousand years ago enjoyed a vast advantage over his wolf competitor through his bow and arrows and other implements, but his advantage was slight compared with that enjoyed by the hunter of today. There is ground for doubt whether even this slight advantage was enjoyed by the human huntsman at the dawn of his hunting career so far as that is known to us by his rude weapons of the stone age. The wolf may have had somewhat the better of it for centuries even after man began his weapon-making and weapon-using career.

Marvelous were the possibilities for the future in the fact that man could do anything at all toward weapon-making. If he could make weapons he could make thousands of other things. That was his supreme advantage. But how could he do these things when his wolf competitor could not? Beyond question his superior ability was due to the fact that primitive mankind had in his hands the physical members available for such making whereas dog-kind had no members which could be thus used. Man at the very dawn of his career as man had physical members which he could spare from other uses and by which he could take hold of such external objects as sticks and stones, and move them about to his pleasure, and shape them to some extent the better to serve his needs.

As to all the activities on which human culture and civilization mainly depend, no animal below the primates could come much nearer equaling man in actual performance than they now do, even were they his equal in mental endowment. Several writers before the Darwinian era and Darwin himself saw this matter in a clearer light than many professed followers of Darwin have seen it. The importance of the diversity of uses to which human hands can be put was recognized to some extent as far back in the history of human culture as the time of Aristotle. This earliest of philosophical naturalists tells us: "Much in error, then, are they who say that the construction of man is not only faulty, but inferior to that of all other animals; seeing that he is, as they point out, bare-footed, naked, and without weapon of which to avail himself. For other animals have each but one mode of defense, and this they can never change; so that they must perform all the offices of life and even, so to speak, sleep with sandals on, never laying aside whatever serves as a protection to their bodies, nor changing such single weapon as they may chance to possess. But to man numerous modes of defense are open, and these, moreover, he may change at will, as also he may adopt such weapon as he pleases, and at such times as suit him. For the hand is talon, hoof, and horn, at will. So too it is spear, and sword, and whatsoever other weapon or instrument you please; for all these can it be from its power of grasping and holding them all." [4] Aristotle goes on to speak of the powers of the hand, particularly the grasping power as dependent upon the fingers. He duly appreciates the great importance of the thumb from being opposable to all the other digits, and comments on the "no less skillfully contrived" nails.

Perception of the importance of hands reached its culmination in the pre-Darwinian period in a whole volume devoted to the subject, and appearing as Number IV of the Bridgewater Treatises.[5] While much of the speculative part of this work has become obsolete by the advance of knowledge, the philosophical standpoint from which it was written encouraged comprehensive treatment of the functional importance of human hands. As a consequence we have here one of the fullest, most adequate descriptions of these members that has ever been written. A single passage, part of which is quoted by Darwin, will sufficiently indicate Bell's general view so far as anatomy and physiology are concerned. "With respect to the superiority of man being in his mind," he writes, "and not merely in the provisions of his body, it is no doubt true; but as we proceed, we shall find how the Hand supplies all instruments, and by its correspondence with the intellect gives him universal dominion." [6]

[4] *De Partibus Animalium,* William Ogle, translation 687a, 25, 30, and 687b, 5.
[5] *The Hand, Its Mechanism and Vital Endowments as Evincing Design,* by Sir Charles Bell.
[6] P. 38.

Following his quotation from Bell, Darwin says: [7] "But the hands and arms could hardly have become perfect enough to have manufactured weapons, or to have hurled stones and spears with a true aim, as long as they were habitually used for locomotion and for supporting the whole weight of the body, or as long as they were especially well adapted, as previously remarked, for climbing trees. Such rough treatment would also have blunted the sense of touch, on which their delicate use largely depends. From these causes alone it would have been an advantage to man to have become a biped; but for many actions it is indispensable that the arms and the whole upper part of the body should be free; and he must for this end stand firmly on his feet. To gain this great advantage, the feet have been rendered flat and the great-toe peculiarly modified, though this has entailed the almost complete loss of the power of prehension." [8]

Darwin the evolutionist saw, as his special-creationist predecessors could not see, that adaptive changes in different parts of the body would follow in accordance with the principle of organic correlation. The special-creative theory implies the special and independent creation of the different organs of the body as well as the special and independent creation of the species. The evolution theory on the other hand implies the origin of organs from other organs and their dependence on other organs and on the whole organism, as well as the origin of species from

[7] This bringing together of the views of Bell and Darwin illustrates a very important principle. Bell, though so distinguished an anatomist as to be sometimes ranked second only to Harvey, was not a believer in the derivative origin of man, while Darwin was committed soul and body to this belief. Nevertheless the two were in close accord as to all sorts of facts in man's structure and as to many general conclusions such as on that here referred to, concerning the importance of human hands. The principle illustrated is this: We can know vast numbers of facts and reach broad generalizations about the structure and functions of man and other organisms, wholly independently of anything we may believe or even know about the origin of the organisms.

[8] *The Descent of Man*, Appleton edition, 1897, Vol. I, pp. 51-52.

other species. But unqualifiedly as the evolution theory has long been accepted, its implications as to the dependence of the organs of the body on one another in evolution as well as in function seems not to have been very clearly seen.

This case of the human head and hands is strikingly in point; and Darwin went some distance in calling attention to the coördinated changes which have occurred in different parts of the body. The pelvis has become broader, the spine peculiarly curved, and the head fixed in an altered position. It has even been claimed that the powerful mastoid processes of the human skull are the result of man's erect position.

The idea that human head and human hands are derivatively as well as functionally interdependent and that both are adaptive to the needs of the human organism is the standpoint of this discussion.

Although several evolutionists of today, writing on the nature of man, have recognized something of the strategic place held by the head-and-hands combination, it is surprising that the hand member of the combination should have received so little attention. A few striking exceptions are found to the general rule. One of these is J. M. McFarlane in his volume *The Causes and Course of Organic Evolution,* 1918. This author's appreciation of the functional significance of the human hand runs close to that of Darwin and Bell. We read: "Possibly no more graphic method could be devised for bringing before us the enormous, the wholly preponderating, importance of the forelimbs than by asking ourselves the question: What would man be without his arms? By these he secures, cooks, and eats his food; cleans his body; grows, collects, weaves, shapes, and puts on his clothes; digs, cuts, or hews material for his home; prepares it often elaborately, pieces it together, and roofs in the whole; fashions and places lights for its illumination. He internally decorates it with materials at times of the most delicate and elaborate hand workmanship; he prepares the soil, sows, waters, reaps, garners, and distributes his grain, straw, fruits, etc.; he fashions instruments of musical harmony, of mechanical skill, of space-penetrating power, of microscopic exploration, of wholesale destruction. He so operates on the body of his neighbor, surgically taking it apart, and placing it together again, as to convert that body truly into a living machine; he catches, tames, pens up, and uses the animals below him as he wills, to ride on them, to be drawn by them, and to use them in many other ways for his purposes. Like the beaver he builds dams; digs canals, and drains or floods countries. He puts together machines that chain and store heat, chemical energy, mechanical energy and electricity. He expands even on all of the above in endless manner, so that he can correctly proclaim himself 'Lord of Creation.' " [9]

All this, so patent that no one questions it, is equivalent to saying that nearly everything distinctively human which is done or ever has been done on this earth never could have been done without human hands. Even the vast and noble edifice of pure mathematics, perhaps the least dependent upon hand work of all earthly creations, would have been impossible without the aid of hands in devising and using the written language of mathematics. Unaided thought and memory would have been quite incompetent to carry through the long and highly complicated operations involved in the creation of this science.

From his possession of the head-and-hands combination each and every person is equipped with amazingly varied capacity for accomplishment. The sociologist F. Müller-Lyer has called attention, though hardly adequately, to this as follows: "In the hand man has a number of organs corresponding to the number of tools he possesses. . . . The hand that clasps a knife is practically another organ to the same hand that holds a paint brush, an auger, a drinking

[9] P. 574.

vessel, pen, hammer, or pistol." [10] The full meaning of this great range of possible activity by the human hand is recognized only when the matter is viewed psychobiologically as well as structurally. That is to say, the full meaning of the varied possibilities of hand activity is not recognized until cognizance is taken of the realities of such activity exhibited by the human species as it exists on earth now and in past times has existed. Reflect comparatively on the variety of hand work presented in the beautifully fashioned and decorated pottery of the Pueblo Indian women of New Mexico, and in the delicate laces of the Indian women of old Mexico. There is no reason for supposing the difference between these two kinds of production is dependent in the slightest degree on inherent differences in the hands by which they are produced. So far as these members are concerned no physiologist would entertain any doubt that the young girl of New Mexico could be trained to produce lace as perfect and beautiful as can her sister of old Mexico. So far as hands are concerned the maiden of old Mexico could become just as good a potter as the maiden of New Mexico. Compare the Navajo rug at its best, woven on a simple form of the hand loom, with the finest, most elaborately figured modern Paisley shawls, woven on the power loom at the climax of its perfection. Does any one imagine that there could be found anywhere among the hands which contribute to the making and using of power-loom, silk-worm filaments and pattern of marvelous intricacy, differences of structure in the hands involved in producing the rugs, which would be at all comparable to the difference between the two products? It is doubtful if the most expert anatomist could discover anything, no matter how far he might push his examination of hand structure, that would enable him to distinguish rug-producing hands from Paisley shawl-producing hands.

[10] *The History of Social Development*, p. 55.

Compare the famous Zeiss optical works of Germany with the equally famous Clyde shipbuilding works of Scotland, and these again with Krupp's munition works in Germany. Let the comparison cover the products of these great "works" as well as the works themselves. *Almost the entire vast and varied material fabric of civilization, alike the parts designed for upbuilding, for peace and happiness, and the parts designed for down-tearing and war, for suffering and misery, is wholly dependent upon the activities of human hands all so nearly identical in structure and basic function that almost any given pair could be as well trained to do any one part as any other part of the work involved!*

Special emphasis must be put on man's hands and arms as contrasted with his feet and legs because of the preëminent part taken by the former in making tools and machines; that is, in making instruments to assist in doing other things. No phase of human activity has contributed so much to man's mastery over nature as has his ability to supplement and augment his very ordinary physical strength, manual dexterity, and sensory power, by mechanical contrivances. Reflect, for instance, on what he is able to do as a traveler by water through his having developed the ocean liner, in comparison with what he could ever do as a mere swimmer: Almost the whole of the physical activity involved in this and innumerable other developments has been performed, directly and indirectly, by the hands.

While thus recognizing the enormously preponderant rôle of the fore limbs in bringing civilized man to his present stage of advancement it must not be forgotten that the hind limbs have also played a distinct and positive part. Ability to move about independently in space is quite distinct from ability for creative work. Although it must be assigned an inferior place in human significance its importance is still great. While it is undoubtedly justifiable to think of the feet as having developed historically in organic coördination

with the hands, we must also think of them as having taken
their form and function partly on their own account, having
an office strictly their own.

EVOLUTIONAL ASPECT

Anatomists and embryologists have dwelt at length on the
fact that the human form presents many structures which
are primitive in character. By this it is meant that the
structures resemble the corresponding parts possessed by
species relatively low in the zoölogical scale. Thus the
single-chambered stomach of man is regarded as more primitive than the four-chambered stomach of the ox. In no part
of man's bodily structure is this primitiveness more pronounced and significant than in his hands. To find what
may justly be called a prototype of the human hand we have
to go clear down the zoölogical scale to the amphibians, for
it is not until we descend this far that we come to hands in
which the digits are freely and fully present (though no
living amphibian possesses a fully developed thumb) and are
unarmed with claws. The absence of claws is favorable for
the later development of finger-ends, the outer surface of
which may be covered by nails, and the skin of the inner
surfaces may become sensitive tactile organs. This is
equivalent to saying that nowhere in the series of four-footed
animals below the primates do we find the fore arm, the
palm of the hand, and the disposition and structure of the
fingers such as to become readily modifiable into the human
hand, until we reach the amphibians. The hand of the
human foetus resembles more the hand of a typical amphibian than that of any other adult vertebrate below the
primates. A moderately critical layman might say: "If your
suggestion that resemblance among animals indicates actual
genetic kinship and thereby gives greater concreteness to
the idea of the web of life, what about jumping from the

primates way back to the amphibians? What about all the
four-footed species that intervene, zoölogically, between the
primates and the amphibians?   Where do the numerous
orders and genera of lower quadrupedal mammals and reptiles come in? Must their place in the web be regarded
dubiously because their fore limbs have less resemblance
to man's than have those of the amphibians? What of
whales, birds and snakes, creatures whose fore limbs have
almost no likeness at all to those of man? Are they to be
wholly counted out?"

These are legitimate questions and are susceptible of a
fairly satisfactory answer. The answer would take us much
farther into the well-known but highly elaborate and technical facts of comparative anatomy and embryology of the
vertebrate limbs than we can go in a work like this. The
general direction in which the answer lies is better shown,
I believe, by F. W. Jones than by any other writer with
whom I am acquainted.[11] The absence of anything in the
way of solid, horny structures from the fingers and toes of
amphibians is likely to strike unzoölogical readers as a rather
trivial fact; and so it is from some points of view. When,
however, we reflect on it as evidence that there once existed
a group of vertebrates having hands and feet so constructed
that they could readily (developmentally speaking) become
transformed into human hands and feet, the fact is
seen to be very far from trivial. Such reflection would
properly run something as follows: For an evolutional
course which could lead to man or any creature comparable
with him (as the anthropoid apes) it was absolutely essential
that the fore limbs should be rescued from becoming devoted
exclusively to locomotion whether on land, in the water, or in
the air. Something of their original pliability had to be
maintained.

Many authors call attention to the structural similarity

[11] *Arboreal Man,* 1916.

between the human hand, especially in its early embryonal stages, and the typical amphibian hand. No one, so far as I am aware, has made much of it from the standpoint of activity except Jones in the book just mentioned. Jones' central hypothesis is that the wide-swinging powers characteristic of the human and other primate arms, and the rotative and grasping powers peculiarly characteristic of human hands were evolved in connection with tree-climbing and locomotion among the branches of trees after the fashion of many present-day monkeys. The very beginning of habits of this sort he believes must have been among animals as far down the vertebrate scale as the amphibians. In support of this he calls attention to the expertness of Tree Frogs as climbers, and notes the clambering abilities of some of the tailed amphibians. "It may seem," he writes, "a long way to go back when attempting to unravel the influence of tree-climbing among the Primates, to appeal to the clambering activities of the water-newt. And yet the anatomical condition of the limbs of man demands a shifting backward of the inquiry to some such stage as this. I believe that the truest picture of the evolution of Primate climbing starts with such a scene as we are depicting now." [12]

This hypothesis appeals to me the more strongly from observations of my own made years ago on a tree climbing salamander.[13] The long-tailed amphibian referred to was discovered to deposit and hatch its eggs typically in decay holes in oak trees, some of the holes utilized being thirty feet from the ground. This hitherto unheard-of breeding habit of salamanders together with the unusual alertness of this species on its feet, its ability to use its tail as a clinging organ, and other departures from the orthodox ways of salamanders are certainly suggestive of the possibilities

[12] P. 16.
[13] "Further Notes on the Habits of Autodax lugubris," *Amer. Naturalist*, 1903, Vol. XXXVII, p. 883.

there are in such lowly, generalized animals as the tailed amphibians. The suggestion is not at all that such off-type habits are really on the road to man or any other higher animal. Given man and other higher animals, such cases do suggest how, functionally, these higher animals may have started.

No aspect of living nature is more interesting than that which involves problems of yet unrealized possibilities; problems of what actions and developments are still possible and what are impossible. It is difficult to see how the front feet of any typical land-dwelling four-footed animal, a lizard, a bear, or a squirrel, could change into hands like those of men. But there is little difficulty in seeing how such a hand as is possessed by a typical amphibian could be so changed.

The vertebrate limbs offer a striking illustration of that principle of evolution of structure according to which, once a part becomes sharply fashioned for performing a particular function, its capacity for performing any other function or of being modified for taking on additional functions, is almost wholly gone. Think how little else a horse or ox can do with its legs than to use them for moving around! Beyond the limited use of the fore limbs for striking and the somewhat less limited use of the hind limbs for kicking, the story of the utility of these members is thus wholly told. Many of the rodents have a great advantage over the hoofed animals in this. The fore limbs of mice and rats, besides being highly efficient for locomotion, are efficient for digging, climbing and gathering up and handling objects, as for food. In man alone are the structure and relations of these members such as to secure the greatest possible variety of useful activity combined with the greatest possible efficiency in each particular activity, and also the greatest possibility for future development. Taking advantage of the more or less legitimate custom of personifying nature we may state the evolutional task nature set for herself, the achievement of which is man: Having discovered that activity of the sort definitive of animal organisms is an effective means of securing well-being, that is to say, is an effective means of adaptiveness, the question of how this means could reach its highest effectiveness presented itself for consideration. The answer to the question was soon seen to hinge on the working together of two different categories of structure, one for the actual performance of movements by the organism, the other for the guidance of the movements. In other words the two categories of muscular structures and nervous structures were produced. In order to make these basic categories workable each had to be supplemented in various ways, especially by supporting and prehensile structures on the muscular side; and by sensory, conducting, and selective structures on the nervous side. As operating structures, especially those devoted to moving the organism from one place to another and those devoted to grasping and holding objects, became more effective for their special purposes, they also became more restricted to the particular actions in question, and less effective for performing other kinds of action. In order to secure the highest measure possible of adaptiveness through activity, operative structures, especially for grasping and holding objects, having the maximum range and maximum effectiveness in themselves, had to be produced in combination with directive structures having also the maximum range and effectiveness of action.

The organism thus produced is the human organism, its arms and hands being first in importance on the operative side of its activities, and its brain of first importance on the directive side of its activities. This statement, the meaning of which may be rather obscure because of the wide range of the generalizations involved, may be helped to objective clarity by an illustration.

The example to be used is from observations of my own. It is chosen because of the goodly number and range of the elements in the purely operative aspect of the generalization. It concerns the activities, especially of the fore limbs and hands, by representatives of four mammalian species rather widely separated from one another in the class of mammals as a whole. These representatives were an airedale dog, Laddy by name; a marmoset of the genus *Midas,* called Sir Henry (after the noted West Indian buccaneer and Jamaican governor); a Capuchin monkey, Jimmy by name; and a four-year-old boy nicknamed Bobby. The incident extended over a period of about three weeks, the locus of it being a yacht making its way leisurely from Panama to San Diego, California.

A better example of a graded biological series as viewed from the standpoint of the structure and use of the arms and hands it would be hard to find; and so far as could be made out by the rough means of testing that could be applied, the intervals between the four members of the series were about equal. At the lower end stood Laddy. There could be no doubt about that. It was pathetic to see his relative help- lessness in this way, especially when he came into close comparison with Jimmy and Bobby. Only in their capering about on the floor was Laddy in it at all with the other two. So far as there was a chance for a straightaway run he had a clear advantage. Since the chances for this were limited by the small floor-space, most of their activities had to go in other directions. In ball-playing, for instance, poor Laddy could do nothing except chase the ball, pick it up with his mouth and carry it around. He could not throw it at all. Bobby, on the contrary, had great fun in not only chasing it, but picking it up with his hands, throwing it, bouncing it on the floor or against a wall, and catching it when it was thrown by some one else. Jimmy, while he could not compete with Bobby in throwing the ball, could do almost as well as Bobby in catching it, and could do better, if anything, in chasing it and picking it up. Com-

pared with Laddy he was a great success as a ball player
and at handling all sorts of objects. And when it came to
getting around over the ship generally—well, neither of the
others were in Jimmy's class at all. So extremely capable
and active was he in this way that he had to be kept chained
most of the time.

In hardly anything was Jimmy's manual ability displayed
to greater advantage than in such uses of his fingers as in
parting the hair of his own body and picking (or pretending
to pick) fleas. This very familiar monkey performance
he appeared to think it his duty to perform on Laddy as
well as on himself. The cautious way in which he would
begin by touching the hair at its tips, pulling it a little, and
finally coming to closer quarters in the business, was highly
diverting to the human onlookers. A very erroneous notion
about the limited opposability of thumb and fingers in monkeys and apes appears to be widespread. Of the erroneous-
ness of the notion anybody can convince himself by watching
carefully the activities of almost any species of monkey in
any good collection of the creatures. I will interrupt this
narrative enough to mention the performance of a large
chimpanzee in the national zoölogical park at Washington.
When eating sunflower seeds the fellow would hold the seeds
in one hand nicely cupped, and with the other pick up the
seeds one by one between thumb and forefinger, and put
them into his mouth quite as skillfully as any human being
can do it. It would be interesting to know at what age a
child becomes as capable in this way as the ape was.

Wonderfully skilled as Jimmy obviously was in several
manual activities, even as compared with Bobby, when it
came to certain other activities Bobby's superiority was unmistakable. These other activities were of such a nature
as to entitle Bobby to the highest place in the series. For
example, he would busy himself very intently in building
houses, castles, and bridges out of wooden blocks, causing

them to resemble certain pictures furnished him as patterns to go by. Anything of this sort was utterly beyond Jimmy, though it looked as though so far as hands in themselves were concerned, he might have done almost as well as Bobby. While there was this very striking difference in Bobby's favor between him and Jimmy, another striking resemblance was in the great number of things they both seemed to feel they must touch, get hold of, and look at. Apparently the only way either could endure for long without doing something of the sort was by lying down and going to sleep. Here too enough difference could be seen to confirm Bobby's claim to the highest place in the series. He could hold himself to the same job for longer periods than Jimmy could.

The most striking difference of all remains to be noticed: When Bobby got tired of one plaything and wanted another, he could demand what he wanted in so many words. Furthermore, in his running about and touching, handling, and pulling different objects he could facilitate the gratification of his curiosity about them by asking questions about them. Abilities of this sort Jimmy was wholly without. Yet as to voice ability, voice culture, we may call it, there was considerable likeness between them. In the quantity of vocal noise each could make whenever anything displeasing crossed his path, neither was much behind the other. Had Jimmy been among his own kind as Bobby was, he would have been at much less disadvantage as compared with Bobby in making his wants, likes and dislikes, and so forth known by his voice than was the case in the actual conditions.

Now what of Sir Henry? Nothing has yet been said about his place in the series. It was perfectly clear that he belonged between Laddy and Jimmy. While he could use his hands in several more ways and to distinctly greater advantage than Laddy could, he was far behind Jimmy on this score. For one thing, he would almost always utilize his hands to good purpose while eating. To illustrate, when pieces of banana, his favorite food, were offered him, although he very rarely failed to take them in his mouth first, immediately thereafter he would raise his arm toward his head, take the large piece in his hand and hold it there while he bit off one mouthful after another till the whole was gone. He almost never failed to use his right hand for this purpose, the left being occupied as a support. When he was on his perch, for which place he seemed to have special liking, the use of the left hand in this was a clear advantage. Beyond this use of the hands over and above their regular use in locomotion, Henry was not much better off than Laddy. He could scratch himself with them as Laddy could not; but any such digital deftness in handling things, as hair and food, so strikingly characteristic of Jimmy, was quite beyond him. Restricted as was the usefulness of Henry's two hands in comparison with Jimmy's and Bobby's two, it was considerably greater than is that of a squirrel's or other rodent's two hands. These latter animals have very little ability to use one of the hands independently of the other. For instance, a squirrel is rarely seen to hold a piece of food in one hand while he does something else with the other. Typically he uses both hands at the same time and in the same way for holding his food.

Now the activities presented by this numerically short mammalian series are strictly correlated with and dependent on a certain structural series, namely the fore-limb series. One does not need to be at all learned in comparative anatomy, to recognize this correlation and dependence. However, in the preceding pages devoted to the structural parts of man on which depend his supremacy over all other creatures, we have examined the facts involved not only in this short series but in a much longer series, with a view to gaining a deeper and clearer insight than by cursory observation we can gain, into just wherein man's place in the series gives him the advantage he obviously has. In order thus to improve our insight we looked at the structural series in its evolutional as well as in its anatomical aspects, the presumption that the series actually is a developmental series being based on what we learned in Chapters 3 and 4 of this volume.

In these examinations of structural series and activity series, almost all the attention bestowed upon details has been given to limbs, especially arm-and-hand. Although the fundamental inseparableness of arm-hands and head was insisted upon, no details whatever of head structure and activity were entered into. Manifestly this leaves our examination woefully defective. Nobody now questions that head, using the term in the general sense indicated above, is not only an exceedingly important element in the combination we have been considering, but that it is an exceedingly complex structural element, performing correspondingly complex activities of its own; and that the limb activities (and all other body activities) are very intimately connected with the head structures and activities. So enormously complex and detailed and subtle are the structure and the activity of the "head" and the connection of limb and general body structure with head structure and activity, that nothing short of a whole volume as large as the one just now being completed will suffice for this part of our enterprise. That is how it happens that this, *The Natural History of Our Conduct,* is to have as a companion book *The Natural Philosophy of Our Conduct.*

BIBLIOGRAPHY

AGASSIZ, ALEXANDER. 1869–71. "Notes on Beaver Dams," in *Proc. Boston Soc. Nat. Hist.,* Vol. XIII.

ALDER, W. F. 1922. *The Isle of Vanishing Men.*

ANSON, GEORGE. *Voyage around the World in 1740.*

ARISTOTLE. *The Parts of Animals,* trans. by Ogle.

BAIRD, SPENCER F.; BREWER, THOMAS M., AND RIDGWAY, ROBERT. 1874. *A History of North American Birds,* Vol. II and Vol. III.

BANTA, ARTHUR M. 1914. "Sex Recognition and the Mating Behavior of the Woodfrog, *Rana sylvatica,*" in *Biol. Bull.,* Vol. XXVI.

BARNARD, E. E. 1915. "A Mistaken Butterfly," in *Nature,* Vol. XCV.

BARROWS, W. B. 1917. *Michigan Bird Life.*

BEAL, F. E. L. 1907. "Birds of California in Relation to the Fruit Industry," *Bull. 30, Biol. Survey,* U. S. Dept. of Agric.

BELL, SIR CHARLES. 1836. "The Hand, its Mechanism and Vital Endowments as Evincing Design," Bridgewater Treatises, No. IV.

BELT, THOMAS. 1874. *The Naturalist in Nicaragua,* second edition.

BETHE, ALBRECHT. 1899. "Dürfen wir den Ameisen und Bienen psychische Qualitäten zuschreiben?" in *Arch. f. d. ges. Physiologie,* Vol. LXX, No. 15. (See Caswell Grave.)

BLAIR, W. REID. 1920. "Notes on the Birth of a Chimpanzee," in *Bull. of the Zoological Society of London,* Vol. XXIII.

BRUCE, JAY. 1923. "The Black Bear in Relation to Stock," in *Calif. Fish and Game Com. Bull.,* Vol. IX.

BUTLER, AMOS W. 1892. "Notes on the Range and Habits of the Carolina Parrakeet," in *The Auk,* Vol. IX.

BUTTEL-REEPEN, H. VON. 1900. "Sind die Bienen Reflexmaschinen?" in *Biol. Centralbl.,* Vol. XX.

CHASE, STUART. 1925. *The Tragedy of Waste.*

CLODD, EDWARD. 1911 (July). "Primitive Man on His Own Origin," in *Quar. Review.*

COMSTOCK, J. H. 1912. *The Spider Book.*

CONSERVATION COMMISSION, STATE OF NEW YORK. Report for 1919.

COUCH, JONATHAN. 1877. *A History of the Fishes of the British Isles,* Vol. I.

CRAIG, WALLACE. 1921. "Why Do Animals Fight?" in *Internat. Jour. of Ethics,* Vol. XXXI.

CUNNINGHAM, ALYSE. 1922. "Letter on John Gorilla," quoted by Hornaday in *The Minds and Manners of Wild Animals.*

DARWIN, CHARLES. *The Origin of Species,* sixth edition.

—— 1897. *The Descent of Man,* Appleton edition, Vol. I.

—— 1882. *The Formation of Vegetable Mould through the Action of Worms.*

—— *Journal of Researches,* Appleton edition.

DEANE, W. 1921. *Fijian Society.*

DITMARS, R. L. 1907. *The Reptile Book.*

DUGMORE, A. R. 1914. *The Romance of the Beaver.*

326 BIBLIOGRAPHY

FABRE, J. H. C. On the Sphex moth, quoted by Kellogg, *Amer. Insects.*
—— On the Sitaris beetle, quoted by D. Sharp, *Camb. Nat. Hist.*, Vol. VI.
FINN, FRANK. 1919. *Bird Behavior.*
FLOWER, W. H., AND LYDEKKER, R. Article "Lemmings," in *Encyc. Brit.*
FORBUSH, E. H. 1917. *Birds of North America,* in Nature Lovers' Library, Vol. II.
FOREL, AUGUSTE. 1908. *The Senses of Insects,* trans. by Percival MacLeod Yearsley.

GALTON, SIR FRANCIS. 1908. *Inquiries into human faculty,* Everyman's Library.
GOLDMAN, E. A. 1921. "Rats in the War Zone," a paper read at the meeting of the American Soc. of Mammalogists.
GOLDENWEISER, A. A. 1922. *Early Civilization.*
GRAVE, CASWELL. 1898. "Psychical Qualities of Ants and Bees," in *Amer. Naturalist,* Vol. XXXII. (See also BETHE.)
GREGORY, WILLIAM K. 1910. "Studies on the Evolution of the Primates," in *Bull. Amer. Mus. of Nat. Hist.,* Vol. XXV.
GRINNELL, JOSEPH, AND DIXON, J. S. *Fur-Bearing Mammals of California.* (In preparation.)

HAMILTON, G. V. 1925. *An Introduction to Objective Psychopathology,* with foreword by Robert M. Yerkes.
HASBROUCK, E. M. 1891. "The Carolina Paroquet, *Conurus carolinensis,*" in *The Auk,* Vol. IX.
HENSHAW, H. W. 1921. "The Storage of Acorns by the California Woodpeckers," in *The Condor,* Vol. XXIII.
—— 1902. *Birds of the Hawaiian Islands.*
HERMAN, OTTO, AND OWEN, J. A. 1909. *Birds Useful and Birds Harmful.*
HORNADAY, W. T. 1887. *The Extermination of the American Bison.*
—— 1922. *The Minds and Manners of Wild Animals.*
—— 1904. *American Natural History.*
HOWARD, L. O. 1923. *The Insect Book.*
HRDLIČKA, ALEŠ. 1907. "Physiological and Medical Observations among the Indians of Southwestern United States and Northern Mexico," in *Bull.* VIII, *Bur. of Amer. Ethnology.*
HUDSON, W. H. 1892. *The Naturalist in La Plata.*
—— 1919. *The Book of a Naturalist.*
—— 1920. *Birds of La Plata.*

JONES, F. W. 1916. *Arboreal Man.*
JORDAN, DAVID STARR, and others. 1898-99. *The fur-seals and the fur-seal Islands of the North Pacific Ocean,* Vol. I.
JUDD, SYLVESTER D. 1917. *Birds of a Maryland farm,* in Nature Lovers' Library, Vol. III.
—— 1898. "The Food of Shrikes," in *Bull. No. 9 of Biol. Survey,* U. S. Dept. of Agric.

KEEN, W. W. 1922 (June 9). "Surgical and Anatomical Evidences of Evolution," in *Science.*
KEITH, ARTHUR. 1911. "Klaatch's Theory of the Descent of man," in *Nature,* Vol. LXXXV.
KELLOGG, VERNON. 1905. *American Insects.*
—— 1908. *Insect Stories.*
KEYNES, J. M. 1921. *A Treatise on Probability.*
KLUGH, A. BROOKER. 1921. "Notes on the Habits of *Blarina Brevicauda* in Ontario," in *Jour. of Mammalogy,* Vol. II.
KÖHLER, WOLFGANG. 1925. *The Mentality of Apes.*

LANG, ANDREW. 1899. *Myth, Ritual, and Religion,* Vol. I.
LINDSAY, W. LAUDER. 1879. *Mind in the Lower Animals,* Vol. II and Vol. III.
LIPKING, E. K. 1922. "Is the Dove Bag Limit too Large?" in

Calif. Fish and Game Com. Bull., Vol. VIII.

LULL, R. S. 1917. *Organic Evolution.*

LUMHOLTZ, K. S. 1920. *Through Central Borneo*, Vol. II.

MACE, HERBERT. 1912. "The Influence of Weather on Bees," in *Nature*, Vol. LXXXIX.

MANNING, F. E. 1922. *Old New Zealand.* (See also PAKEA MAORI.)

MATHEWS, G. M. 1910. *Birds of Australia*, Vol. VI.

MATTHEWS, W. D. 1913 (Sept.). "Evolution of the Horse," in *Amer. Mus. of Nat. Hist. Guide Leaflet Series* No. 36.

MCCOLLUM, E. V. 1925. *The Newer Knowledge of Nutrition.*

MCDONNEL, JOHN. 1918. *Mammals of North America*, in Nature Lovers' Library, Vol. IV.

MCFARLANE, J. M. 1918. *The Causes and Course of Organic Evolution.*

MERRIAM, C. HART. 1921. "A California Elk Drive," in *The Scientific Monthly*, Vol. XIII.

MILL, J. S. 1874. *A System of Logic.*

MILLS, ENOS A. 1923. *In Beaver World.*

MOFFATT, C. B. 1903. "The Spring Rivalry of Birds," in *The Irish Naturalist*, Vol. XII.

MOOREHEAD, W. K. 1914. *The American Indian in the United States.*

MORGAN, C. LLOYD. 1896. *Habit and Instinct.*

MORGAN, L. H. 1868. *The American Beaver and His Work.*

MOSELEY, H. N. 1892. *Notes by a Naturalist. An Account of Observations Made during the Voyage of H. M. S. "Challenger" round the World in the Years 1872-76.*

MOSSO, ANGELO. 1896. *Fear*, trans. by F. Lough and F. Kiesow.

MÜLLER-LYER, F. C. 1920. *The History of Social Development*, trans. by Elizabeth Coote Lake and H. A. Lake.

NELSON, E. W. 1921 (Apr.). "The Big Game of Alaska," in *Bull. of Amer. Game Assoc.*
—— 1925 (Aug.). "Status of the Prong-Horned Antelope, 1922-24," in *Bull.* No. 1546, U. S. Dept. of Agric.

OSBORN, H. F. 1913. *The Horse Past and Present.*

PAGET, SIR STEPHEN. 1914. *Pasteur and After Pasteur.*

PAKEA MAORI. 1922. *Old New Zealand.* (See also MANNING.)

PECK, MORTON E. 1921. "On the Acorn-Storing Habits of Certain Woodpeckers," in *The Condor*, Vol. XXIII.

PECKHAM, GEORGE W., AND PECKHAM, ELIZABETH G. 1898. "The Instincts and Habits of Solitary Wasps," in *Wisconsin Geolog. and Nat. Hist. Bull.* No. 2, *Science Series* No. 1.

PITT, FRANCES. 1920. "The Stoat," in *The National Review*, Vol. LXXV.

PORTER, J. H. 1924. *Wild Beasts.*

RACEY, KENNETH. 1921. "The Murrelet," in *Bull. Pacific Northwest Bird and Mammal Club*, Vol. II.

RAU, PHIL. 1915. "The Ability of the Mud-Dauber to Recognize Her Own Prey (*Hymen*)," in *Jour. of Animal Behavior*, Vol. V.

READ, CARVETH. 1920. *The Origin of Man and His Superstitions.*

RIDGWAY, ROBERT. 1901. *Birds of North America*, Vol. I.

RITTER, WILLIAM E. 1921. "Acorn Storing by the California Woodpeckers," in *The Condor*, Vol. XXIII.
—— 1897. "The Life-History and Habits of the Pacific Coast Newt (*Diemictylus Torosus Esch*)," in *Proc. Calif. Acad. Science*, Vol. I, No. 2.
—— 1903. "Further Notes on the Habits of *Autodax lugubrius*," in *Amer. Naturalist*, Vol. XXXVII.

ROBINSON, LOUIS. 1897. *Wild Traits of Tame Animals.*
ROMANES, GEORGE J. 1883. *Animal Intelligence.*
—— 1884. *Mental Evolution in Animals.*
ROOSEVELT, THEODORE, and others. 1902. *The Deer Family.*
ROTH, W. E. 1924. "An Introductory Study of the Arts, Crafts, and Customs of the Guiana Indians," in *Thirty-eighth Annual Report of the Amer. Bur. of Ethnol.*, 1916–17.

SCAMMON, C. M. 1874. *The Marine Mammals of the Northwestern Coast of North America.*
SCHNEIDER, G. H. *Der thierische Wille.*
SETON, ERNEST THOMPSON. 1909. *Life Histories of Northern Animals*, Vol. I.
SHARP, DAVID. 1895. "Insects," in *Camb. Nat. Hist.*, Vol. VI.
SPENCER, SIR BALDWIN, AND GILLEN, F. J. 1904. *The Northern Tribes of Central Australia.*
STORR, FRANCIS. Article "Duel," *Encyc. Brit.*

TAYLOR, J. H. 1906. *Beavers, Their Ways, and Other Sketches.*
THOMPSON, WILL F. 1919. "The Spawning of the Grunion (*Leuresthes tenuis*)," in *Calif. Fish and Game Com., Fish Bull.* No. 5.
TWAIN, MARK. *A Tramp Abroad*, quoted by Howard in *The Insect Book.*

TYLER, JOHN M. 1923. *The Coming of Man.*
TYLOR, E. B. 1924. *Primitive Culture*, Vol. I., sixth edition.

VALLERY-RADOT, RENÉ. 1923. *The Life of Pasteur*, trans. by Mrs. R. L. Devenshire.

WALLACE, A. R. 1856. "Some Account of an Infant Orang-Utan," in *Annals and Magazine of Nat. Hist.*, Vol. XVII.
WARBURTON, CECIL. 1912. *Spiders.*
—— *Cambridge Natural History*, Vol. IV.
WHEELER, W. M. 1910. *Ants.*
WILDER, B. G. 1893. "The Habits and Parasites of *Epeira riparia*, with a Note on the Moulting of *Nephila plumipes*," in *Proc. Amer. Assoc. Adv. Science*, Vol. XXII.
WILLIAMS, THOMAS. 1860. *Fiji and the Fijians.*
WILLOUGHBY, CHARLES H. 1920. "Beavers and the Adirondacks," in *The Conservationist*, Vol. III, No. 5.
WILSON, J. F. "The Sheep-Killing Dog," in *Farmers' Bull.* No. 935, U. S. Dept. Agric.
WRIGHT, WILLIAM H. 1909. *The Grizzly Bear.*

YERKES, ROBERT M. 1915. "Maternal Instincts in a Monkey," in *Jour. of Animal Behavior*, Vol. V.
—— 1925. Foreword to *An Introduction to Objective Psycho-Pathology*, by G. V. Hamilton. (See also HAMILTON.)

Pugnacity: of sticklebacks, 166.
Pupa: as stage in development, 29.

Rabbits: petrified by fear, 235.
Racey, Kenneth: quoted on habits of Franklin grouse, 211.
Rage: self-injury due to, among animals, 237; among chimpanzees, 251.
Rattlesnake: alleged charming ability of, 235.
Rau, Phil: quoted on activities of mud dauber wasps, 126, 162 et seq.
Read, Carveth: quoted on use of names, 28; on man as hunter, 39; on adoption of hunting life, 306.
Reality: independent of our knowledge, 21; observational, 26.
Reason: and alternative possibilities of action, 93.
Recognition: individual, among insects, 165.
Reflexes: of lower animals, 79.
Relation: between man and celestial objects, 5; man and physical objects, 6; genetic, between man and lowest animals, 58.
Relationship: genetic, 18.
Religion: and science, 63, 94; and the guidance of instinctive activities, 287.
Remorse: absence of, among animals, 181.
Reproduction: maladaptive human activity in, 288; not dependent on sex, 289; sexual, extent of, 289; sexual, as mode of curtailing excessiveness of propagation, 290; and sex, importance of distinction between, 293; basic, and basic sexuality, dependent on different stimuli, 294.
Reproductivity: checks on, 291.
Resemblance: the principle of, 32; man and primates, 35, 37, 42; and difference, 49.
Revelation: divine, as to man's origin, 24.
Ritter, W. E.: quoted on work of California woodpeckers, 128 et seq.; on cannibalism among salamanders, 169; on tree-climbing salamander, 317.
Robert: as individual name, 25.
Robinson, Louis: quoted on animal treatment of helpless companies, 175.
Robbing: a form of maladaptive activity, 267.
Romanes, George J.; 162, quoted on mating habits of stickleback, 167; on fear in horse, 233.
Roosevelt, Theodore: quoted on fight-

ing among deer at mating time, 177; on pronghorn antelope, 228.
Roosters: crowing of, 86.
Roth, W. E.: quoted on festivities of Guiana Indians, 259; on use of nose-string in Guiana Indians, 265, 266.
Rubbish: collected by ants, 120.
"Running a good thing into the ground": 272.

Salamanders: cannibalism among, 168; tree-climbing, illustrative of prototype of hands, 317.
Safety: need of activity for, 74.
Salvation: human, dependent on man's superior adaptive capacity, 300.
Savages: a kind of monkeys, 36; maladaptivity among, 255.
Scammon, C. M.: quoted on elephant seals, 232.
Schneider, G. H.: on mistakes of insects, 162.
Schwarz, E. A.: quoted on habits of shrikes, 139 et seq.
Scepticism: proper rôle of in science, 50.
Science: and religion, 63, 94; and poetry, 195; in the correction of maladaptive activity, 284; in the attainment of welfare, 287.
Scientists: attitude of toward scepticism, 50.
Seal: elephant, deficiency of fear in, 230.
Sea lions: training of, 115.
Self-control: of Fijians, 271.
Self-destruction: among Fijians, 271.
Self-guidance: of instinctive activities, 287.
Self-injury: maladaptive activity resulting in, 182; among birds, 198; due to rage, 237; among high-cultured people, 278; war a form of, 282.
Self-restraint: 272.
Self-torture: among savages, 271.
Series: mammalian, illustrating grades of manual activities, 320.
Seton, Ernest Thompson: quoted on fighting among deer, 178; on death of buffalo by venturing on rotten ice, 225.
Sense: common, in using individual names, 27.
Senselessness: in food habits of domestic animals, 216.
Sentiment: in interpretation of animal activity, 95.
Sex: maladaptive human activity in, 288; instinct, periodicity of, among animals, 291; and reproduction, importance of distinction between, 293.

For Product Safety Concerns and Information please contact our EU
representative GPSR@taylorandfrancis.com
Taylor & Francis Verlag GmbH, Kaufingerstraße 24, 80331 München, Germany

9 780815 367475